Free limited time bonus

Stop for a moment. We have a free bonus set up for you. The problem is this: we forget 90% of everything that we read after 7 days. Crazy fact, right? Here's the solution: we've created a printable, 1-page pdf summary for this book that you're reading now. All you have to do to get your free pdf summary is to go to the following website:

https://livetolearn.lpages.co/enthrallinghistory/

Once you do, it will be intuitive. Enjoy, and thank you!

Contents

Part 1: Sparta

An Enthralling Overview of the Spartans and Their City-State in Ancient Greece along with the Greco-Persian Wars, Peloponnesian War, and Other Conflicts Involving the Spartan Army

Introduction

Every unit of society is connected to untold stories from thousands of years ago. This means that there is a lot of knowledge to discover in the pages of history. This knowledge gives us a fuller sense of ourselves and where we stand in the world.

History has always been more than tedious academia that sometimes feels as if it serves no practical purpose in real life. Every generation of humanity has passed down their tales of existence and experiences to the next. This took diverse forms: stories, folklore, traditional songs, and paintings, just to mention a few. And the brilliant efforts of historians, both ancient and modern, have continually gifted humanity with discoveries of the past that we need to appreciate the present.

How can we truly understand the world we live in if we do not know how it came to be?

The ancient world saw the rise of many civilizations, and their impact can still be felt to this day. If we trace this connection in regards to Greece, it will take us as far back as the classical era—which is precisely the period when most of the key events in this book took place.

The classical era started and ended at different times in different parts of the ancient world, but in Greece, it happened between the 6th and 4th centuries BCE.

That's a very long time ago—around three thousand years ago, in fact. It can be hard for some to realize that we are talking about real people who lived and breathed and did these great deeds, not some amazing character created in the pages of a novel.

Want to read all about it? Settle down for an extraordinary trip to ancient Greece, home to some of the most extraordinary societies in the history of the world.

Our main destination is Sparta, a city set in the southeastern part of the Peloponnese. It was home to some of the greatest warriors to ever walk the earth. They were involved in more drama than you like to think. The Spartans were a people who would brag about their freedom, and rightfully so!

So, whether you are already a huge fan, an enthusiast who wants to learn more about them, or a beginner looking to start from scratch, this book documents all there is to know about Sparta.

With clear, straightforward words strung together in an intriguing, easy-to-read narrative, you won't find a better story!

Part One: The Rise of Sparta (1100 BCE–500 BCE)

Chapter 1 – From Myth to Reality

Much of ancient Sparta's lush history is enmeshed in the glorious acts of her legendary kings. Their vaunted triumphs in battle, their pretzelled love stories, and their brilliant feats in ancient politics took a Doric Greek city-state located in the southeastern Peloponnese to prominence.

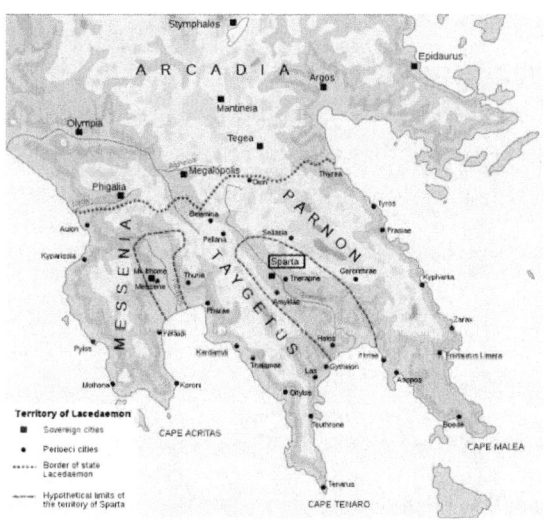

A map of ancient Sparta.
(Credit: https://en.wikipedia.org/wiki/Sparta#/media/File:Sparta_Territory.svg)

It is important to examine the early mythical beginnings of Sparta to understand its growth. Much of what you will read in this chapter is based on legends, but many legends have a ring of truth to them. For instance, the Trojan War likely didn't see the aid of gods and goddesses on the battlefield, but the people at the time would have thought this to be true, which is why they often feature so prominently in the stories of the war.

As far as origins go, Sparta had not always been called "Sparta." The city-state was formerly known as Lacedaemon, and in some texts, it is referred to as Laconia. The historians Herodotus and Thucydides often referred to Sparta as Lacedaemon in their works. This was because it emerged from the ancient Laconian capital of the same name located in the south of Greece.

Around 1600 BCE, Lelex, the son of Poseidon (Greek god of the ocean), was the first mythical king of Laconia (or Sparta). While some ancient traditions cite Lelex as the offspring of the sun god, Helios, or Poseidon, others believe that Lelex was an autochthon, a mortal formed from the earth and trees. He was married to a river nymph named Cleocharia, and she birthed many sons, one of which was his heir, Myles.

Myles went on to father Eurotas, who did not have a male heir to cede his kingdom to. He gave the kingdom to Lacedaemon, the son of Zeus. He married one of Eurotas's daughters named Sparta, which is how this kingdom got its name.

Little did King Lacedaemon know that the name Sparta would be used to reference one of the mightiest city-states in all of ancient Greece.

King Tyndareus

Hippocoon's Rebellion

You may have happened upon the legend of King Tyndareus when reading about the famous Oath of Tyndareus. This happened during his political quest in the marriage of his stepdaughter, Helen, who would later become known as Helen of Troy.

According to Greek tradition, Tyndareus was the son of Oebalus, the king of Sparta, and his wife, Gorgophone. Other sources assert that he was the son of Messenian King Perieres and Gorgophone, his queen. Despite the variations to Tyndareus's pedigree, it is commonly agreed that he had several siblings, notably Hippocoon and Icarius.

Tyndareus was crowned as the king of Sparta, but Hippocoon coveted the throne. He believed that since he was the oldest, the crown should be his. In his first attempt, Hippocoon usurped the throne of Sparta and sent its former occupant, Tyndareus, into exile, along with his other brother, Icarius (who would become the father of Penelope, the wife of the famous Odysseus).

The exiled brothers found refuge among the inhabitants of Aetolia. These inhabitants were the legendary Curetes, and they were in the heat of war against their enemies, the Calydonian hunters, at the time. In other sources, Tyndareus spent his exile in a quaint Laconian town along the Eurotas River, Pellana.

Tyndareus may have remained in exile were it not for the intervention of Heracles, the famous son of Zeus. Heracles's military campaigns in the Peloponnesian Peninsula targeted the ruler of Pylos, King Neleus, and all his allies. After King Neleus and his sons were vanquished, his allies, including the reigning Hippocoon, suffered the same fate. With Hippocoon and his sons gone, Tyndareus returned to Sparta and reclaimed his throne.

Leda and the Swan

Gods often interacted with mortals by appearing to them in different forms. When King Tyndareus ascended the throne of Sparta, his beautiful queen, Leda of Aetolia, bore him four children: Clytemnestra, Helen, Pollux, and Castor. But they weren't all his children.

According to ancient sources, Zeus, the god of the sky, was smitten by Leda's beauty. His desire for her moved him to descend from Mount Olympus in the form of a swan, and he slept with her on the night she was to be with her husband, the king.

Queen Leda got pregnant, and she birthed two eggs, with each egg holding two children. Since Leda also laid with her husband the same night, there are conflicting versions on whose children belonged to Zeus and Tyndareus. Regardless, they were raised by King Tyndareus as his own.

William Butler Yeats would compose a sonnet for this encounter in the 1920s, and the legend of Leda and the Swan would be portrayed in paintings, sculptures, murals, epic poems, and other forms of art.

Leda and the Swan, a 16th-century copy based on the Michelangelo painting that is now lost.

Oath of Tyndareus

Helen (yes, the famous Helen of Troy) is thought to be one of the children of Zeus, the king of the gods. She was written to be as lovely as Queen Leda, although many say she was the most beautiful woman in the world. Her status in divinity was an accessory to her irresistible charm, which attracted the attention of a horde of eligible bachelors throughout Greece.

Helen of Troy *by Dante Gabriel Rossetti, 1863.*

As a young girl, Helen was abducted by Theseus of Athens (the famous slayer of the Minotaur). Since he believed himself to be divine, it was only right that he marry someone who was divine as well. And you can't get much better than the daughter of Zeus. He hid her away with his mother, Aethra, and then went on an expedition to the underworld with his friend.

His absence was a window of opportunity for Helen's brothers, Castor and Pollux. They captured Athens and took their sister back to Sparta. As punishment for his affront, the city was sacked, and his mother was taken as a slave.

When Helen came of age, suitors flocked King Tyndareus's palace, each fervently requesting her hand in marriage. Odysseus, Ajax the Great, Menestheus, Patroclus, Menelaus, and

Agamemnon (some sources say Agamemnon was there to represent Menelaus) were some of the many men who sought to marry Helen.

Luxurious gifts were presented to the royal family of Sparta by all the suitors, but King Tyndareus was unsure who to choose. If he was not diplomatic enough about the selection, he risked offending the suitors, provoking war and conflict. Times were delicate, and the situation was dicey, making caution an imperative for Tyndareus.

Odysseus of Ithaca, one of the suitors, saw the Spartan king's plight and offered him a solution. He would figure out a diplomatic way to settle this in exchange for the hand of the king's niece, Penelope. King Tyndareus eagerly took Odysseus's offer, and as promised, a solution was proposed. All of the suitors would sign a pact of non-hostility toward the chosen suitor, which included the promise of taking up arms against anyone who'd pose a threat to the chosen suitor and his wife.

The suitors agreed to swear the oath, which became known as the Oath of Tyndareus, as it would keep them in line for Helen's hand in case the chosen one faltered. Menelaus, Prince of Mycenae (pre-Dorian Sparta), was selected to be Helen's husband, and his older brother, King Agamemnon of Mycenae, married Helen's sister, Clytemnestra.

However, Helen's marriage to Menelaus was about to take a twist when a certain handsome Trojan prince came into the picture.

King Menelaus

Menelaus and his brother Agamemnon were born in the heat of a murky power tussle between their father, Atreus, and their uncle, Thyestes. The contention was so intense that their father died at the hands of their cousin, Aegisthus, and Thyestes assumed the throne of Mycenae.

Their tyrannical uncle forced Menelaus and Agamemnon to live out their youth in exile. When the exiled brothers met King Tyndareus, they harnessed their military strength, and with his help, they took back their homeland from Thyestes. Agamemnon became the king of Mycenae, and Menelaus married King Tyndareus's stepdaughter, Helen.

Sometime after their union, King Tyndareus and his wife, Leda, stepped down from their positions as king and queen of Sparta. Menelaus and Helen took over, and their first daughter, Hermione, was born.

The Trojan War

Prince Paris (also known as Alexander) had not been one of the suitors who swore the Oath of Tyndareus. But he also did not desire Helen—at least that is until he met the goddess Aphrodite. As a reward for choosing her as the most beautiful goddess, Aphrodite promised Paris that the most beautiful woman in the world would be his wife.

After his encounter with the goddess, the prince of Troy reunited with his family and embarked on a diplomatic trip to Sparta—or so it seemed. Paris's real mission in Sparta was to find Helen and make her his with Aphrodite's blessing. He found that Queen Helen was as lovely as the tales said, and the Trojan prince fell in love with her.

When Paris learned that Helen's husband was in faraway Crete to attend a funeral, he eloped with Helen to Troy. Traditional accounts give varying details about Helen's elopement to Troy. Some infer that she was forcefully removed from her palace by a lust-drunk Paris, while others claim that Helen, by Aphrodite's intervention, fell in love with Paris and willingly left Sparta with him.

Helen's migration to Troy, coerced or voluntary, was sealed by marriage to Paris. She was no longer Helen of Sparta but Helen of

Troy, and this laid the precedent for the most legendary war in the annals of Sparta: the Trojan War.

Herodotus writes that it wasn't the first time the wife of a reigning king was snatched by another. Helen's elopement was one of many such incidences at the time, so Paris likely anticipated mild or no consequences for his actions.

Contrarily, King Menelaus was furious to return home to an empty bed. The unprecedented event had also left his daughter, Hermione, dispirited.

The *Iliad*, the famous Greek poem written by Homer that centers on the Trojan War, highlights that King Menelaus's initial action was to lead a diplomatic mission to Troy to solicit his wife's return.

Paris and the Trojans refused, fanning the flames of fury and revenge in Menelaus. A prince of Troy had insulted the king of Sparta and, indeed, Sparta itself. Unlike others who had gotten away with taking the wives of other kings, Prince Paris's defiance would not be overlooked.

Menelaus rallied his men and, through Agamemnon, summoned all of Helen's suitors who had taken the Oath of Tyndareus to uphold their pact. With the kings, princes, and nobles from the Peloponnese on his side, Menelaus forged a formidable alliance. He could call upon his brother Agamemnon, the wily Odysseus, and the legendary war hero Achilles, just to name a few. Together, they marched on Troy, which is believed to be in present-day Turkey, and laid siege to its fortress in the 12th or 11th century BCE.

In some versions, the Trojan War is presented as one of the ways for Zeus to reduce the human population on Earth. Although we know this was not the reason for the war, it is easy to see why the people of the time thought this. After all, the Trojan War caused massive casualties.

The Trojan War is thought to have lasted for ten years, and thousands were killed in battle, while hundreds more deserted. The Trojans held an advantage over their enemies since their city was protected by nearly impenetrable walls. They also held more knowledge of the terrain than the warring foreigners.

However, the Greeks had more men fighting, but after Achilles was killed in battle, the Greeks realized they needed a strategy that would put an end to the war once and for all in their favor.

Odysseus came up with another brilliant solution.

The next morning, the Trojans woke up to the news of Menelaus's surrender. After laying siege to the gates of Troy without any success, the Greeks had sailed back home. The war was over. The Greeks left a gigantic wooden horse on the shores of Troy as an offering to Athena.

A replica of the Trojan Horse from the movie Troy. *Some have posited that the Trojan Horse might have actually been a ship!*

The men of Troy celebrated, and they moved the monument into the city as a trophy for their triumph in battle. It seemed as if Helen of Troy no longer had to return to Sparta.

Unknown to the Trojans, the Trojan Horse was a ploy of the Greeks, and their lethal plan would be launched that night. Menelaus and the finest warriors in Greece were hiding inside the Trojan Horse. While the Trojans slept, the Greeks snuck out of their hiding place and opened the city gates for the rest of their troops.

Troy was ruthlessly plundered, and the Trojans were massacred. Indeed, the Trojan Horse was not the victory symbol that the Trojans had envisaged. It was an instrument in the fall of Troy and was actually the trophy of Menelaus and his allies.

The Dorian Invasion and the Dawn of the Greek Dark Ages

Heracles, the son of Zeus and Alcmene, was a Greek demigod and the progenitor of the Heracleidae (or Heraclids).

King Eurystheus, the last Mycenaean king in the Perseid Dynasty, was a sworn enemy of Heracles, and his hatred extended to Heracles's descendants. According to Greek ancient traditions, Eurystheus had them all expelled from their lands in the Peloponnese.

The banished Heracleidae were received by King Aegimius of Doris, and they were integrated into the Dorian community. Doris was a small region in central Greece, and the people spoke Doric, one of the major dialects in classical Greek.

Unlike the neighboring Achaean Greek cities with their elaborate cultural lifestyle and magnificent structures, the Dorians preferred simple communal pastoral living. They worked the fields as farmers and herders, and their men were skilled in warfare.

Many generations later, the descendants of Heracles, now fully Dorians, returned to the Peloponnese to reclaim their homeland.

This act is historically referenced as the Dorian invasion, and it took place in the early 11th century.

The term "invasion" describes the migration of the Dorians to Mycenaean Greece, and it was not a typical war. However, the qualifier was adopted as a result of the violent nature of the Dorian occupation of Greece.

As revenge for their exile, the Dorians, armed with swords, raided the city of Mycenae, which was the epicenter of the emerging Greek civilization, and destroyed its buildings. They also took Laconia, Argolis, and Messenia, and they ventured farther into the southern Aegean Islands. The former occupants of the captured Greek cities fled to the mountains of Arcadia, and others sought asylum in Asia Minor and Attica.

The Dorians took their settlement campaign far beyond the shores of Greece to parts of Italy and North Africa while holding the fort down in Sparta, Argos, and Corinth. The sudden conquest of a nearly obscure rural tribe potentially ended the Mycenaean era in Greece and heralded an epoch of rapid cultural decline.

Details of these times have remained in the dark because historical records written during the Mycenaean era were lost during the Dorian invasion. This is why historians call it the "Dark Ages."

After the Dorians made themselves the ruling class in the Peloponnese, their language, Doric, became the dominant dialect throughout the Peloponnese.

With the population of Greeks widely diminished and cultural structures dismantled, the wealth of pre-Doric Greece would suffer a great decline. Written historical documents were misplaced, trade and socio-economic systems collapsed, and the glory of the Bronze Age was buried beneath the debris of destroyed palaces and temples.

The end of Mycenaean Greece gave prominence to Sparta as the seat of political power. The 7th-century Heraclids (or

Heracleidae), justified by their status as the only remaining descendants of Zeus, took over the reins of political affairs.

Amid the chaos of the Greek Dark Ages, a new government rose. Two ruling dynasties would emerge from among the descendants of Zeus: the Agiads and the Eurypontids. Two kings would rule Sparta.

This was one of the provisions of the new Spartan Constitution, the Great Rhetra, which was formulated by a sage lawgiver who went by the name Lycurgus.

Chapter 2 – Lycurgus's Reforms

Lycurgus of Sparta

Greek biographer and historian Plutarch gives the most detailed existing account of the life of Lycurgus, a Spartan statesman of the 9th century, in his work titled "The Life of Lycurgus." Lycurgus is credited with founding the post-Doric Spartan political order, which guided Sparta out of the turbulent Greek Dark Ages.

Little is certain about Lycurgus's pedigree or actual existence, but some legends hold that he may have been the human manifestation of the god Apollo. This, however, contradicts Plutarch's account in which Lycurgus makes sacrifices to Apollo at some point in his life. Plutarch establishes Lycurgus as a descendant of Heracles and a prince from one of the two ruling houses of Sparta.

The intricacies of his roots remain debatable; however, historians agree that Lycurgus's journey to prominence began with the death of his older brother, Polydectes of Sparta. Polydectes left his son, Charilaus, in Lycurgus's care. Lycurgus made the child king, and the news of his deed spread throughout Sparta.

The more famous Lycurgus grew for his humility and belief in justice, the more the queen, Charilaus's mother, loathed him. She was convinced that Lycurgus's generosity was a façade and that he secretly nursed desires to seize the throne.

Lycurgus was unable to convince the queen and her people of his sincerity to Charilaus, so he decided to leave Sparta. He embarked on a long journey that took him away from the young king until the latter was old enough to sire an heir.

The Voyage

After forfeiting an elevated political position in Sparta, Lycurgus's first stop was Crete, a Greek city-state that had also been taken over during the Dorian invasion.

Crete was rapidly recovering from the tumult of the Dark Ages. It had once been ruled by King Minos, son of Zeus and Europa. Minos was an excellent legislator, and Lycurgus would model his reforms on Minos's work.

Thales, a musician and lyric poet, was an acquaintance of Lycurgus in Crete. Thales was skilled in making beautiful, calming music, and his renditions had an almost magical effect on people. Supposedly, every time Thales performed in a banquet hall, his listeners would put aside their differences and commit to being virtuous people. Lycurgus saw the influence of Thales's music as potentially being useful in preparing the hearts of his people for the reforms he would bring back to Sparta.

Next, Lycurgus visited Ionia. To his fascination, their lifestyle varied profoundly from those of the Dorians. The Ionians, which was one of the four major ethnic tribes of ancient Greece, were culturally sophisticated. Their art and philosophy had significantly advanced, leaving those of the austere Dorians several laps behind. In Ionia, Lycurgus happened upon the works of Homer, which he studied extensively and popularized. Plutarch highlights that Lycurgus made a quick stop at Egypt as well, where he gained refined military knowledge. He also reached Spain and India, noting the unique elements of their society and politics.

Due to Lycurgus's exposure to foreign cultures and civilizations, his passion for reforming the political foundations of Sparta heightened. There was no better time to receive a written note from the people of Sparta pleading for his return.

"Homecoming King"

Lycurgus was welcomed back to Sparta in a celebratory fashion. It seems the people's admiration for him had only increased since his departure. His nephew, King Charilaus, was terrified at the news of his homecoming, fearing that Lycurgus had come to usurp the throne of Sparta.

Fortunately, Lycurgus had bigger fish to fry. He headed for the Temple of Apollo, which housed Pythia, the high priestess and Oracle of Delphi. There, he surrendered himself to the god, seeking his counsel and blessing for his mission to reform Sparta.

The Oracle endorsed Lycurgus, and this translated into tremendous support for Lycurgus because the Oracle was greatly revered among the people. Lycurgus's followers increased throughout Sparta, and his reforms would go on to forge the most famous city-state in Greece.

A drawing of Lycurgus of Sparta

Lycurgus's Reforms

A politically stunted Sparta was in dire need of a new set of laws to operate on. After receiving the blessings of the Oracle, Lycurgus was inspired to formulate a body of laws known as the Great Rhetra. Supposedly, Lycurgus said there would be no written constitution, so it is believed the Great Rhetra was passed down orally. However, it is possible that it was written down at some point, as we know quite a bit of what it entailed.

Under the new constitution, Sparta would be ruled by two kings instead of one, and the power would be equally shared.

The Gerousia

The Gerousia was a council of elders, which was comprised of thirty men in total: twenty-eight men and the two kings of Sparta. According to the Great Rhetra, members of the Gerousia were called *gerontes* and had to be at least sixty years old.

Once elected, a member of the Gerousia, excluding the kings, would serve in the council for life. Candidates were typically chosen from the aristocracy and voted for by the Spartan citizenry. Voting was done vocally, and despite its many flaws, it remained in use in ancient Sparta for many generations.

Collectively, the Gerousia wielded immense judicial power, including veto power over the Spartan Assembly (the Apella). In the words of Plutarch, the creation of the Gerousia was a break from the anarchy and tyranny that had characterized most of the Greek Dark Ages. The power of the kings could then be checked, and the citizens could truly be heard.

The Redistribution

"For there was an extreme inequality among them, and their state was overloaded with a multitude of indigent and necessitous persons, while its whole wealth had centered upon a very few. To the end, therefore, that he might expel from the state arrogance and envy, luxury and crime, and those yet more inveterate diseases of want and superfluity, he obtained of them to renounce their properties, and to consent to a new division of the land, and that they should all live together on an equal footing; merit to be their only road to eminence."

These words by Plutarch sum up the background of Lycurgus's land reforms in Sparta. The totality of Sparta's land was divided into equal parts and given back to the people. This brought an end to the plague of hegemonic land ownership by the greedy elite.

Next, Lycurgus addressed the coinage system of Sparta. The nation was ridden with wealth laying in a few hands (the full citizens of Sparta, known as the Spartiates) and exploitative corruption.

In his wisdom, Lycurgus believed that a direct measure against the hoarded wealth of the minority elite would overturn the relative stability in Sparta. Instead, he focused on the existing coinage system—the source of their ill-gotten wealth. At his behest, a ban was declared on the possession of gold and silver. Sparta's new currency was made from iron and coated with vinegar, making it frail and worthless to foreign traders.

What use was a currency that could not be spent in other states in Greece? Trade relations soon dwindled, as did the wealth of the corrupt elite. With their access to luxuries cut off, there was little desire to attain wealth through illicit means, just as Lycurgus had predicted.

More importantly for Sparta, the people began to depend on internal goods. This means that Sparta did not have to interact with foreign powers as much, allowing the society to be self-sustainable in almost everything.

The Institution of Messes

Public mess halls in Sparta were only frequented by those at the bottom of the social chain. The rich preferred to dine in the comfort of their elaborate homes on fatted pigs served on gold-rimmed platters. They ate the rarest, most exotic fruits and the best wine. They were obsessed with private, gaudy displays of sparkling tableware crafted from silver and gold.

Lycurgus unveiled his third reform, which mandated that every man of Sparta, regardless of social status, would eat in the public mess halls. This system was called the syssitia.

The rich, even the kings of Sparta, would no longer dine extravagantly or in private with their wives but on a simple diet.

The meat shared in the mess halls came from the animal sacrifices made to the gods, as a portion of the sacrifice would be saved for the mess hall. Meat also came from hunts, as men had to send part of the animal for these common meals. There were few circumstances that allowed men to be absent from the table.

Military Reforms and Legacy

Lycurgus was an ardent believer in military discipline and physical fitness, so he incorporated elements of the knowledge he gleaned during his sojourn to Egypt and other nations into the existing Spartan structure.

Before the reforms, the Spartan military embodied tough, brave men of war. Lycurgus foresaw the significance of training the minds and bodies of young Spartans so they could bring glory to Sparta. Young men needed to be absorbed into the art of warfare, and young women had to train their bodies to produce strong Spartan men.

For the men, a military educational program called the agoge was introduced. Once Spartan boys attained the age of seven, they would be taken away from their families to undergo rigorous training. In the early days of the agoge, Lycurgus was a trainer to the boys. As the system evolved, more skilled trainers joined.

Lycurgus believed that the process, similar to making the finest quality gold, would be survived only by the finest Spartan men. The boys were taught, punished, and tested under the hardest conditions and thoroughly examined by the elders of Sparta.

The agoge was highly competitive, and it instilled brute discipline and unrivaled vigilance in young Spartan men. These values were believed to be the core tenets of a true warrior, and the highest honor for a young man in Sparta was the completion of his training and being ready for battle.

Under Lycurgus's watch, the women of Sparta were not left out of physical activities. They wrestled, boxed, and participated in other sports to stay in top shape for motherhood. They believed that by doing this, their bodies could only produce children that were neither ill-formed nor diseased.

Lycurgus knew that an enemy of Sparta could master all of their military strategies during a prolonged battle. Hence, he discouraged repeated warfare against the same enemies. The military techniques of Sparta could not become common knowledge, or else Sparta stood the risk of a crushing defeat.

A few historical sources credit some marriage reforms to Lycurgus, all of which centered on temperance and sexual restraint. Undoubtedly, Lycurgus yearned for a Sparta devoid of corruption, gluttony, and debauchery, whether that person was male or female, rich or poor.

The annals of Sparta describe Lycurgus as a visionary leader who prioritized the collective prosperity of the people over selfish personal gains. He was highly pragmatic in his approach to Spartan politics, and with the backing of the Oracle of Delphi, he won the hearts of many Spartans.

Twenty-first-century historian John Lewis Gaddis uses the phrase "a fox with a compass" to describe Lycurgus's astute personality. By choosing to leave Sparta for peace to reign rather than kill his infant nephew and the queen, Lycurgus established himself as a man averse to greed. This trait was one he dedicated his life to, as he sought to impress it on his fellow people.

Of course, there are some critics. Some historical accounts accuse Lycurgus of being a perfection-obsessed fascist who advocated the dreaded practice of dumping sickly infants into Kaiadas, a cave. Under Lycurgus, Spartans reportedly saw no use for such children in the agoge or other state-sponsored training. Archaeologists who excavated Kaiadas have refuted this claim, declaring that no infant remains were found in the pit. However, since this legend has carried on to this day, there might be some truth to it; after all, other societies around the world abandoned babies if they could not care for them properly. Thus, Sparta might have done this as well, although it wouldn't have been out of a need to purge their babies to create a perfect Spartan society.

The End of the Road

Lycurgus's life is steeped in legends. One story says that after having accomplished his aspiration of setting the precedents for contemporary Spartan society, Lycurgus was stoned in the marketplace by the nobles and decried for his measures to make the people more equal.

Lycurgus fled the marketplace, and Alcander, one of the nobles, gave chase. He attacked Lycurgus and struck him in the eye, blinding him.

The other nobles found the two, and they were shocked at what had happened. Moved with piercing guilt for their ill-treatment of Lycurgus, the Spartans gave Alcander to Lycurgus.

Lycurgus took the young man and dismissed the people, but rather than take his revenge, Lycurgus pardoned Alcander. He took Alcander in and mentored him to greatness. The news of this act spread throughout Sparta, and the people looked at Lycurgus with more admiration than ever before.

One day, Lycurgus gathered the people of Sparta, both friends and foes, for an important occasion. In light of the growing unrest in Sparta about his administration, he had decided to do something, the same thing he had done when accused of being a threat to his nephew Charilaus.

Lycurgus was leaving Sparta.

Before his departure, Lycurgus made the Spartans swear to uphold his reforms. He had shown them grace by not allowing the Great Rhetra to be written down, giving them room to modify it.

After the Spartans swore to keep his laws, Lycurgus left, never to be seen or heard from again. Lycurgus's later life and death is so shrouded in mystery that some sources in classical Greek mythology describe it as a "disappearance from history." Others posit that he starved himself to death to seal the oath sworn by the Spartans.

Lycurgus's numerous followers formed a hero cult in his honor, and for many generations, he was seen as a shining beacon of Sparta's ideals. Many credit Lycurgus for bringing Sparta to prominence in the pages of history.

After all, the city of Sparta would never be the same after Lycurgus's reforms.

Chapter 3 – The Messenian Wars

Following the Dorian invasion of Greece, Sparta sought to expand Dorian political control, cultural domination, and land ownership. Naturally, the first stage of this expansion was to nearby city-states in the Peloponnesian Peninsula: Argos to the northeast and Messenia to the west.

Messenia was home to beautiful, fertile fields that quickly captured the desire of the Dorians (Spartans). Land was a great measure of any nation's wealth, and a people as pastoral as the Dorians knew this all too well. It was true that they had taken most of Messenia during their invasion, but the political power of the region remained in the firm hold of the Achaeans. Consequently, the Spartans created a mandate to seize it.

The Spartan quest to annex Messenia, as well as the historic reactions provoked in the course of this quest, is documented by Pausanias as the Messenian Wars.

The Catalysts

Wars rarely break out on impulse alone. Typically, tensions build up, sometimes for generations, and rise like hot volcanic magma to erupt at the slightest trigger. According to ancient Greek travel writer Pausanias, this was true of the Messenian Wars—a series of battles between Sparta and her neighbor Messenia.

The Saga of Kings

The foundation of the dissent between these two Greek city-states was their contrasting ethnic dispositions. The Achaeans could never accept the imposition of a Doric commander, Cresphontes, as the new king of Messenia. After all, he was of the "unsophisticated" Heraclid clan that had expunged many Greeks from their homelands during the Dorian invasion.

Cresphontes's position as king was not accepted until he took Merope's hand in marriage. Merope was an Arcadian princess and the daughter of Achaean King Cypselus. The Achaeans were friendly neighbors of the Arcadians. Obviously, the marriage was a diplomatic attempt at consolidating Cresphontes's power.

Did it work?

No, not really. It seemed as though the Achaeans could see right through the king, and the marriage of convenience was not enough to appease them forever. In the eyes of the Achaeans, Cresphontes remained a threat to Achaean political supremacy in Messenia.

Eventually, the Achaean nobles plotted and executed a bloody coup that saw the death of King Cresphontes and all his sons except one: the young Prince Aepytus.

Prince Aepytus was spared because he had been socially assimilated into the Achaean culture. He had been schooled in Arcadia. He thought, acted, and spoke like an Arcadian. Essentially, the young prince was only Dorian by blood.

Upon rising to the throne, Aepytus became the first king of a new Messenian ruling dynasty known as the Aepytidae.

The Dorians who occupied parts of Messenia were enraged at the "Achaeanization" of King Cresphontes's only remaining heir, but they were a minority in the region. There was little they could do.

Subsequently, they turned to their mother state, Sparta, for aid. By then, the Spartan expansionist campaign in Argos had proven successful, leaving Messenia yet to be subjugated.

The Virgins of Artemis's Temple

Twenty-five years before the outbreak of the First Messenian War, an event occurred in a temple of Artemis that acted as another catalyst for war.

Artemis, the daughter of Zeus and the twin sister of Apollo, was revered in Greece as the goddess of the hunt, the moon, and chastity. Her temple was sacred, forbidding any form of violence against man or woman.

One day, during the reign of Phintas, there was a grand festival at the Temple of Artemis, which was located on the border between Messenia and Laconia.

The festival saw the attendance of prominent Messenians and Spartans alike, including King Teleklos of Sparta. Somehow, terrible violence broke out that day. Pausanias tells two versions of the story, which come from both the Spartan and Messenian historical records.

Spartan tradition asserts that the attending Messenians unduly attacked the virgins who worshipped at Artemis's temple and raped them. The Messenians also murdered King Teleklos of Sparta, defying what was sacred ground.

On the other hand, the Messenian version states this was a counterattack against Teleklos, who had disguised young armed men as virgins. Allegedly, this was a strategy to gain access to the temple. They would more easily be able to attack and slaughter the Messenian nobility.

The truth is unknown, but the day ended the same way. King Teleklos and his army of virgins or poorly disguised men were attacked and killed by the Messenians in Artemis's sacred abode.

The fires of war between Sparta and Messenia had long been stoked; all that was left was a final spark.

This rising animosity would outlive an entire generation and be passed on to the next.

The Trigger

When Polychares, a Messenian athlete, won the *stadion* ("stadium") race and was named champion at the 764 BCE Olympic Games, his fame spread far and wide throughout Greece. He must not have known that he would be involved in the skirmish that would trigger a war between rival neighbors.

Euaiphnos, a Spartan, loaned some grazing lands to the Olympic champion. This meant that Polychares could use the land for growing crops and rearing cattle while paying Euaiphnos.

One day, without consent, Euaiphnos sold off Polychares's cattle to merchants and kept the money for himself. When confronted by Polychares, Euaiphnos said that there had been a raid by pirates, who carted the cattle away.

Unfortunately for Euaiphnos, his lies were revealed when one of Polychares's herdsmen, who had barely escaped a bad ordeal with the merchants, told his master the truth. Repulsed by his dishonesty, Polychares confronted Euaiphnos again. Euaiphnos was instantly apologetic. He requested that Polychares send his son to recover the money that had been illicitly made from the cattle sale. Polychares agreed, thinking Euaiphnos was willing to make things right.

However, Euaiphnos again betrayed Polychares's trust by murdering his son when they were well outside the borders of Sparta. Euaiphnos had no genuine intentions of returning the money.

When Polychares heard of his son's murder, he swore bitter vengeance, not just on the Spartan who had done him wrong but on as many Spartans as he could find. He petitioned the Spartan government for justice. But that took too long. Polychares decided to take justice into his own hands and embarked on a murder spree.

The Spartan government swung into action now, demanding that Polychares be extradited for his murder of Spartans. The Messenian government threw its weight behind Polychares, demanding punishment for Euaiphnos first.

Attempts at a diplomatic resolution were thwarted by an internal conflict between the two kings of Messenia: Androcles and Antiochus. The kings and their supporters were unable to agree on the extradition of Polychares. King Androcles, who was for extradition, was assassinated by Antiochus's overzealous retainers who were against the extradition.

King Antiochus did not live long enough to fulfill his plans. When his son, Euphaes, became the king of Messenia, King Alcmenes of Sparta declared war on Messenia.

The First Messenian War (743 BCE–724 BCE)

War was where fine strategies, brute strength, and the best-crafted weapons of destruction met to determine the victorious and the vanquished. An unprecedented attack from the Spartan camp was the first act of war, and you may find that the First Messenian War might have had its victor crowned at its inception.

Spartan King Alcmenes, the son of the murdered King Teleklos, set out on a campaign to seize Ampheia in a surprise night attack.

Ampheia was a Messenian town believed to be set upon the hills of the Spartan border. It was the perfect military base for Alcmenes and his troops. So, under cover of night, the Spartans snuck into the open, unguarded gates of Ampheia and ruthlessly sacked the town, awakening the slumbering natives to meet their brutal deaths.

Shocked and unprepared for this invasion, the people of Ampheia fled for their lives. Some went to temples, while others fled out of the city gates to escape the wrath of the Spartans. For the unfortunate who could not escape, they faced a hard life of slavery or brutal death.

The Spartans made themselves at home in their new base. They would proceed into other parts of Messenia from Ampheia. They would not stop until the entire city-state acknowledged Spartan dominion.

News traveled fast to King Euphaes, who resided in the capital of Messenia, Stenykleros. Euphaes moved swiftly to address his people about the dire situation. Their enemy, Sparta, had made the first move, and Ampheia had fallen captive because of neglect and unwariness—a mistake that could not be repeated.

King Euphaes mobilized Messenians from far and wide to fortify their cities. Citizens were thoroughly trained in the art of wielding weapons and other defensive tactics.

Euphaes's strategy was simple: avoid launching an offensive against the Spartan forces. The Messenians had the geographical advantage as occupants of the invaded land. They could remain safe behind their garrisoned city walls until the Spartans gave up and left.

Unfortunately, the Spartan army blazed on for two years, raiding parts of Messenia and taking money and grain to their base in Ampheia. The Messenians were wrong to assume that the Spartans weren't on their land to stay.

In time, the people realized that King Euphaes's defensive strategy was not going to work. The Spartans were unrelenting in their campaign and had taken over most of the Messenian countryside.

Being prisoners in their own land for years made the Messenians distraught. With limited and quickly depleting supplies came the realization that they could not hide behind the city walls forever, especially since their farming lands were under Spartan authority. King Euphaes decided that the time had come to face the Spartan invaders once and for all.

There is no doubt that the Spartans were frightening men of war, even though they had yet to reach the peak of their military prowess. Still, the Messenian troops had spent all those years sharpening their swords and skills for battle. They actually stood a chance against the stubborn invaders.

In 739 BCE, an elite Messenian army marched out of the capital in the name of King Euphaes. They headed toward the Spartan-occupied Ampheia.

A few miles away from their destination, the Messenians set up camp. King Euphaes's superior warfare tactics were instrumental in the successful attack of Spartan troops that ambushed them while they crossed into the mountains of Ithome.

Would this small victory change the course of the war? Time would tell.

King Euphaes, who was advanced in years, gave Cleonnis command of the Messenian troops. Sparta's King Alcmenes would die around the same time, and his son, Polydorus, took the throne.

One historic day, the Messenians went into battle against the Spartans on the lowlands of Taygetus, which was somewhere near Ampheia.

Pausanias thinks that the military strategies and battle formations of the Spartans were more organized than those of the Messenians. The Spartans used a formation called the phalanx, which was a rectangular formation consisting of heavy infantry who used spears and other similar weapons and shields.

An illustration of what a phalanx formation would look like.

The Messenians charged, with little regard for formation, but they could not break the Spartan lines or conquer them on their first attempt. Or the second. Or the third—or the many attempts that followed after.

It seemed as if the Spartans were impenetrable.

Eventually, the Messenians retreated, seeking refuge in the natural fortress of Mount Ithome. They knew they were losing the war, so they turned to the gods for aid. They consulted with the revered Oracle of Delphi, who revealed that a royal virgin must be sacrificed to assure their triumph over their enemy.

Aristodemus, a Messenian war hero, stepped forward to sacrifice his virgin daughter. The royal sacrifice supposedly kept the Spartan forces at bay for several more years.

Upon hearing the word of the Oracle of Delphi, the Spartans suspended their incursion into Messenia. Eventually, though, they became restless and continued on. The Spartans marched on Messenia once again and managed to kill their king. Aristodemus was crowned as the new ruler.

The Spartans were so merciless that Aristodemus, overwhelmed with shame and humiliation, took his life at his daughter's grave, and the vanquished Messenians either were plunged into slavery or found some way to flee.

The Second Messenian War (c. 684 BCE–650 BCE)

As you might already know, a distinct feature of ancient societies was human inequality. Not every man or woman was born free or remained free. War determined the fate of almost everyone, from freeborn to slave to royalty.

After the First Messenian War, the vanquished Messenians were to witness a fall in their social status under the new overlordship of the Spartans. They would go from being freeborn citizens to helots.

A few classical records suggest that the first helots in history were Spartan-colonized Laconians in the Peloponnese and that they were soon joined by the captured people of Messenia.

Now that the Messenians were under Spartan rule, the Messenian helots were barely better than slaves. However, unlike slaves, helots were not an individual's property. They were owned by the state, and each helot was assigned to a household for duties ranging from domestic and administrative to economic and military purposes. During the war, helots served the Spartans as fighters and rowers on warships.

However, even if the helots proved outstanding on the battlefield, attaining their freedom was rare. On some occasions, a helot could buy their freedom, but that did not happen often. Helots were free to have their own families and practice their religion, but this wasn't enough for the Messenians, who yearned for their freedom.

Since the Spartans were very involved with their military efforts, the men of Sparta were away from home quite a bit, proving their worth on the battlefield in their quest to expand Sparta. A result of this was fewer Spartan births than those of the Messenian helot population.

Subsequently, the Spartans could not ignore the idea that the more helots there were, the higher the chances of a rebellion.

Preemptively, the Spartan elected leaders known as the ephors used brutal means to keep the helots in check, such as routine massacres to "trim" the population. They especially targeted those helots who attempted to challenge Spartan authority.

In Greek author Myron of Priene's historical account, he describes the plight of the repressed Messenian helots:

> "They assign to the Helots every shameful task leading to disgrace. For they ordained that each one of them must wear a dogskin cap and wrap himself in skins and receive a stipulated number of beatings every year regardless of any wrongdoing so that they would never forget that they were slaves. Moreover, if any exceeded the vigor proper to a slave's condition, they made death the penalty, and they allotted a punishment to those controlling them if they failed."

For forty years, the Messenian helots endured hardship under Spartan rule—until one day Sparta's biggest fear finally reared its ugly head.

The Battle of Deres and a Messenian Hero

The helots had had enough of being ill-treated by the Spartans. They largely outnumbered their overlords, and according to Xenophon of Athens, they hated their masters so much that they would gladly eat their flesh.

Hatred and malice led to unorganized riots and increased attempts at escaping captivity. When the Messenians' rebellious cause found a champion in a man named Aristomenes, a new war was under way.

Aware that their fears had finally materialized, the Spartans moved to quell the helot revolt with the Battle of Deres in 684 BCE. The battle ended without a clear winner, but the Messenians had made their defiance of Spartan rule known.

Encouraged by the outcome of their first battle, the Messenians offered the crown to their leader, Aristomenes. He was a descendant of the royal house of Aepytus, the former king of Messenia. Apparently, he refused the crown but took the title of commander-in-chief.

Soon, the news of the Messenian revolt spread to Arcadia and Argos, which allowed them to make allies with the repressed peoples there—they were all united against Sparta.

The Battle of the Boar's Grave

Aristomenes took command of the Messenian troops. During the reign of Kings Anaxander and Anaxidamus of Sparta, Aristomenes lured the Spartan troops into an ambush at a place called Boar's Grave, which was located in Messenia's capital.

The Spartan army, which had troops from Corinth and Lepreum, as well as mercenaries from Crete, pursued the Messenians but only found defeat at Boar's Grave.

Legend has it that the victory of Aristomenes and his men had been predicted by a Messenian seer by the name of Theoclus. To be assured of victory, Aristomenes was warned that he could not go past a pear tree in the plain where they battled the Spartans.

The oracle's warning stood the test of time as a slight breach of it nearly cost the Messenians their victory. In the euphoria of their success, Aristomenes and his men raided small parts of Laconia and terrorized the Spartans as they advanced.

Aristomenes fought ruthlessly on the battlefield, singlehandedly decimating the enemy's army. The Messenians spoke of him as the scourge of the Spartans.

The Battle of the Great Trench

The fires of war between the protesting Messenian helots and their Spartan masters who sought to subdue them raged on for many years. The Messenians, led by Aristomenes, were unrelenting in their quest for freedom, but their determination found a match in the Spartans, who were valiant men of war and masters of strategy.

The Battle of the Great Trench (also known as the Battle of the Great Foss) saw an assembly of allies for Messenia, including the Arcadians, who were led by their shifty king, Aristocrates.

Unknown to the poor helots, Aristocrates had been bribed by the Spartans to pull out his troops mid-battle. The Messenians were shocked at the Arcadians' sudden retreat. Aristocrates would later pay with his life for his betrayal, but the deed was done. The Spartans took advantage of their confusion. They raged against the puzzled Messenians, chasing Aristomenes and his men into the mountains.

Mount Eira was a haven for the Messenians, but it wasn't home. Aristomenes and what was left of his troops stayed in a city there, occasionally raiding small towns under Spartan dominion. One day in the latter years of the war, Aristomenes was captured by the Spartans. He was to be killed as an example to anyone who dared defy Sparta's rule.

However, it seems that fate had other plans. With the help of a Messenian servant girl in Sparta, Aristomenes escaped captivity and returned to Eira. He was received with much jubilation, and for eleven years, Messenians, whether they were men, women, or children, rallied against Sparta.

The day of the final onslaught approached, and there would be neither a retreat nor concession from Sparta. They invaded Mount Eira, as they had done to Mount Ithome during the First Messenian War, and once again defeated the Messenians.

Prior to this final campaign, the Spartans sought direction from the Oracle of Delphi and were told to appoint a general from Athens. A martial songwriter and poet named Tyrtaeus was appointed to bring the Spartan troops a victory. He reminded the Spartans that they fought for their country and families and that this was essentially a fight to the death.

Invigorated, the Spartans ravaged Mount Eira, and many Messenian rebels were captured. As for their champion,

Aristomenes, legend tells that he was snatched out of harm's way by the gods. In the end, Aristomenes found refuge in a city in Rhodes, Ialysos, where he lived out the rest of his days.

Similar to the aftermath of the First Messenian War, attempts of another Messenian uprising were crushed. The Messenians were brought to their knees before the Spartans' supremacy and once again assumed their status of being helots.

Sparta reemerged as the most powerful political and militaristic Greek state in the Peloponnese. However, her power would soon be tested again by a formidable enemy.

Chapter 4 – The Peloponnesian League

Foundations

With their rebellious adversaries brought to heel, the 6th-century Spartans realized more than ever the importance of consolidating their political and military power. The helot uprising was all but a taste of the woes to befall Sparta if she failed to rise to the challenge.

Argos and Arcadia, Sparta's neighbors, eventually began to pose a considerable threat to Sparta's supremacy. It was a problem that called for urgent action. Sparta was also in need of more land and resources for its growing city-state.

It was time to invade Arcadia once more.

Herodotus recounts that prior to their campaign against Arcadia, the Spartans had been assured of its victory over many parts of the region by the Oracle of Delphi. Unfortunately, the Spartans had misinterpreted the Oracle's message. Tegea, an Arcadian province, was not part of the regions of Arcadia that the Oracle had spoken of. Ignorantly, Sparta marched on Tegea around 550 BCE, taking fetters to bind the Arcadians once they were defeated. The doomed Arcadians would join the Messenians in helotage, and the news of Sparta's might would spread to the rest of her enemies in the Peloponnese.

In an epic twist, the warriors of Sparta were met with a crushing defeat at the hands of the Arcadians and were bound with the same fetters they had brought with them. For several centuries, the Spartans' fetters were on display at the Temple of Athena in Tegea.

This was a big lesson for Sparta. Not all of Arcadia was going to be easily conquered. Perhaps it was time to give up the old ways of exerting Spartan influence in the Peloponnesian Peninsula and explore new methods.

The battle between Sparta and Tegea—the Battle of the Fetters—was the beginning of a historic pact between the victor and the vanquished. Tegea could not risk another campaign against Sparta since they had just barely won the Battle of the Fetters. Also, since Sparta was undoubtedly the emerging giant of Greece, it was best to remain on her good side for protection from aggressive Argos. These sentiments were shared by the people of Corinth and Elis.

Greece would soon enter an era of political divide: on one side, there was Sparta, and on the other side was Argos.

The scramble for domination of the Peloponnese continued, sometimes exploding in small wars. But once Tegea joined the Spartan bloc, it gave Sparta an edge over Argos, at least according to Herodotus.

Sparta saw a rare opportunity to unify its allies under a confederation. It would be a league of city-states unlike any before it.

The Peloponnesian League

Friend or Foe?

"The league was founded so that Sparta might protect itself against both a possible uprising of Sparta's helots and regional rival Argos."

These words of Thucydides in his work titled *History of the Peloponnesian War* summarize the reasons for the formation of the Peloponnesian League.

Indeed, the formation of the league cemented the plight of the Messenian helots. Their prospective allies were now aligned with Sparta, and the Argives were no better than the Spartans; they might have been even worse.

With more city-states flocking to Sparta's side, Argos knew that its days as one of the top dogs were numbered.

Around 519 BCE, King Cleomenes I ascended the throne of Sparta. His brilliant policies finally displaced Argos, leaving Sparta as the undisputed master of the Peloponnese. Sparta's allies—Elis, Corinth, Tegea, Kythira, Mantinea, Pylos, Melos, Boeotia, Lefkada, Ambracia, and Epidaurus—became pioneers of the Peloponnesian League.

Despite being defeated by the Spartans in battle, Argos refused to be a part of the Peloponnesian League. Sparta did not push it; all that mattered was that the Argives were no longer a threat.

Historians mutually agree on the uniqueness of the Spartan-led Peloponnesian League. It was not a "league" in the actual sense of the word any more than it was purely "Peloponnesian." Collectively, the ancient Greeks referred to the league as the Lacedaemonians (Spartans) and their allies, inferring that the league centered around Sparta.

This wasn't far from the truth, considering that Sparta was not obliged to reciprocate its loyalty to its allies. On the other hand, members of the league swore allegiance to Sparta in return for protection. They were not required to pay tribute but were tasked with offering military contingents to Sparta in times of war. This army could be commanded by either one of the two Spartan kings or a Spartan general.

More interestingly, this military obligation was not strictly binding to high-standing members of the league like Corinth. As a matter of fact, the Corinthians enjoyed more freedom than any other member of the Peloponnesian League. This was because of their vast military reserves and repute as a wealthy city-state.

The Spartans were aware of the resources at Corinth's disposal, as well as the importance of keeping the Corinthians close. This very likely accounts for why Sparta took no notice of Corinth waging war against a fellow league member, Mantinea, as recorded by Thucydides.

Despite their political and social duties to Sparta, the members of the Peloponnesian League could run religious affairs without any interference.

Another distinct feature of the Peloponnesian League was its atypical legislative body, although meetings held between Sparta and other members of the league were rare. Only Sparta reserved the authority to call for this congress, and the Spartans were the ones who presided over it. The league members could send representatives to attend it.

This congress, known as the Congress of the League, made decisions based on a voting system. Each state had one vote; however, the votes were not the ultimate deciding factor—Sparta's resolution was.

History further implies that rather than exert this authority blatantly and render the votes useless, the Spartans would influence some members of the league, typically the small city-states, to vote in their favor on matters. In the unlikely event that the majority vote differed from what Sparta wanted, Sparta was not compelled to follow the congress's decision.

The Peloponnesian League would prosper since all of its members stayed true to their oath of allegiance and loyalty, but what about Sparta, which swore neither?

The decline of the Peloponnesian League (traced to the 4th century BCE) would take a long time. Sparta was a menacing enemy, and breaking away from the league was tantamount to declaring war—it was a path that had to be treaded with caution, if at all.

Most historians agree that the Peloponnesian League outlived the Peloponnesian War, but when Athens, which was forced to join the expanded league (known as the Hellenic League), began to rebel against Spartan hegemony, the wall of solidarity cracked.

The Peloponnesian League would face the Athens-led Delian League in a series of wars called the Peloponnesian War.

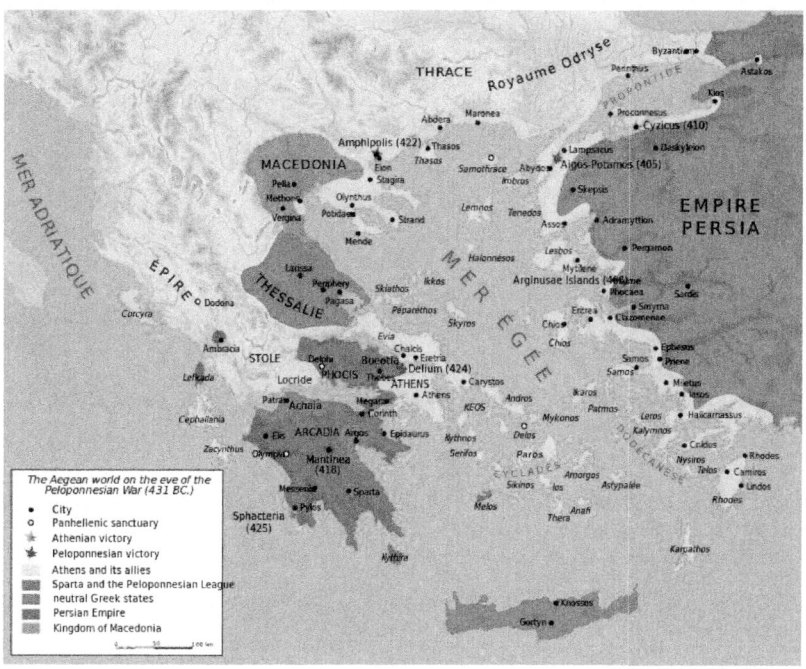

A map of the Peloponnesian League during the Peloponnesian War.
(Credit: https://en.wikipedia.org/wiki/Peloponnesian_League#/media /File:Map_Peloponnesian_War_431_BC-en.svg)

But before this happened, the whole of Greece would be consumed with fighting an army of foreigners from ancient Iran.

Part Two: Sparta and the Greco-Persian Wars (499 BCE–449 BCE)

Chapter 5 – The Hellenic Alliance

Sparta's Choice

The term "Hellenic Alliance" is used to describe the coalition of city-states in Greece against the Persian invaders during the Greco-Persian Wars, which rocked 5th-century Greece.

You will find that this alliance was fleeting, but it proved that all of Greece could be united for a common cause after all. The events leading up to these conflicts are intricate yet incredibly fascinating. At the center of it all was Sparta, whose actions and inactions would shape the new century's history for good.

By 500 BCE, there was no question of Sparta's fame and might. A tiny Laconian kingdom founded by the legendary King Lelex had become a fierce Greek city-state through wars, conquests, and diplomacy. The proud Spartans would speak highly of their motherland to their children, passing on their strength and dedication to preserve Sparta's good fortune.

In history, the forging of an empire (or, in this case, city-state) is never glorious at its inception, as it takes years of expansion to make a power seem mighty. However, with expansion comes additional challenges, like keeping the people in faraway territories happy. The Spartans were a people of war and tact, though. They saw the Peloponnesian League as a powerful weapon that, if finely wielded, could keep the member city-states in Greece and beyond under Spartan control. As such, internal conflicts were inevitable, but none could overcome Sparta or displace her as a superpower in the Peloponnese.

Another significant accessory to Sparta's hold on power was the people's knowledge of which battles were theirs to fight. Despite demanding and receiving the allegiance of their ally states to fight for Sparta and "inherit" all her enemies, the Spartans were under no such oath to any of their allies in return. This was a perk for being the most powerful city-state in the Peloponnese. Sparta would only go to war if it aligned with her interests.

The first major conflict that Sparta would not become involved in was the Ionian revolt, which broke out at the dawn of the 5th century BCE.

The Ionian Revolt

The Ionians, like the Dorians of Sparta, were a major ethnic division in classical Greece. While the Dorians seized power in Sparta and extended it to other city-states in the Peloponnesian Peninsula, the Ionians were subjugated by the Persians around 540 BCE.

During the reign of King Cyrus the Great, the Ionian regions of Greece were forced to become part of the Persian Empire (also known as the Achaemenid Empire). The Persians, a culturally sophisticated people, were working on building the largest empire in the world. After conquering Ionia and other parts of Asia Minor, the Persians began to hear of the famous Spartans and wanted the growing city-state for themselves.

The power-hungry Persians may never have found their perfect pretext to butt heads with the Spartans and invade their land were it not for the choices of Sparta's sister state, Athens.

To tell the story properly, we have to go back in time a bit. The Greek Dark Ages that followed the Dorian invasion saw the mass migration of Ionians to some coastal cities of Caria and Lydia. These settlers founded twelve Ionian cities and sought to live out their lives independent of foreign control.

These city-states made a pact with each other, but their independence would not last forever. In 560 BCE, King Croesus of Lydia invaded and conquered the Ionian cities to extend his power. However, this victory would be snatched out of his hands by King Cyrus the Great at the Battle of Thymbra, which happened around 547 BCE.

After the capture of the Lydian capital, Sardis, the other Ionian cities fell one by one, becoming part of the Persian regime. The Persians were ruthless and unforgiving, but this was mainly because there was no elite group that would ally with the Persians to help them rule the Greek city-states. The Ionians had refused to stand with Cyrus the Great against the Lydians during the Battle of Thymbra, and as punishment, the Ionians would suffer being ruled under Persia's terms.

Tyrants were appointed by the Persians—one in every Ionian city to enforce Persian rule. These tyrants were Ionian, but they were loyal only to the Persian Empire and were hated by their kinsmen for it.

One of these tyrants led to the Ionian revolt. Around thirty years later, during the reign of King Darius the Great, a certain Ionian tyrant named Aristagoras was placed in charge of Miletus. He wanted to make his position more secure and prove his allegiance to Persia, but his plan backfired. To save his skin, he incited a revolt against the Persian authorities. Herodotus emphasizes that this act was a means to shield himself from the consequences of his failed campaign, as he had promised he would help expand the Persian Empire but failed to follow through. Fortunately for Aristagoras, the Ionians had harbored bitterness against their Persian overlords for so long that he didn't have to do much to provoke an insurrection.

In an act of war, Aristagoras cunningly gathered his kinsmen, announced he was stepping down as tyrant, and declared Miletus an independent democratic state. Aristagoras was well aware that Miletus lacked the military and financial resources for a battle against the Persians, but he stoked the flames anyway.

It is thought the revolution spread throughout all of the Ionian city-states. Knowing war was imminent, Aristagoras defied the harsh winter and set sail across the Aegean to seek help from a worthy opponent: Sparta.

The year was 499 BCE, and King Cleomenes I was a very hospitable host. He received Aristagoras and heard his appeal. Sparta and her allies in the Peloponnesian League could match the wrath of the Persians, but it wasn't the first time that King Cleomenes had heard such calls for help. Barely two decades earlier, King Maendrius of Samos, another Ionian city, came to solicit Sparta's aid in warding off the Persians.

King Cleomenes I knew that what affected Ionia did not affect Sparta, at least not directly. And if the Persians came to the Peloponnese, the city-states there would come together to fight them off. Thus, his reply was the same as the one he'd given the king of Samos: No. Sparta would have no part in the Ionian Revolt.

Aristagoras knew his revolt would be doomed if he sailed back home without a powerful ally, but King Cleomenes had his mind made up. Worse still, his decision had been supported by the Spartan ephors. Aristagoras stood no chance of convincing the Spartans, so he turned to the Athenians, who were already in a soured political relationship with the Persians. Aristagoras was better received there, and because his kingdom, Miletus, had identified as a democratic state (just like Athens was), the Athenians were moved to support the revolt.

The people of Eretria came on board soon after for two reasons. First, they had long perceived Persia to be an obstacle to Eretria's control of the trade routes in the Aegean. Joining forces with the Ionians could boost the chances of a successful revolt, ridding the Eritreans of the problematic Persians once and for all. Another reason highlighted by Herodotus was that Eritrea owed favors of allegiance to Athens and Miletus because both states had helped Eretria in past war endeavors.

Having succeeded in his quest, Aristagoras could confidently sail home and prepare for war. As agreed, Athens and Eretria rose to the occasion and offered naval aid to the Ionians' cause. In a grand gesture, Athens provided a fleet of twenty ships, while Eretria provided five.

However, the war against Persia would end in defeat, and it would have rippling consequences not just for Athens but also for all of Greece. It remains uncertain if the outcome would have been different if Aristagoras had won the support of Sparta on that winter's day.

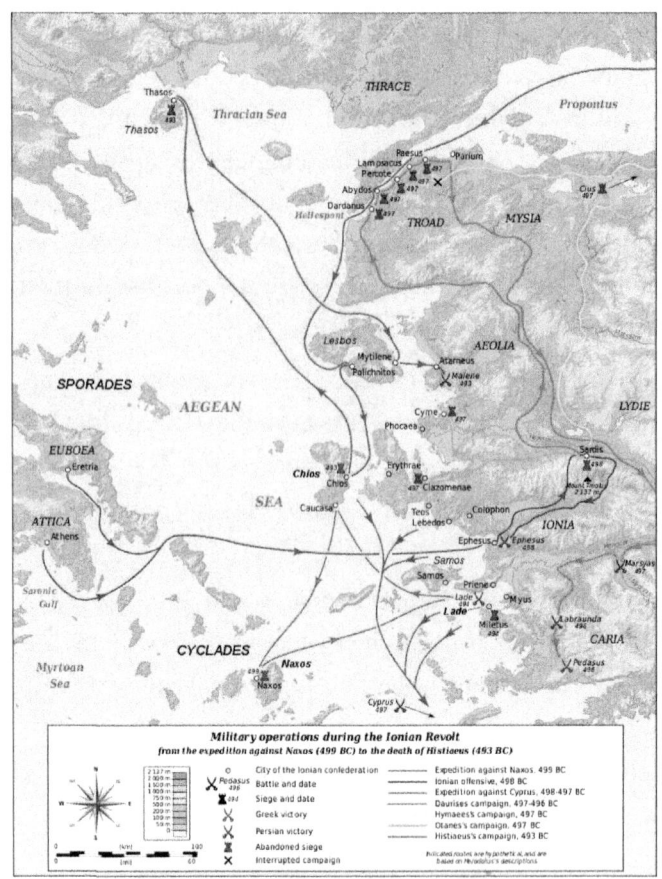

A map of the Ionian revolt.
*(Credit: https://en.wikipedia.org/wiki/File:Ionian_Revolt_*
Campaign_Map-en.svg)

The Battle of Marathon

You have heard of "marathon" as a word used to describe a long-distance race, one that is typically over twenty miles. But do you know its origin?

Simply put, Marathon was the historic scene of the decisive bout of the First Greco-Persian War.

When the Ionian revolt failed, King Darius of Persia had finally secured his long-sought-after justification to attack Greece. He masked the Persian invasion as revenge for the support that Athens had lent to Miletus during the Ionian revolt. Supposedly, he ordered his servants to remind him every night at dinner to think about the Athenians. This would keep his ambition burning until he would go to war with Greece.

A successful venture into Athens and the rest of Greece required a traitorous gatekeeper who would hand the Persians the keys to the city. The Persians found this in Hippias, a former Athenian tyrant who had been dethroned and exiled. Hippias had run away to Persia, where he was welcomed.

Evidently, Hippias was still malicious toward his countrymen and the Spartans, who had invaded Athens in 510 and drove him out. What better way to get revenge on them than by holding hands with the Persian invaders as they watched Greece burn?

The "key" to the city of Athens given by Hippias was his counsel on how best to penetrate the city. King Darius of Persia would use Hippias's grievances to expand his great empire. In 492 BCE, the Persian force, led by Darius's son-in-law, Mardonius, re-subjugated Thrace (southeastern Europe) and Macedonia.

The following year, Darius tried a more diplomatic approach. Although most city-states gave into the Persian demands, Athens refused, going as far as killing the diplomats. Sparta, in the meantime, had internal crises, which led to Cleomenes being killed. He was succeeded by Leonidas, his half-brother.

Darius realized this was the perfect time to take his vengeance on Athens and Eretria. On their way, the Persians attacked city-states that had not yet submitted. In 490, Eretria fell.

This led to the first major battle of the Greco-Persian Wars, and it would be the one that would end this first invasion. The Persians sailed down the coast of Attica and landed at Marathon, which was about twenty-five miles from the city of Athens.

Miltiades, an Athenian general, stepped up to the challenge of stopping the encroaching Persians from reaching the city. He had led expeditions against the Persians in the past and learned a few tricks. However, the Athenians knew that their chances would be much better if they could find people who were experienced on the battlefield. They knew they needed the Spartans.

Miltiades and his people had to get a message to Sparta to request reinforcements as soon as possible. They could only stall the Persian troops for a short time since the Persians outnumbered them almost two to one. A long-distance runner named Pheidippides was sent on a 150-mile run from Athens to Sparta. It would take him two days to do it.

This act begs a few questions in contemporary discussions. Why did they only send one man? Why didn't the Athenians send a group of horsemen? It seems rather foolish to send only one man on foot to Sparta, doesn't it?

First, no horse in Athens could endure the two-day journey to Sparta. Greece was (and still is) one of the most mountainous regions in Europe. The grounds had nothing for the horses to feed on, and with a mission this urgent, the horses would need that extra endurance.

Second was the problem of trust. Sending multiple messengers with such a sensitive message would do the Athenians no good, considering that bribery and treachery were common at the time. Since Miltiades had gone to battle with the Persians in the past, he knew that they were capable of buying untrustworthy men.

Ancient Greek athletes were known for their unique diet: olives, dried meat, figs, and a small plant called sea buckthorn. These were believed to boost stamina and endurance. Pheidippides must have taken more than a handful for his special journey.

For two days, he raced to Sparta.

A modern drawing of Pheidippides en route to Sparta.

Upon his arrival in Sparta sometime in the early fall, Pheidippides found the Spartans enjoying a feast in honor of the god Apollo Karneios. It was Carneia, a traditional Peloponnesian festival. The Spartan men and women were hardly in the mood for war. Besides, it was the law that Sparta could not wage war during Carneia until the next full moon.

The Spartans had to send Pheidippides away with the same answer they gave Aristagoras: No. Sparta would yet again take a neutral stance and not participate in the Battle of Marathon.

Pheidippides would run back to Athens. Then, he would run to the battlefield at Marathon, where he would witness the outcome of the battle. He then ran back to Athens, where he supposedly died of exhaustion. Of course, this story is questioned today because it has an overly romantic quality. But regardless, our modern-day marathon stems from the distance he ran from Athens to Marathon.

The Athenians were disconcerted when they received the news of Sparta's refusal to join them in battle. Other historical accounts suggest that it wasn't an outright refusal. Instead, the Spartans promised that they would come later after their festivities, which means they would not arrive for another ten days. Regardless, it seemed as if the odds, more than ever, were in favor of the Persians.

One day, Athenian sentries saw a huge cloud of dust coming from the north. The Persians were coming to destroy them. Alarmed, the Athenian troops gathered, armed and ready to defend their motherland to the death.

Surprisingly, the incoming men were not Persians. They were troops from Plataea, another Greek city-state, and they had come to fight to protect Greece. Plataea had sent one thousand men, and they were welcomed with gratitude by the Athenians.

The Plataeans had come when they were most needed, and Athens would be eternally in their debt. However, the Persians still outnumbered the Greeks at least two to one. King Darius had infantry and cavalry forces that were so vast that it bordered on impossible that the Greeks could win.

The first five days of the war ended in a stalemate. Neither the Greeks nor the Persians were prepared to sacrifice their men just yet.

In time, Miltiades took the lead, and the Greeks launched a ruthless offensive against the unsuspecting Persians while their cavalry was away from the battlefield. This audacious affront dazed the Persians, and in the time that it took them to form ranks, the Greeks had entrapped them on both flanks.

The scantily armored Persians suffered a great onslaught and were forced to retreat. Thousands of Persians died that day, while the Greeks lost only around two hundred. This victory, despite the non-involvement of Sparta, was a sign that overcoming the Persians was a possibility.

The triumphant Greeks were invigorated, and they returned home to strategize. They knew the Persians would return and more furiously than the last time. It became imperative that the Greeks set aside their differences and unite.

The Meeting on an Isthmus

An isthmus is a narrow strip of land bordered by water on both sides; it is a common geographical feature in Greece. There was one near the prosperous city of Corinth. The Isthmus of Corinth was home to a famous moment in Greek history, for King Leonidas of Sparta believed it to be the perfect place for a meeting.

That year, 481 BCE, a second Persian invasion was on the horizon, and the Greeks wanted to be assured of their victory.

Invitations went out from the gates of Sparta to all the city-states in Greece. There was to be a meeting at the Isthmus of Corinth in springtime to discuss pressing affairs.

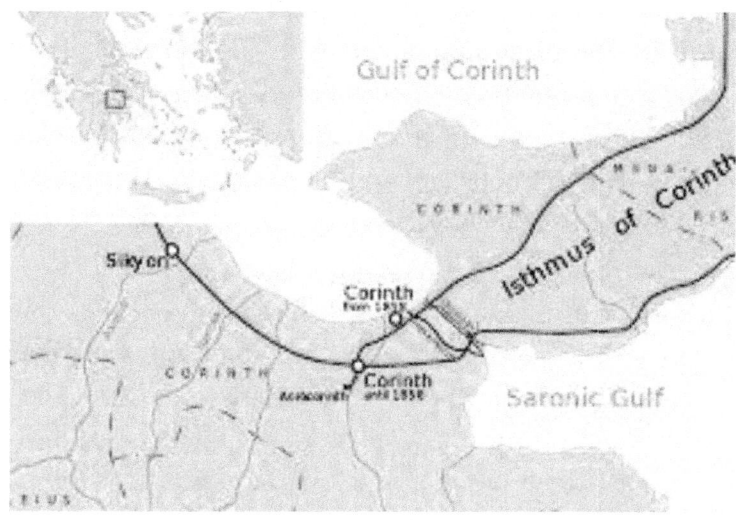

Location of the Isthmus of Corinth.

Out of about seven hundred Greek city-states, only seventy attended the congress presided over by Sparta. The matter at hand was obvious: how to rid Greece of the Persians for good.

It was mutually agreed that Sparta would take command of the troops and fleets of Greece; however, in a gathering of such prominent city-states, a power play was inevitable. Athens was the first to have a swing at it. The Athenians could not simply agree to leave the control of all the armies of Greece in the hands of the

Spartans alone. They wanted an equal share of command; after all, Athens was as famous as Sparta.

This raised some arguments during the congress, but subsequently, Athens, which was represented by a brilliant politician and war strategist named Themistocles, agreed to submit to the command of Sparta. Themistocles's decision, though initially criticized by Athenian council members, was eventually accepted. It was necessary at the moment. Athens also agreed to suspend the ongoing conflict over maritime domination with its neighbor Aegina.

King Gelon of Syracuse and Gela declared his support by offering his massive fleet of ships and thousands of men in exchange for the highest command of Greece's troops. It was an offer so ridiculous that some Greek historical accounts imply that it was made on purpose. Apparently, King Gelon was aware that he would be rebuffed, but he wished to use it to justify his withdrawal from the Greek alliance to focus on the Carthaginians ravaging his country.

Other consensuses were reached during the congress, but the Greeks in attendance could not help but notice the absence of the other states, namely Thebes. All hands had to be on deck to achieve the goal of a truly united front against Persia. On top of this, there was always the chance that those absent city-states might join the Persians. For instance, Argos ended up siding with Persia. And some city-states refused to join the war, like Crete.

Nevertheless, a large group of city-states gathered together. This group became known as the Hellenic League. This league would represent Greece in a legendary battle against the Persians.

Chapter 6 – The Battle of Thermopylae

The Antecedent

Thermopylae has an important spot in Greek history as the theater for an epic battle against the Persians. Thermopylae, a narrow, mountainous pass on the east coast of central Greece, has many aliases, the most common of which is "the hot gates" or "the gates of fire." These names came about because of Thermopylae's hot sulfur springs.

Many explanations exist for the "hotness" of the waters at Thermopylae. Some Greek traditions assert that it's because the pass was one of the many portals to Hades, the underworld in Greek mythology. Another tradition states that during the Labors of Heracles (or the Romanized Hercules), Heracles bathed in the waters of Thermopylae to cleanse himself from the poison of a serpent monster named Hydra. This bath left the coastal waters of Thermopylae hot.

The hot springs of Thermopylae.
(Credit: Fkreasar; Wikimedia Commons)

Although neither account is logically accurate, what does it matter? It does not take away the importance of Thermopylae as a strategic location and the most brilliant place to tackle the Persians.

To recap the events that had already occurred, in 491 BCE, King Darius I of Persia sent envoys to Greece to demand their submission to Persian authority. Sparta would make an example of King Darius's messengers and toss his envoys into a well, where they met their death. Athens responded similarly and had the Persian envoys executed. Any city-state that defied Persia knew that they were essentially declaring war.

The Persians raided parts of Greece in 490 BCE, destroying Eretria. This was followed by the Battle of Marathon, in which Athens led the Greeks to victory. The Persians returned home after their defeat at Marathon, and it would take the rest of King Darius's life (four years) to prepare for another invasion.

He would never take on Greece again. Rather, his son, Xerxes, took the Persian throne and continued his father's legacy of making all of Greece bow to Persian supremacy.

As King Xerxes was about to find out, though, he was up against a formidable enemy.

By Sea and Land

War was nearly here, and the Greeks had never heard of an army so great.

The size of Xerxes's army has been speculated as having between a hundred thousand and three million men—a testament to the vastness of the Persian Empire. It seems likely that the Persians brought somewhere between 200,000 and 500,000, which is still a formidable force. It is thought that the Greeks only had around 150,000 men during this second Persian invasion.

After watching his father suffer humiliation at the hands of the proud Greeks at Marathon, Xerxes must have been resolved to spare no man or ship in his quest to seize their land. The Persians would attack Greece by land and sea simultaneously, and they would not stop until every single Greek city-state became Persian vassals. Xerxes expected that the Greeks, upon hearing of the might of his army, would tremble at their impending doom and surrender. In fact, in 481, he sent envoys to Greek city-states to see if they would pay tribute; Athens and Sparta were excluded.

Meanwhile, back in Greece, the Hellenic League had been formed, and Athenian General Themistocles had offered a brilliant war plan. The allies of united Greece would split into two: half to face the Persians at sea and the other half on land.

Themistocles would lead the naval campaign, commanding an allied Greek fleet of 271 warships against Xerxes's 1,200-ship armada on the cape of Artemisium. This would prevent the Persians from passing Thermopylae via the sea.

At the same time, the Greeks would be blocking the pass of Thermopylae, which was the only way for the Persians to reach southern Greece (the Peloponnese). King Leonidas of Sparta took the charge here.

The Greeks knew the Persians had the numerical advantage. However, Persia was bringing the war to Greek soil, meaning that the Greeks held the geographical advantage. Greece's terrain could be weaponized against the Persians and their huge numbers, and there was no better place to make it happen than the pass of Thermopylae.

The Persian numbers would mean nothing if they could be lured into the narrow pass. Only a handful of soldiers would go in at a time, giving the Greeks some leverage.

The Persians advanced slowly from the north. But there was a problem. The Spartans were again celebrating Carneia, which means the Spartans couldn't fight. The Olympic Games were also taking place, during which military activity was forbidden. This military ban was known as the Olympic truce, and it was designed to protect traveling athletes and spectators from attack.

However, this time, even the ephors agreed that Sparta could not sit idly by and watch Xerxes reduce Greece to ruins.

In reverence to the Olympic truce and Carneia, King Leonidas decided to take only three hundred men—the finest soldiers in all of Sparta. Along the way, they would try to recruit other Greeks to join them.

Three hundred men against Xerxes's hundreds of thousands of soldiers seems like insane odds. It was a suicide mission, but for the Spartans, there was no greater glory than dying in defense of Greece.

Also, the three hundred Spartans were convinced that they could stall the Persians long enough for the festivities at home to be over and reinforcements join them. They also thought it was possible for Xerxes to run out of supplies for his men.

On the road to Thermopylae, the valiant Spartans were joined by 6,700 patriotic Greeks. The Spartans' spirits were lifted at their increasing chances of victory. Together, the united Greeks made for Thermopylae. The errant Persians were going to get what was coming to them.

A Glorious Defeat

Sometime in mid-480 BCE, the troops of united Greece arrived at the pass of Thermopylae and awaited the Persians. King Leonidas and his seven thousand men fortified themselves, making camp at the "middle gate," the narrowest part of the pass. When Leonidas heard that there was another path that went around Thermopylae, he sent some forces there but kept the bulk of his men at Thermopylae.

Finally, on a fine August morning, the Greeks saw the Persians. Some Greeks argued that they should retreat and head to the Isthmus of Corinth. Leonidas shot those ideas down.

Xerxes sent a Persian to the Greeks, but he was not a soldier. He was an emissary with a written note from Xerxes himself. Its content was similar to King Darius's message to the Greeks a decade earlier: "Hand over your arms."

Leonidas and his battle-ready men must have laughed at this. The Spartan king's legendary reply was just as brief: "Come and take them."

Herodotus records that the wrath of Xerxes was unleashed four days after, signaling the start of a battle for the ages.

Archers and Immortals

Xerxes's army had soldiers from every part of his empire, including India, Egypt, Media, Elam, Libya, Cappadocia, Macedonia, Thrace, Ethiopia, and the Arabian Peninsula. This afforded him the luxury of sending army contingents one at a time to battle the smaller Greek troops.

In his first offense, Xerxes ordered an army of five thousand Persian archers to rain arrows on the Greeks. The Greeks were hardly scathed, thanks to their bronze helmets and aspides (large shields made from wood and coated with bronze).

There would not be another attempt at shooting arrows. Instead, Xerxes ordered a full-force attack, sending waves of ten thousand men to destroy the Greeks.

Leonidas swiftly moved to counter, ordering his men to their signature formation, the legendary Greek phalanx. With their raised, overlapping shields and their sharpened spears sticking out from beside each shield, the Greeks battled the Persian troops, whose spears and shields were no match. The narrowness of the path greatly aided the Greeks, as they didn't have to commit all of their men at once.

A 19ᵗʰ-century depiction of the Battle of Thermopylae by John Steeple Davis.

The Greeks slaughtered the Persians. Xerxes, who was watching from his elevated throne, shook with rage. He supposedly stood up three times due to his outrage.

That same day, the aggrieved king of Persia unleashed his most elite infantry unit, who also doubled as the king's imperial bodyguards: the Immortals. The Immortals were feared throughout the known world as fierce men of battle, and they always stood at ten thousand in number. Any Immortal soldier who was killed, sickly, or wounded had to be immediately replaced to preserve the strength of the infantry, which explains the name "immortals."

The Immortals were skilled in hand-to-hand combat, archery, and the use of their spears. Each Immortal had been taken away from his parents at the age of five and built for a single purpose: to destroy Persia's enemies in battle.

The Greeks must have balked at seeing the Immortals advance. And after a heated battle, the Greeks moved to retreat. The Immortals pursued them farther down the pass; they knew that no Greek would be spared.

Xerxes's victory was finally within reach, and he basked in the euphoria of seeing Leonidas fall—until it all faded into oblivion. All along, the Greeks' retreat was fake; it was just an attempt to lure the Immortals to their doom, and they had fallen for it.

To Xerxes's chagrin, the Immortals could not bring the Greeks to their knees. By the day's end, the Greek lines stood strong.

Do or Die

At the crack of dawn the next day, the soldiers of Persia woke up to a decree from King Xerxes the Great. Any Persian soldier who dared retreat would suffer the penalty of a painful, disgraceful death.

Xerxes quickly proceeded to send a new wave of attacks. He assumed that since the Greeks had spent the day before warding off his endless troops, they would be wounded and/or too tired to endure another round of battle.

But he was wrong. Very wrong.

As the next batch of Persian infantry bore down on them, the Greeks stood at the ready. The harder they fought, the stronger and more invincible they seemed to become. Part of this was due to the fact that the Greeks on the front lines were regularly swapped out, allowing the weary men to rest before jumping back into the battle again.

Xerxes would yet again bear witness to the valor of the men of Greece. Reality must have hit him. The pass of Thermopylae was the Greeks' fortress. As long as they remained there, the size of his army would count for nothing.

However, there was no going back. Who would believe that the great king of Persia had cowered before the lesser numbered Greek men?

The second day ended not very differently from the first. The Persians sounded the retreat, and Xerxes retired to his camp, consumed with desperate anger. The Greeks mourned their few dead and celebrated another day's victory.

That night, the air reeked of the blood of the thousands of Persians who had fallen. But it also smelled of something else.

The Stench of Betrayal

King Xerxes could not sleep. How could he shut his eyes when the Greeks slowly but surely decimated his troops? What manner of men were the Greeks? Every breath that Leonidas of Sparta and his men still drew was an indignity to Xerxes's greatness, and he wouldn't have it.

Later on the second day, the balm to Xerxes's wounded pride walked into his camp. It was a Greek man from Trachis.

His name was Ephialtes, and he was a local shepherd. He requested to be brought before the king of Persia since he had important information that could win the Persians their victory.

Xerxes granted him an immediate audience, and Ephialtes expressed his desire for a big reward in exchange for this vital information. Xerxes was one of the wealthiest kings in the world, and he promised the Greek all the riches he could ever dream of.

Ephialtes revealed that there was a small mountain trail that went around the pass of Thermopylae called the Anopaia Path. If the Persians took this route, they could get behind the defensive line of Leonidas and his men and attack from behind.

Xerxes was pleased by this news and sent a contingent that evening, which was led by one of his finest commanders, Hydarnes the Younger.

King Leonidas had envisaged such a move; this was the path that he had sent men to guard before the battle even began. The Phocians were guarding it, and there were only about one thousand of them. On the morning of the third day, the Persians came upon the Phocians, who fled to a nearby hill to make their stand. However, the Persians had a single aim, and they were not about to be distracted by the Phocians. They sent out a volley of arrows and continued on their way.

When Leonidas received news that Greece had been sold out and that the Persians were quickly advancing, he called a council. As it stood, their defensive line had been rendered useless, and defeat was inevitable.

For his treachery, Ephialtes's name would become synonymous with betrayal. It came to mean "nightmare."

The Last Stand

Leonidas of Sparta is a monumental figure in Greek history, and this is owing to his display of courage and selflessness for his motherland. He had left his kingdom, his Queen Gorgo, and their son, knowing that a glorious victory awaited him in battle—that or a glorious death.

After small victories against the enemy, the actions of one man had suddenly turned the tables against the Greeks. Nonetheless, Leonidas had sworn to protect Greece from destruction. If he ordered all of his men to stand down or retreat, Greece would burn for sure. On the flip side, if he ordered all the Greek soldiers to stand and fight, the Persians would encircle them and have them all killed.

Leonidas had no time to waver on his decision. He had to decide what would be best for Greece and his men. This was why he called the council.

Two historical accounts exist for the events that followed. The first version tells of how many of the Greek allies panicked and fled, leaving Leonidas and the Thespian general Demophilus behind with their men to face the Persians. Another account explains that it was Leonidas who ordered most of the Greek troops to return to their homes. There would be no judgment passed on those who left, but those who remained would fight to the death to stall the Persians.

Regardless of what happened, King Leonidas and his three hundred men stood their ground. There were also nine hundred helots, seven hundred Thespians, and four hundred Thebans (it is thought that most of the Thebans surrendered to the Persians at some point in the battle). Herodotus famously described the Greeks as displaying "the best strength they had against the barbarians, fighting recklessly and desperately."

Leonidas took these men and moved to meet the Persians in battle, this time in a wider part of the pass. In the intensity of the battle, King Leonidas fell to his death.

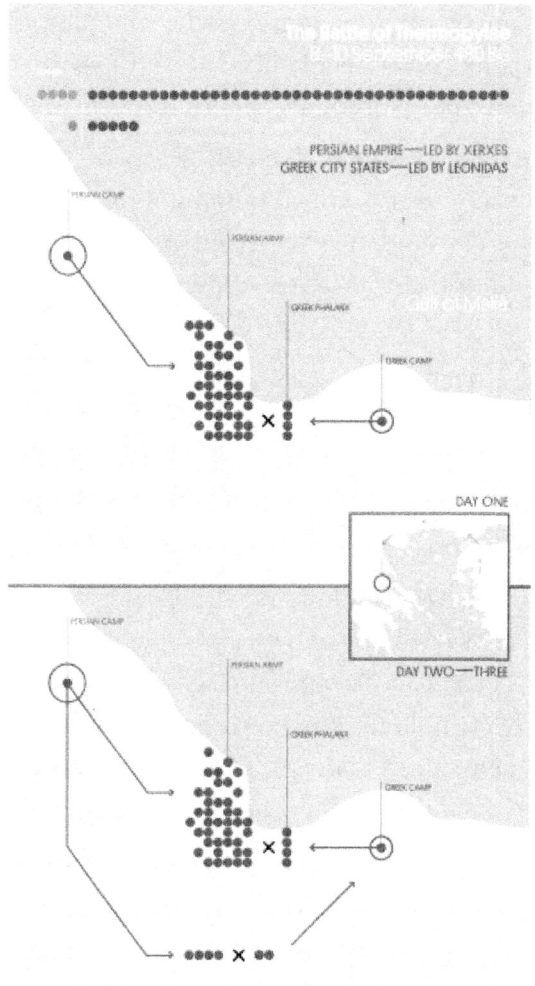

How the battle unfolded.

A Beautiful Death

The Persians teemed in number, closing in on the weary Spartans from every side to seize Leonidas's corpse. The Greeks were able to keep the body with them. The remaining Greeks fled to a nearby hill, but they were not safe there. The Persians surrounded the hill, shooting arrows at the Greeks until they were all dead.

The Persians took Leonidas's body, and a vengeful Xerxes ordered that the corpse be beheaded and put on a stake. His corpse would not be returned to Greece for forty years.

According to Herodotus, Xerxes's victory at Thermopylae had come at the cost of over twenty thousand of his troops. The Greeks most likely lost around two thousand men out of their original seven thousand, with most of these men dying on that final day of battle.

For them, a death in Greece's defense was the greatest honor. This is why you may find the defeat of the Greeks at Thermopylae appraised in history as a conquest in itself. The sacrifice of Leonidas and the brave Greeks, especially the Spartans, would be retold for generations to come.

News reached Artemisium, and the Greeks grieved the loss of their brothers. With Thermopylae breached, there was no point blocking the Persians at Artemisium. On top of this, although the Greeks had been holding their own at Artemisium, the numbers were not on their side. Themistocles commanded the retreat of the Greek navy to Salamis, where fortune awaited the Greeks.

Drunk on his victory, Xerxes saw to the destruction of Thespiae, Plataea, and Athens. In his account, Herodotus describes that the Persians plundered the Temple of Athena, vandalized sacred statues, and razed the Acropolis.

Before the Persians stormed Athens, many Athenians had been evacuated from the city to Salamis with the help of Themistocles and his men. Others escaped capture by a hair's breadth but not for long. Eventually, they were captured and put to death or, worse, put in chains.

Fortunately, the Greeks were able to garrison the Isthmus of Corinth, the birthplace of the Hellenic League and the gateway to the rest of the Peloponnese. With this, the Persians could advance no farther.

Unknown to Xerxes, the Battle of Thermopylae was not the defining event in the Greco-Persian Wars. Only time would tell that victory could be just as fleeting as defeat.

Chapter 7 – The Battle of Plataea

Mardonius of Persia

After Thermopylae, the Hellenic League was torn apart. The Greek allies of Attica, Boeotia, Phocis, and Euboea were conquered and forced to defect to Persia's side. They would battle their fellow Greeks, who were led by Themistocles, in an epic naval conflict called the Battle of Salamis.

Against the appeals of Artemesia, the queen of Halicarnassus, to have the Persian troops stand down, Xerxes followed his trusted general Mardonius's counsel to pursue the Greeks to Salamis. This was partly because the latter's advice was more appealing to Xerxes's ambitions and partly because General Mardonius of Persia was no ordinary man. His father, Gobryas, had been a prominent nobleman in the courts of King Darius. As his father had served King Darius, Mardonius served King Xerxes.

Mardonius had championed the expedition against Greece on the battlefield as a commander, and Xerxes held him in high regard as his counselor, general, and brother-in-law. Together, they had razed a deserted Athens to rubble.

Mardonius was also aware that nothing mattered to the king of Persia more than having the Athenian Themistocles meet the same fate as Leonidas.

At Salamis, however, King Xerxes and his allies were met with a crushing defeat despite having three times more warships than the Greeks. As it turned out, Themistocles's genius war strategies were superior to the menacing Persian armada.

Xerxes had seen enough, and he returned to Asia with most of his men. Apparently, he was worried that the Greeks would move up north toward the Hellespont, where he had erected pontoon bridges that had helped his large army move from Asia to Europe. If the Greeks destroyed these bridges, his troops would be trapped in Europe and decimated by war or starvation.

Since Mardonius had pushed for the Battle of Salamis to happen in the first place, Xerxes put him in charge of completing the campaign against Greece. He had also been left to administer the Persian-conquered Greek states as a satrap (governor).

Mardonius, a man described by Herodotus as "mischievous," held power, wealth, and, most importantly, the pride of Persia in his hands. What became of these would be determined at the Battle of Plataea.

Pausanias of Sparta

The death of King Leonidas left a vacuum in one of the thrones of Sparta: one that Leonidas's son, Pleistarchus, was too young to fill. Queen Gorgo knew she would have to preserve the throne through a regency until her son came of age. Gorgo, who was reputed to wield influence in the high power chambers of Sparta, sought to select a man she could entrust with the regency.

King Leonidas's nephew, Pausanias, was chosen for the job (no, not the same Pausanias who documented the First Messenian War). Pausanias assumed office during one of the most chaotic times in the annals of Sparta. In 479 BCE, the stubborn Persians were still on Greek soil, and they sought to take it for Xerxes.

As a Spartan man and descendant of the Agiads, there was no doubt that Pausanias was a great man on the battlefield. He would prove his mettle against Mardonius and lead Greece to another victory.

But first, he had to repair the Hellenic League.

Much of Greece had become vassals of Persia, but with King Xerxes and most of his troops gone, Mardonius could only control so many states. For instance, the people of Athens had taken back their city when Mardonius retired to Thessaly for the winter.

Pausanias took advantage of this and worked hard to rally as many Greek city-states as possible to drive out the foreigners who had more than overstayed their welcome.

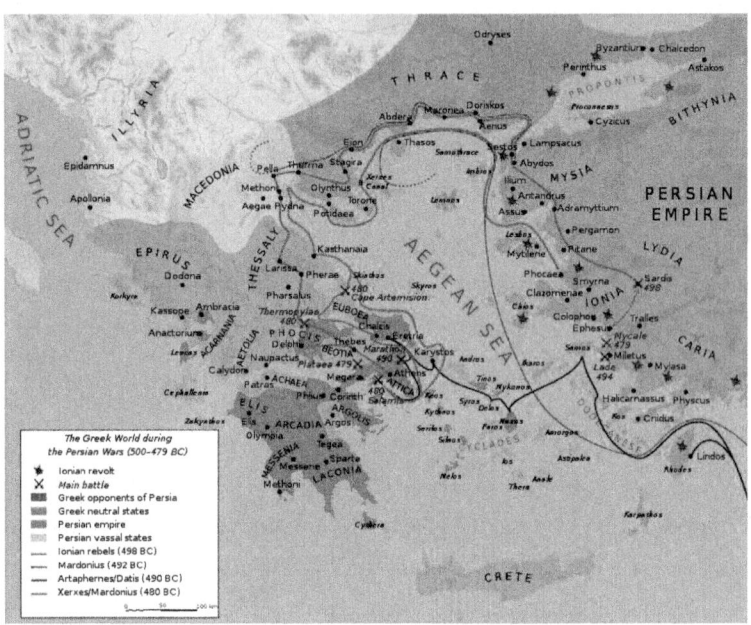

The Greek world during the Persian Wars. (Credit: https://en.wikipedia.org/wiki/Battle_of_Plataea#/media/File:Map_ Greco-Persian_Wars-en.svg)

War at Plataea

The Tensions Within

The Athenians got busy rebuilding their city, but they were still vigilant. Mardonius and his troops might return one day and force them to relive the horror of watching their beloved city burn.

Athens had requested the other Hellenic allies to help fight off the Persians once and for all, but none of them responded, despite knowing that Athens was the most vulnerable to another Persian attack.

Like the Persians, "united" Greece was in a stalemate for the remainder of the winter season. With springtime came some activity. Athens received a special guest, King Alexander I of Macedon, which was a Persian vassal. Alexander had been sent by Mardonius with an interesting offer for the Athenians. Indeed, the Persian general had been privy to how the Athenians were being neglected by their fellow Greeks and sought to take advantage.

Mardonius, through his messenger, offered the Athenians a hand of friendship in exchange for becoming a vassal of Persia. As tempting as the entreaty sounded, an experienced Athenian statesman like Aristides the Just would not be fooled. Supported by a delegation from Sparta, Aristides's answer was crystal clear: "As long as the sun holds to its present course, we shall never come to terms with Xerxes."

Mardonius took great offense at the Athenians' rejection of his diplomacy, and he was left with one other option: war. So, the Persians once again laid siege to Athens, which was again evacuated beforehand. Herodotus notes that Mardonius wreaked more havoc than the first time, saying, "Mardonius burnt Athens, and utterly overthrew and demolished whatever wall or house was left standing."

The reconstruction efforts would be led by Themistocles after the face-off at Plataea.

Call to Action

The Athenians had had enough of Persian aggression and the indifference of their so-called allies. Despite the pact at the meeting at the Isthmus of Corinth, Athens had been ignored in her time of need, left to the mercy of the ruthless Persians.

During the second destruction of Athens, many citizens fled to Salamis. Mardonius knew where to find them, but rather than attack, he sent word to the surviving Athenians, extending them a hand of friendship.

The Athenians were desperate. What use were their Greek allies if they would not come to their aid? To them, it seemed as if all their efforts at alerting their allies to the danger at hand had proven unsuccessful.

Perhaps a threat would do the trick.

The Athenians sent a delegation, joined by men from Plataea and Megara, to Sparta. If the Greek allied forces remained impassive to their plight, Athens would join hands with Persia.

Whoever thought up this idea as the means to snap the other Greeks out of their nonchalance was right. In a matter of weeks, Pausanias of Sparta rose to the occasion and led an elite troop of five thousand Spartans toward the Persians. Altogether, though, it is thought the entire Spartan force numbered around forty-five thousand, which included helots and hoplites from other parts of the peninsula.

Back in demolished Athens, Mardonius learned that the Spartans were making their move. He quickly finished off what was left of Athens and headed to Thebes, one of the pro-Persian Greek states under his governance. From there, he moved toward Plataea, where he built a massive military base. Since Pausanias and his troops were advancing toward them, Mardonius thought he could lure the Greeks near the Persian base, where they would hold the advantage.

Pausanias approached, and every day, more men joined the Greek allied forces. Aristides joined with his eight thousand men, and the swelling Greek army marched to the plains of Plataea. Other Greek allies, such as Corinth and Megara, among others, joined the Spartans and Athenians for the Battle of Plataea.

Collectively, it is believed there were around eighty thousand Greeks. It was the largest army the Greeks had ever assembled since the inception of the Greco-Persian Wars. Yet, the great Persian army still outnumbered them. It is believed they had around 100,000 men.

The Waiting Game

In an era dominated by frequent wars and skirmishes, it was ironic that both sides wanted minimal bloodshed. Mardonius's plan to bait the Greeks into his territory did not yield the results he wanted. The Greeks established their camp a few miles away from where he wanted them and in terrain that favored Greek battle techniques.

This should have been expected, considering that the Greeks had always displayed superior skills in strategy. Still, the Greek army was outnumbered, and unlike the Persians, the Greeks had no cavalry. An offense would cost them the lives of more men than they could afford to lose.

Mardonius and his men shared similar sentiments. Over the past war-torn decades, they had witnessed firsthand the excellence of the Greek defense. The Battle of Thermopylae had been a lesson to never attack the Greeks when the terrain favored them.

A waiting game thus ensued.

The Persians would not move out of their territory to attack the Greeks and vice versa. A few historians think that another reason for Mardonius's reluctance was that, deep down, all he wanted was for the Greek alliance to break apart. The cracks were already there, and it was only a matter of time before another internal conflict arose. Then, he could get a powerful Greek city-state like

Athens on Persia's side, and the rest of Greece would fall once and for all.

The Greeks, on the other hand, were counting on the Persians to harry them first. In previous military engagements, the Persians were usually on the offensive. This time, however, Mardonius and his men seemed to be stalling for something.

In some historical records, Mardonius indeed sent out his cavalry to attack the Greeks when they first arrived, but Athenian archers struck them down. After inflicting some casualties on the Greek forces, Mardonius reportedly lost the cavalry leader, Masistius. The Greeks moved forward due to their victory.

But both sides still refused to move on the other. A whole week whirled by, and not a peep came from the Persian camp—until one day, Mardonius's men breached the right flank of the Greek camp and captured their supplies. It seems that Mardonius's big strategy was to cut off the Greek supply lines and force them out of their stand-off.

This chokehold yielded results within a few days; the Greeks finally made a move, which was to retreat to a better position near Plataea.

The Wild Chase

Mardonius woke up to the news of the Greek retreat. Now, he could pursue the Greeks and end the war.

The Greeks had planned to retreat before dawn, but by morning, the Athenians, Spartans, and Tegeans hadn't even left yet, as they were guarding the rear of the retreat. When they were sent off to join the rest of the forces that were retreating, they didn't follow the directions closely enough and split up. The Athenians were under attack by troops from Thebes, one of the pro-Persian Greek city-states. The Spartans and Tegeans, who had moved farther into the hills of Plataea, realized they could not outrun the cavalry led by Mardonius.

The Persians caught up with the Spartans and Tegeans near the Temple of Demeter, and the battle began.

Pausanias had offered sacrifices and prayers to the gods for a Greek victory, but a few minutes into the battle, the Persians were destroying them. In signature fashion, the Persians let their arrows fly in thousands upon their enemies.

Since the numbers were not in their favor, the Greeks knew to rely on their superior weapons and the legendary phalanx formation. After forming a shield wall to protect themselves from the raging Persian arrows, the Greeks moved quickly across a small river, with the Persians hot on their trail.

The battle slowly began to turn. The Greeks pushed back, and they slowly but surely made progress. The Spartans were closing in.

Mardonius rode his white horse, surrounded by one thousand bodyguards, doing his best to shout out orders. He urged the tired Persians to fight on and boosted their falling morale.

Plutarch records that a certain Spartan soldier named Arimnestus grabbed a heavy rock. He hurled this rock at Mardonius, who fell off his horse and died.

The Persian army realized that their champion had fallen and fled the field. It was the Greeks' turn to pursue, and they did not stop until every Persian they caught was slaughtered, including Mardonius's security detail.

In the battle between the Athenians and Thebans, the Athenians had won but were unable to pursue their enemies. This was because they had to catch up with the Spartans and Tegeans.

With Mardonius and his army out of the way, the Greeks were joined by the remaining allied forces and stormed the Persian camp. The Persians left at the camp put up a weak resistance to the Greek army. It is believed that the Greeks killed nearly all of the Persian soldiers in the camp. Supposedly, only a few thousand Persians were allowed to live. This was likely done so the men could tell the tales of the Greeks' wrath in battle and to show

Xerxes that his plans to conquer Greece would never see the light of day.

Retribution

When large-scale wars like the Second Greco-Persian War come to an end, the victorious side often takes measures to ensure that the defeated is unable to wage war against them again. This accounts for why the Greeks were not caught up in celebrations after raiding the Persian military base. There was still much to do to rid their soil of the "barbarians."

On the same day of the Battle of Plataea (at least according to Herodotus), Spartan King Leotychides had sailed to Samos. There, Persian ships were beached due to the poor state of their ships.

The Greeks were met with a force of about sixty thousand Persian soldiers who had been assigned to guard the area, but their numbers counted for nothing when the Greeks struck. That afternoon, the Persians were annihilated, and their ships were razed to ashes.

King Xerxes's campaign was finished. The Persians had lost the battle on land and sea.

Artabazus, the Persian general now in charge, quickly fled to Asia Minor by land since their ships had been burned. He lost many men, but he succeeded in making it to a safe spot in Byzantium.

Now that the Persians were gone, at least for the most part, the Greek allied army turned on Thebes, the Greek city-state that had chosen the side of Persia. It would take three more decades until the Greco-Persian Wars finally came to an end. But this time around, the Greeks would be on the offensive.

Part Three: Sparta in Greek Affairs (460 BCE–222 BCE)

Chapter 8 – Peloponnesian War: The First Phase

After the Persians were vanquished at the battles of Plataea and Mycale, the allied Greeks sailed as far as Sestos and Byzantium to free the Ionian Greek cities from Persian domination.

In 478, allegations arose against Pausanias after he allegedly released some prisoners of war to curry the favor of Xerxes. Pausanias refuted these charges, claiming he had no hand in how the prisoners had escaped from captivity, but the Athenians and other allies of Greece did not believe him. Rumors of Pausanias's newfound alliance with the Persians spread like wildfire, and it was only quelled when Pausanias was recalled from Greek command.

Soon after his recall, it became clear that the Spartans were not invested in continuing the fight. They were more concerned about Athens' growing power.

So, now that the Greeks had the Persians off their backs, would they stay united, or would they pick up their tribal conflicts from where they had left off?

The Delian League

Apart from Themistocles, there was one other Athenian commander who had played a significant role in the Greco-Persian Wars, notably at the Battle of Mycale. His name was Xanthippus, and one day, he got wind of some momentous news.

King Leotychidas of Sparta had come up with an idea to free the remaining Ionian city-states from the claws of the Persian Empire once and for all. They should migrate to Europe.

According to Leotychidas, if the Ionian Greeks in Asia Minor migrated to Europe, they would be safer and more easily protected. Then the allied Greek city-states could get back to running their internal affairs sovereignly, just as they had before.

But Xanthippus considered this idea absurd. The Ionian city-states had been under Athenian rule, and agreeing to a move like this might mean they would fall under Sparta's control. It was their job to protect the Ionians. So, on behalf of Athens and a few Greek allies, Xanthippus rejected the Spartan king's proposal.

With the conquest of Byzantium complete, it seemed as though Sparta would not proceed with the campaign against Persia. Athens quickly stepped up to fill the role as leader.

Unknown to the Spartans, their withdrawal would cost them the loyalty of some members of the Hellenic League. An urgent congress was scheduled to be held on the sacred island of Delos, which was believed to be the birthplace of the god Apollo and his twin sister Artemis.

Sparta was not invited, of course, but nearly every Ionian Greek city-state was. Athens presided over the meeting. This gathering in Delos saw the formation of a brand-new league: the Delian League.

The Delian League purportedly sought to take revenge on the Persian Empire for terrorizing and ravaging Greece during the Greco-Persian Wars.

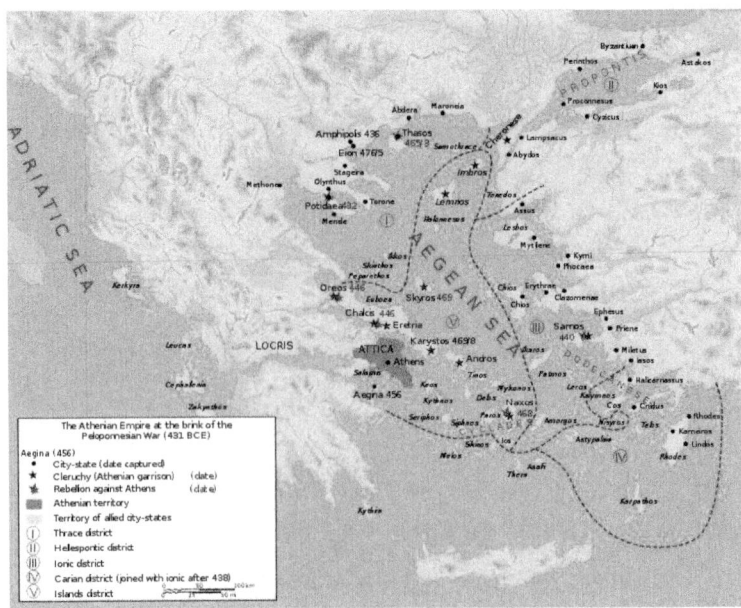

Although it took time for the Delian League to grow this large, the map gives you a good idea of how many allies Athens could call on.
(Credit: https://en.wikipedia.org/wiki/Members_of_the_Delian_League#/media /File:Map_athenian_empire_431_BC-en.svg)

The members swore an oath to be enemies to each other's enemies and to have the same allies as one another, just like the Peloponnesian League. Meetings would be held routinely in Delos, and each member would have the power of one vote for decision-making.

Athens held most of the power. As part of membership obligations, each member paid dues and tributes to Athens. These funds would be used to enlarge the league's navy, which was under Athens' control, as well as sponsor military expeditions if the need arose. While rebuilding their city walls, the Athenians expanded their naval power by using the tributes paid by the Delian allies.

Although it seemed as if the Delian League had been created to make Persia pay for the invasion of Greece, Athens' imperialist ambitions would shine through in the years to come.

The Third Messenian War

The Spartans realized that Athens was strategically positioning herself to dominate Peloponnesian Greece. The Delian League stood as an opponent to Sparta's Peloponnesian League, which was regathered after the end of the Second Greco-Persian War. Eventually, some city-states, such as Megara, defected from the Peloponnesian League to join the new Athens-led league.

If strong allies of the Peloponnesian League like Corinth ever held hands with Athens, Sparta would be toppled. Sparta needed to keep Athens' growing prowess in check, but Sparta had a bigger problem at hand: the Third Messenian War.

Quakes and Shakes

The people of Sparta were going about their daily business on one fine day in 464 BCE. Boys in the agoge were wrestling in the dirt, and the girls were at school. Suddenly, the ground began to shake. The Spartans must have been worried, but all they could do was wait.

The tremor increased, shaking the foundations of Sparta and other nearby city-states to their core. It was an earthquake. It was one of the most destructive in ancient times, and it was not something that the Spartans could fight with spears.

Natural disasters could not always be predicted, so it is unlikely the Spartans were prepared for it. They scrambled for their lives as the ground cracked and split, crumbling walls to dust. Temples, statues, monuments, city halls, and private houses were reduced to ruins, trapping thousands of people. It was a severe blow to the population of Sparta. It is thought that around twenty thousand people died in the quake.

A depiction of the earthquake in ancient Sparta.

Amid all the chaos, a certain group of people saw an opportunity: the repressed lower caste of the Spartan society, also known as the helots.

The helots had never seen their prideful Spartan masters in such panic. For a people who had been thoroughly humiliated and defeated in the First and Second Messenian Wars, it seemed as though Mother Nature herself had presented them with the chance of a lifetime: a narrow path to lasting freedom.

Quickly, the helots rallied and drew their swords, signaling a bloody revolt. They wouldn't miss this opportunity for the world. They charged against their perplexed masters, wading and sprawling through chunks of falling walls and decapitated statues.

The Spartans saw that another revolt was upon them and that their confusion was fuel to the rioting helots. Immediately, they sent word to their neighboring Greek city-states, requesting military reinforcements and aid to quell the rebellion.

But the Messenian rebels were unstoppable. They fought their way out of Sparta and made for the fortress in Mount Ithome, where their ancestors had repelled the Spartan forces in the past. The helots believed that the historic fortress would grant them cover from the wrath of the Spartans and, eventually, victory.

Meanwhile, back in Sparta, their allies had swiftly responded to the call for help. Troops arrived at the gates of the devastated city of Sparta to join in subduing the errant helots. Among them was a contingent of four thousand men from Athens, who offered a hand of assistance, but the Spartans spat on it.

Indeed, the tensions between Sparta and Athens had been put on ice during the Greco-Persian Wars, but Athens' new power experiment with the Delian League had ticked off the Spartans. They could not shake their suspicions that Athens had treacherous intentions of siding with the Messenian rebels. So, they turned the Athenian troops away, which was a grave insult to Athens.

This event would remove the façade of peace between Sparta and Athens and pave the way for the inevitable: a war to determine once and for all who was the true power of Greece.

Initial Rounds

The Athenian Experiment

Cimon, the Athenian general who had led the four thousand soldiers to Sparta but was sent back, paid for this humiliation with his career. He was left out in the cold from Athenian politics and replaced by his rival, Ephialtes, but this was not enough retribution. They knew the Spartans would have to pay for their insolence.

Considering Sparta's military proficiency, the Athenians knew better than to recklessly declare war on Sparta. They needed formidable allies with similar grudges against Sparta for a chance at victory.

Fortunately, the Delian League was up to the task. All Athens had to do was get more states on her side.

Thus, for the ten years that the Spartans were engulfed in the Third Messenian War, the Athenians embarked on a quest to drum up allies throughout Greece. First, they approached Argos, Sparta's arch-enemy, which readily gave support to the cause. Then, they made allies of Thessaly and Megara.

Megara had belonged to the Peloponnesian League, but it was consumed by conflicts against a fellow member, Corinth, in 459 BCE. Athens offered aid to Megara, and together, they pushed back the powerful Corinthians from the border isthmus they previously controlled.

This act made Athens a direct enemy of the Corinthians, and the Corinthians would respond by strengthening their alliance with Sparta and the other members of the Peloponnesian League. The First Peloponnesian War had begun.

Battle of Tanagra

After the Persians, drunk on their victory against Leonidas and his brave men at the pass of Thermopylae, destroyed Athens, the city of Athens was rebuilt. This time, the Athenians would construct the Long Walls. These walls would go around the city and be directly linked to Athenian seaports.

Themistocles believed that the walls would better fortify Athens against future attacks and serve as escape routes to the sea in cases of a siege. The Long Walls would also secure faster access to the Athenian fleet in cases of war.

When the Spartans heard of the Long Walls being constructed in Athens, they made subtle attempts to dissuade the Athenians from the project but were rebuffed. Historians believe that this confirms the Spartans' beliefs of Athens' ambitions of power, which bred distrust and led the Spartans to reject Athens' help during the Third Messenian War.

Undeterred by Sparta's aversion, the Athenians proceeded with the construction of the Long Walls, which was funded by the joint treasury of the Delian League. Also, the alliance with Megara granted the Athenians control of the sea and the Gulf of Corinth. Once this alliance was confirmed, the Long Walls were built in Corinth and Megara as well.

In 457 BCE, the Phocians declared war on Doris, where the Doric Greeks originated from. Sparta marched 1,500 soldiers to the city's aid, and another ten thousand men joined them. They took on Phocis and won.

Athens heard of Sparta's advance and rolled out to ambush them in Boeotia. They were joined by one thousand men from Argos, and it is believed their total numbers were around fourteen thousand men.

The troops from Athens and Sparta met on the plain of Tanagra, and an epic battle ensued. With the Spartans only slightly outnumbered, it was an intense engagement that resulted in multiple casualties on both sides.

Nonetheless, the great warriors of Sparta pushed back the Athenian allied troops and were able to return home via the Isthmus of Corinth. As for the defeated Athenians and their allies, they retired to recoup their losses. However, the war was far from over. After two months, Athens would return invigorated and seize Boeotia at the Battle of Oenophyta.

The Truce

Over the Top

Despite their victory against Athens at the Battle of Tanagra, the Spartans knew not to advance any further. The Athenians would regret not following the Spartans' example after their victory at the Battle of Oenophyta.

After bringing Boeotia to its knees, Athens took the war to its long-time enemy Aegina, an island near Athens, where the Athenians won another victory. These victories emboldened the Athenians to invade the Peloponnesian coast. Tolmides, an Athenian general, led this campaign in 455 BCE with four thousand men and an elite Athenian fleet of over fifty ships.

First, they besieged a small Messenian village under Spartan control named Methone, but the Spartans would not have it. A Spartan infantry was urgently dispatched to Methone, and the Athenians were forced to retreat.

Next, the Athenians invaded and razed the Spartan port of Gytheion. They continued into the Gulf of Corinth and seized Chalcis, a Corinthian colony. The Athenians wanted to provoke some kind of reaction from Corinth and, by extension, Sparta.

However, the Spartans remained inert. They were still occupied with the war against the rebellious helots, which had dragged on for ten years after the devastating earthquake. In 454 BCE, the Spartans had defeated the last of the helots. Many rebels had lost their lives in the war, and a few survivors who escaped fled to Naupactus near the Gulf of Corinth. There, they were well received by Tolmides.

In order to fulfill the core purpose of the Delian League, which was to take revenge on Persia, the Athenians led their allies to war against Egypt, one of Persia's vassals. The Athenians sought to take advantage of the uprisings in Egypt, but the Athenians were crushed by the Persians.

This humiliating defeat would take the Athenians years to recover. Athens' repute across the Aegean suffered a slight decline, giving impetus to the subjugated peoples of Boeotia to demand independence from Athenian control.

In response, Tolmides and his men made for Boeotia to put the errant vassals in their place at the Battle of Coronea in 447 BCE. There, Athens was defeated yet again, and the vicious cycle of rebellion by Athenian vassals heightened. Megara, Euboea, and Aegina all erupted in revolt against Athenian supremacy.

Now that Sparta was politically stable, it moved against Athens by invading Attica and other Athenian colonies. Athens was torn apart by the war, and its reputation as the emerging power of ancient Greece hung by a brittle thread.

The Athenians suffered many defeats, and they grew weary of the chaotic series of wars against Sparta and her allies. A united Greece under Athenian control was demanding more than they could afford.

One winter day in either 446 or 445 BCE, Sparta received an invitation for a peace treaty from Athens: a proposition for thirty years of peace between the two city-states.

One of the conditions of the treaty was that Athens would hold on to its original territories and hand over control of the Spartan territories in its possession. Neutral states would be free to align with either Sparta or Athens, giving the Peloponnesian and Delian Leagues equal recognition.

The Spartans saw no reason to disagree since the terms were mutually favorable. Sparta would uphold her end of the agreement. But would Athens do the same?

Chapter 9 – The Peloponnesian War: Phase Two

Sparta and Athens had always been politically and culturally divergent. The Athenians would have a hard time holding hands with a nation so blatantly against democracy and all its tenets.

By some cosmic miracle, these two powerful Greek city-states came to an agreement of peace—one that would supposedly last for thirty years. This period marked the end of the seemingly endless skirmishes between the Athenians and Spartans, as well as their allies.

However, the peace would only last for fifteen years. And even during those fifteen years, Greece could not be at peace.

The Dictator

The Peloponnesian League was a militaristic institution, as it allowed member states to run their internal affairs uninterrupted. This freedom was not sustained in the Delian League. As the years went by, Athens interfered more and more in the politics of its members, enforcing the Athenian model of governance—democracy—on each state and forcing them to become vassals.

Worse still, Pericles, an Athenian general and Tolmides's colleague, had long ordered the Delian League's joint treasury to be moved from Delos to Athens. This generated resentment among members of the league, as they found Pericles's decision to be rather shady.

Soon, the Delian League was riddled with suspicions that the resources contributed by the members were being diverted to sponsor Athens' imperialistic interests. Not too long after, Athens, as the leader of the Delian League, promulgated a new method of paying tribute. Members could only make monetary contributions rather than troops, ships, or weapons.

This announcement deepened the distrust felt by the members. Thucydides summarizes the nature of Athens' relationship with its allies:

> "Of all the causes of defection, that connected with arrears of tribute and vessels, and with failure of service, was the chief; for the Athenians were very severe and exacting, and made themselves offensive by applying the screw of necessity to men who were not used to and in fact not disposed for any continuous labor. In some other respects, the Athenians were not the old popular rulers they had been at first; and if they had more than their fair share of service, it was correspondingly easy for them to reduce any that tried to leave the confederacy. The Athenians also arranged for the other members of the league to pay its share of the expense in money instead of in ships and men, and for this, the subject city-states had themselves to blame, their wish to get out of giving service making most leave their homes. Thus while Athens was increasing her navy with the funds they contributed, a revolt always found itself without enough resources or experienced leaders for war."

Athens quickly found itself entangled in internal wars, notably the Samian War in 440 against Samos, an ardent ally of Athens.

The Spartans watched as the alliance between Athens and her allies became strained. Tempting as it was to take a shot at a war-torn, vulnerable Athens, Corinth and other members of the Peloponnesian League voted against going to war.

In the end, Athens would extinguish all of the revolts and put the affairs of its small empire in order.

Old Grudges: The Battles of Sybota and Potidaea

The year was 433 BCE, and there was no love lost between Corinth, Sparta's wealthiest ally, and a small island in the Ionian Sea named Corcyra. Corcyra was a former colony of Corinth, and the animosity between the two had existed for quite some time.

Corcyra sent emissaries to Athens, requesting an alliance. The Athenians moved to their assistance and sent a fleet of 10 warships to join the Corcyreans' 110 ships.

This was too close for comfort in regards to Sparta. It warned Athens that their fleet should not get involved unless Corinth actually invaded Corcyra. Sparta did not get directly involved in this battle, but it was kept apprised of what was happening.

Corinth and Corcyra went head-to-head in one of the largest Greek naval battles at that time. The Athenians also fought, even though the battle itself did not take place on Corcyra. It took place near Sybota, which was close to Corcyra but not close enough to violate the treaty.

The battle was devastating for both sides, and both sides ended up claiming the victory. One year after that naval battle, the Corinthians were provoked yet again by the Athenians.

Potidaea was a small yet strategic city located in the Chalcidice Peninsula. Although it was a colony of Corinth, Potidaea was a member of the Delian League, meaning it paid tribute to Athens but wasn't under her political control.

Knowing that Corinth would retaliate for their role during the Battle of Sybota, the Athenians sprung to action using Potidaea. As the head of the Delian League, Athens demanded that Potidaea renounce its political alliance with Corinth and banish the

Corinthian administrators from the city. They also demanded that a portion of Potidaea's city wall be demolished and that the Potidaeans send hostages to Athens to prove their fealty.

Potidaea rightfully believed that this was an attempt by Athens to reduce the state to vassal status, making it an extension of the Athenian empire. However, one could argue that Athens feared Corinth would spur Potidaea to revolt, just like Macedonia was doing to the Athenian vassals in Thrace.

The Athenian government thus granted a man named Archestratus command of one thousand soldiers and thirty ships for an expedition. He would first go to Macedonia and then to Potidaea to urge the Potidaeans to make up their minds in favor of Athens.

Realizing that neutrality had failed them, the Potidaeans resolved to take a side once and for all. Athens' demands were ludicrous, but the danger of refusing was too great. The Potidaeans sent a diplomatic delegation to Athens to negotiate more agreeable terms, but the Athenians were adamant.

The Potidaeans were cornered, but there was one other state they could turn to: Sparta.

Sparta ratified Corinth's protection of Potidaea from Athenian aggression by appointing a Corinthian general named Aristeus to command the troops of Corinth, which numbered about two thousand men.

Athens was finally at war with Corinth, and to ensure a victory, the Athenians sent out reinforcements led by Callias, who was one of the richest men in Athens.

The Athenian troops and ships outnumbered those of Corinth, and when they clashed at Potidaea in 432 BCE, the Athenians decimated the Corinthian troops and forced Aristeus to retreat.

The Challenge

The Spartans heard about Corinth's grand fiasco during a war council of the Peloponnesian League. Many member states bore bitter grudges against the Athenians. For instance, Megara, which was now realigned with the Peloponnesian League, was grappling with trade sanctions imposed by Athens. The league members expressed dissatisfaction over Sparta's tepidity to Athens' recent activities. Corinth, in particular, reminded Sparta of her duty to protect members of the league and urged the Spartans to take action.

If an important city like Corinth felt so threatened by the Athenians, the Spartans knew something had to be done. They were worried that they would lose Corinth's naval strength or, worse, Corinth's loyalty.

Midway into the meeting, a delegation of visitors walked in. They were messengers from Athens.

They hadn't been invited to the meeting, so this was entirely unexpected, but they had come with a message for Sparta, Corinth, and the other members of the Peloponnesian League: a warning to not dare contemplate going to war with Athens.

In their words, Athens had continued the fight against the Persians while Sparta sat on the sidelines. The Athenians condescendingly admonished Sparta and her allies to remember their place.

The Spartans knew that this was not just a warning. It was a challenge. Once the cheeky Athenians were gone, the Spartans and other allied states must have said among themselves, "We have taken the back seat long enough. Now, we join the war and give these impetuous Athenians a serving of Spartan brutality."

This heralded the untimely termination of the Thirty Years' Peace and a second bout of the Peloponnesian War.

For context, Sparta and Athens had different war strategies. The Athenians commanded a vast naval fleet and had the finest naval commanders in Greece, like Themistocles, who defied the great Persian armada on the Cape of Artemisium.

The Spartans, on the other hand, excelled in land battles. While Themistocles had commanded the Greek fleet during the Second Greco-Persian War, King Leonidas of Sparta had led his three hundred men and other Greeks against a much larger Persian enemy overland.

After fifty years of fighting shoulder to shoulder against a common enemy, Athens and Sparta had turned on each other.

Sparta declared its justification for invading Athens: to free the Greek city-states that had long been oppressed by the Athenians while they expanded their empire. This won Sparta popular support, but more importantly, the war against Athens was a means to reinstate Sparta as the one true master of Peloponnesian Greece.

The second phase of the Peloponnesian Wars was a series of sea and land battles between former allies turned belligerents. The Spartans would win more of the land battles but only a few at sea, as the Athenians remained dominant in that arena.

The Archidamian War

This war, named after King Archidamus II of Sparta, lasted from 431 to 421 BCE. It was the first phase of the Second Peloponnesian War (the Second Peloponnesian War is typically referred to as *the* Peloponnesian War, most likely because it was the more decisive of the two wars).

Sparta's strategy to surround the countryside of Athens and block off farmlands and supply routes forced the Athenians to seek refuge behind the Long Walls.

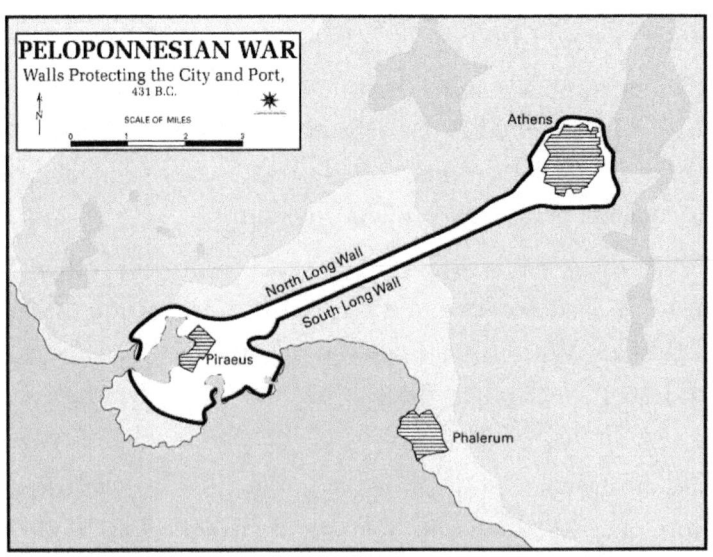

What the Long Walls likely looked like.

At the behest of statesman and war general Pericles, the Athenians declined to leave their city walls and face the Spartans in open battle. Pericles had masterminded Athens' involvement in the Battle of Sybota, as well as the imposition of trade sanctions on Megara—the catalysts that ended the Thirty Years' Peace and triggered the Second Peloponnesian War.

For Athens' survival, Pericles persuaded the Athenians to avoid a land battle against the Spartans unless it was absolutely necessary. Instead, they would prepare for a naval offensive in the Gulf of Corinth.

Eventually, the Spartans realized their siege on the countryside was ineffective since the Athenians still retained access to the sea and maritime routes due to the Long Walls. If Sparta wanted a real war, they needed a new strategy or a miracle.

It would end up being a miracle: a horrid, deadly miracle that would shake the city of Athens from within.

In 430 BCE, the port of Piraeus, Athens' main source of food and other supplies, gifted the Athenians with a deadly epidemic. This horrible plague did not care about a person's status; Pericles and his sons even died. Between one-third to two-thirds of the Athenian population perished, and the plague traveled across the Mediterranean, ravaging every city in its wake.

Meanwhile, the Athenians were trapped behind their own walls, spreading the illness more quickly due to their tight quarters. The Spartans were not excited about contracting the disease themselves, so they abandoned their plans and went home.

However, with Pericles gone, the Athenians could now pursue a more aggressive approach. In 429 BCE, Athens emerged victorious from the consecutive naval battles of Rhium and Naupactus. The Athenians continued to wreak havoc around the Peloponnese, going into areas like Boeotia and Aetolia.

In 425 BCE, Athens discovered a peninsula called Pylos. Demosthenes, the Athenian commander, discovered that it was a strategic position, one they could use to attack Sparta. The Spartans knew something had to be done before the Athenians continued overland to take more of their territory.

The Spartans sent sixty ships to Pylos, outnumbering the Athenians only slightly. But it was not enough. The Athenians destroyed eighteen of their ships; the Spartans only managed to destroy eight Athenian ships.

The Athenians also managed to trap a large number of Spartiate hoplites, probably close to around four hundred, on the island of Sphacteria. About one hundred of these hoplites were fully-fledged Spartan citizens, which roused the Spartan government into action.

The Spartans attempted to find a diplomatic resolution with the Athenians, but it failed. The Battle of Sphacteria followed. For this land battle, Demosthenes was joined by Cleon, a radically thuggish Athenian general who had essentially taken over Pericles's role. Together, they led over three thousand Athenian soldiers against the few hundred Spartans.

The Spartans were forced to surrender. It is believed this was the first time in history that Sparta bowed down rather than fight to the death. This monumental defeat and humiliation dealt a severe blow to Sparta's reputation. And it would take more than the victory at the Battle of Amphipolis for them to recover.

Brasidas of Sparta

Brasidas was a talented warrior. He'd barely survived the Battle of Pylos, and soon after that, he was sent to capture Amphipolis, an Athenian colony in Thrace, as revenge for the Athenian occupation of Pylos.

Rather than sack the city and slaughter all its inhabitants, Brasidas proposed a truce. The people of Amphipolis could stay or leave in peace as long as they surrendered. Time was not on Brasidas's side as Thucydides (yes, the historian, although at this point in time, he was a general) was making his way to the city. Amphipolis decided to take Brasidas's offer. He made the same offer to other towns in Thrace, trying to stay one step ahead of Thucydides. Speaking of Thucydides, he did not fare well in all of this. Many blamed him for Amphipolis's fall, and he was recalled back to Athens, where he was sentenced to be exiled.

Athens was scared of what might happen if all their cities turned against them, so they signed a truce with Sparta in 423 BCE. Athens wanted to buy time, while the Spartans hoped for the return of their prisoners that had been taken during the Battle of Sphacteria.

However, peace was not to be. Brasidas took Scione and refused to return it, even after hearing of the armistice. Cleon set out to take it back, kicking off the Second Battle of Amphipolis in 422 BCE.

Sparta won this battle and even managed to deliver another decisive blow on top of that by killing Cleon. However, Brasidas was also killed due to the injuries he received. He at least lived long enough to hear the good news that they had won. After his death, he was buried in the city of Amphipolis, where he would be revered as a hero and the city's founder.

The Battle of Amphipolis was a defining event in the Peloponnesian War. Sparta supposedly suffered seven casualties; the Athenians suffered around six hundred. Still, both sides yearned for a breather.

King Pleistoanax of Sparta and Nicias, the Athenian commander-in-chief, entered negotiations for peace, and in March 421 BCE, the Peace of Nicias was signed.

This marked the end of the decade-long Archidamian War.

The Battle of Aegospotami

It should come as no surprise that the Peace of Nicias did not last long. Barely two years after the treaty, Sparta and Athens went head to head in the most epic land battle in classical Greece.

It happened in a small Arcadian city named Mantinea in 418 BCE. Parts of Arcadia and all of Argos threw their weight behind Athens, which had a formidable army of eight thousand men. They went up against Sparta and her allies, which numbered around nine thousand. The Spartans defeated the Athenian troops and forced Argos to withdraw its support of Athens.

This victory was celebrated in Sparta as a sign. Despite the demoralizing string of defeats over the years, the Spartans had not lost their mettle after all. The trend continued at the naval battles of Syme and Notium; the Spartans crushed the Athenians without mercy and laid waste to their warships.

In 406 BCE, the Athenians made a minor comeback at the naval Battle of Arginusae, causing the Spartans to lose seventy ships and their commander, Callicraditdas. Athens, however, lost nearly thirty ships, and the city exploded with internal strife as a result of the losses. Six Athenian naval commanders were condemned to death for their ineptitude, as many men died as a result of the battle, although some of this blame could be placed on the storm that took place. It is likely that Athens was feeling the heat and needed to lay the blame on someone.

The Final Onslaught

Back in Sparta, Lysander, who had championed the victory at the Battle of Notium in 406 BCE, was reinstated as a deputy commander of the Spartan navy.

By law, Aracus was Lysander's superior; however, Lysander was practically in charge. Since Lysander had already held office once as the commander-in-chief of the navy (known as a navarch), he could not occupy the position again. However, Sparta needed Lysander's talents to finish off the demoralized Athenians.

Sometime in 407 BCE, before the Battle of Notium, Lysander had single-handedly gained the alliance of a most unlikely acquaintance: Persia. It seems crazy that these two countries would fight on the same side. But the times made unlikely enemies allies. Thus, Lysander of Sparta befriended Cyrus the Younger, the prince of Persia, in the late 4th century BCE. And Persia, which was led by Darius II, lent naval aid to Lysander for the Battle of Notium.

Persia would do it again for the final bout of the Peloponnesian War: the Battle of Aegospotami.

By the time of Aegospotami, Athens was wrecked. Hope was dwindling among the elite. Poverty and hunger made scarecrows of the common folk, and the Delian League's resources were almost depleted. Worst of all, their naval and land troops had lost all courage to pursue the conquest of Sparta anymore.

To truly crush Athens, Lysander knew he would have to strike Athens where it would be felt the most. Athens relied on imported grain and military supplies from Asia via the straits of Bosporus. Lysander's first goal was capturing the important city of Lampsacus.

Lampsacus was a tribute-paying member of the Delian League and a strategic city on Athens' supply route. Lysander and his naval troops occupied the city, as well as Sestos, which was another important city to Athens. The Spartans also raided Salamis, Aegina, and parts of Attica.

The Athenians were distraught to learn that their naval bases had been seized by Spartan troops and that their supply routes were cordoned off. An Athenian general named Conon took around 180 ships and over 35,000 men to the straits of Aegospotami, near the Hellespont, where Lysander and his navy met them for a final clash.

After a long, hard fight, only nine Athenian ships and a handful of men survived the wrath of the Spartans. Athenian historian Xenophon describes the mood of Athens upon receiving the news of this crushing defeat. "A sound of wailing ran through from Piraeus through the Long Walls to the city, one man passing on the news to another; and during that night no one slept, all mourning, not for the lost alone, but far more for their own selves."

The Athenians were right to be fearful.

The Spartans tore down the city walls of Athens and kicked out their democratic government, replacing it with the oligarchy the Athenians so loathed. The golden age of Athens was over, and what was once the cradle of democracy and arts heralded a seismic shift in politics, the economy, and culture.

Lysander and his men sailed home victorious, and Sparta went wild with jubilation at the news of Athens' surrender in 404 BCE.

The Delian League was finished, and every corner of the former Athenian Empire would greet the dawn of a new era, where Sparta—and only Sparta—held the highest power in ancient Greece.

Chapter 10 – The Corinthian War

Background

In light of the greatest events in history, especially warfare, you will discover that there were no permanent friends or foes. One moment, you could be dealing with an enemy; the next, they are your most important ally.

Sparta, the victor of the Peloponnesian War, had been allied with Athens during the Greco-Persian Wars, yet Persia, the common enemy at the time, later became an ally of Sparta. These ironies would continue after the Peloponnesian War, as the Spartans, drunk on victory, would make fatal mistakes that would sour relations with an age-long ally, like Corinth.

The year was 400 BCE, and Sparta's allies all over mainland Greece were not over the blatant ingratitude of the Spartans toward their contributions in the Peloponnesian War. Rather than share the spoils of war with her allies, Sparta had kept it all, despite the fact that these allies had given ships and men to aid her cause. Sparta also hoarded the tributes paid by vassals of the former Athenian empire, as well as other benefits, much to the displeasure of her allies.

Sparta had started on this absurd path barely seven years after the Peloponnesian War. As a personal favor, the war hero Lysander helped his friend, Prince Cyrus, to ascend the throne of Persia, using Sparta's military and naval resources at his disposal, in 401 BCE. However, these efforts failed, and Cyrus was killed in the conflict. Sparta's involvement in enthroning Cyrus would never be forgotten by his brother, Artaxerxes II, who retained the throne.

Sparta's allies watched as the wealth they had collaboratively made available to Sparta was expended on frivolities while they remained estranged.

In 402 BCE, Sparta had turned on one of its allies and a member of the Peloponnesian League, Elis. Elis was forced to become a vassal state of Sparta, which was a breach of Sparta's promise to never interfere in the internal affairs of its allies.

Sparta's other allies, notably Corinth and Thebes, had since feared that Sparta was unraveling as an imperialist nightmare, seeking to bring all of Greece to kneel in servitude—a dreadful similarity to Athens with the Delian League.

A confirmation of their speculation was Sparta's invasion of Ionia in 398 BCE. It was evident that Sparta was targeting her weaker allies in her quest for territorial expansion. It would only be a matter of time before bigger allies like Thebes and Corinth would meet the wrath of the Spartans.

Sparta had to be stopped.

The First Strike

Sometime around 396 BCE, Persia sent a governor named Timocrates to the major cities of Greece, including Athens, Corinth, and Thebes. King Agesilaus II of Sparta had been making inroads in Persia. His invasion, on top of Sparta's aid to put Cyrus the Younger on the Persian throne, must have rubbed the Persian king the wrong way. Timocrates was sent with gold to entice these cities to join Persia in taking Sparta down.

It seems that Thebes lacked the wherewithal to openly defy Sparta, so they cunningly convinced their neighbor, Locris, to raid Phocis, a staunch Spartan ally. Since Thebes was an ally of Locris, it had to step in. The effects rippled as planned, and Sparta declared war on Thebes in 395 BCE, leading to the Battle of Haliartus.

This conflict was just a prelude to another war that would test the might of Sparta: the Corinthian War.

Lysander and another commander named Pausanias were saddled with the task of dealing with the Thebans. Each commander was assigned troops, but Lysander and his man arrived several days earlier.

The city walls of Haliartus were no challenge. Lysander saw no reason to wait for Pausanias, who had undermined him in the past. Lysander ordered a frontal assault, and his men charged at the city walls, ready to pull it down.

Unknown to the Spartans, the Theban army was lying in wait outside the city walls. When the Spartan offensive was launched, the Thebans barreled out of their hiding spots and rained destruction on the Spartan troops.

Lysander was killed in battle, and the remaining troops sustained considerable losses. Pausanias would be punished with exile for arriving late to the battlefield and giving away Boeotia during the negotiations with the Thebans.

Sparta had lost this round, along with two great men. Was King Agesilaus a strong enough leader to steer Sparta through the imminent storm?

King Agesilaus II of Sparta

After Agesilaus's controversial ascension to the Spartan throne around 400 BCE, during which he accused a legitimate heir of being illegitimate, he had his eyes set on Asia Minor. Plutarch and

Xenophon believe that the Spartan king had grand plans of bringing the entire Persian Empire under Spartan control.

King Agesilaus of Sparta.

Ephesus, an Ionian Greek city, became Agesilaus's military base. There, he enlisted mercenaries who had fought for the deceased Prince Cyrus to join his troops in the war against Persia. These mercenaries were loyal to Lysander, and the Spartan king was worried that he would be sidelined.

As a result, he would frequently humiliate Lysander in front of the men to remind him of his place and possibly force him to quit the army. This act of insecurity demonstrated by a Spartan king was repulsive to Lysander. Lysander gave the king what he desperately yearned for and left the king's army.

Now assured that he was truly in charge, King Agesilaus sailed into Anatolia (modern-day Turkey), home to some of the Persian

Empire's most valuable vassals. King Agesilaus's mission was to turn the vassals against Persia and destroy the empire from within.

After numerous victories, Agesilaus proceeded to Sardis, where he encountered its new provincial governor, Tithraustes. The sly Spartan king met his match in Tithraustes, who bribed his way out of engagements with Sparta and redirected Agesilaus to the north.

King Agesilaus is believed to have been a brilliant war tactician, but he was a poor diplomat. The incursion into Asia was interrupted when he received urgent news from home in 395 BCE that his estranged friend, Lysander, was dead and that the allies of Sparta had turned into enemies.

One year later, King Agesilaus would reroute to Sparta and conquer all the delinquents in his way, including the main players of Corinth, Thebes, and Argos, at the Battle of Coronea.

Battle of Coronea

King Agesilaus arrived in the Peloponnese in 394 BCE. Earlier that same year, the Spartans had won a victory at the Battle of Nemea. The coalition troops of Thebes, Corinth, Argos, and Athens had a force of twenty-four thousand hoplites, yet they were overrun by Sparta's eighteen thousand men.

Xenophon recalls that the Thebans ruined the formation by their lack of cooperation, putting the other Greeks at peril. The coalition successfully blocked the Spartans from invading Corinth and advancing to the heart of Greece even though the Spartans won the battle.

Such a setback was not new to Athens, given their experience during the Peloponnesian War. Argos and Corinth, on the other hand, were demoralized. The allied Greeks regrouped and pushed the Thebans forward to lead the next attempt against Sparta.

It is not known for certain how much time passed before the Battle of Coronea, but it is likely it did not happen too much later, as the loss at the Battle of Nemea still weighed on their minds. In the Battle of Coronea, the Spartans were joined by the Phocians and the Orchomenians, numbering around fifteen thousand men altogether. The Orchomenians had been allies of Thebes during the Greco-Persian Wars but had fallen out with the Thebans soon after. The Thebans were present at this battle, as well as the Argives and some other allies. Together, they numbered around twenty thousand men.

The two armies charged at each other, and in a fit of panic, the Argives deserted the battlefield, dooming the coalition Greeks to another defeat. The Orchomenians held off the Thebans with their phalanx, but the Thebans eventually broke their lines and attacked King Agesilaus's camp to plunder his spoils of war from Asia.

They had barely stolen anything when Agesilaus arrived with his elite troops, but they still brutally slaughtered the Thebans. Bloodshed unlike any other was recorded on that day, and the handful of Thebans who escaped Agesilaus's wrath scampered to Mount Helicon, where the Argive deserters had fled to.

The Battle of Coronea, the second major bout in the Corinthian War, ended in a decisive victory for Sparta.

Battle of Lechaeum

The year was 392 BCE, and a group of pro-Spartan Oligarchs had been exiled from Corinth in the aftermath of a civil war against anti-Spartan Democrats. Embittered by their ill-treatment, the pro-Spartan Oligarchs joined forces with King Agesilaus of Sparta to invade parts of the Gulf of Corinth. They captured Lechaeum, a port that housed many Corinthian warships.

With the port secured, King Agesilaus moved a contingent of his troops to raid other parts of Corinth, while a stationary army remained at Lechaeum to guard the port. Among these troops were men from Amyclae, a city-state in the Peloponnese that was allied with Sparta.

Every year, these men had to travel home for the three-day festival of Hyacinthia in honor of Apollo. The festival approached, and soon, the Amyclaean men were ready to leave.

In 391 BCE, the Spartan commander in charge of Lechaeum ordered that six hundred hoplites and a cavalry force escort the travelers. The six hundred hoplites would only escort them to the border of Corinth and return to the base at Lechaeum, while the cavalry would see the men all the way home.

Iphicrates, an Athenian commander in Corinth, heard of the movement and saw an opportunity to attack the six hundred hoplites on their way back to the base. This move had not been predicted by the Spartans because they thought the Corinthians and Athenians would fear their larger numbers.

On their way back from escorting the men of Amyclae, the six hundred Spartan hoplites were attacked by a horde of Athenian javelin throwers (also known as pelstats). Seizing advantage of the Spartans' shock and rare disorganization, Iphicrates and his men bore down on the Spartans and pursued them toward Lechaeum.

The Athenians would throw javelins, wound the Spartans, and make a run for it. This hit-and-run tactic was aimed at wearing out the Spartans and avoiding an organized front where the Spartans would be more powerful.

At the day's end, 250 Spartans were dead, but since they retained control of the port at Lechaeum, the Battle of Lechaeum would have little impact on the Corinthian Wars.

As it turned out, the Athenians' victory, even though it was impressive, was not enough to overturn their defeat at Coronea.

The King's Peace

The Switch

By the late 390s BCE, the coalition of Athens, Corinth, Argos, Thebes, and Persia was at the edge of a cliff.

Corinth had been ravaged by internal strife between a powerful pro-Spartan minority and the majority who wanted out of Sparta's doomed alliance. Argos had taken a back seat in campaigns against Sparta, especially after the shabby display at the Battle of Coronea.

Thebes, like Corinth and Argos, was depending on Athens to continue the fight.

Meanwhile, Athens was reemerging as a threat to the Persian Empire, despite being torn apart by internal issues between the Oligarchs and Democrats. The Persians had supported the rebuilding of Athens and its rapid recovery from the disasters after the Peloponnesian War, but Artaxerxes II quickly came to regret it. He was now worried that he had sharpened Athens' claws at Persia's expense. It was the perfect timing for the Spartans to send a delegation to Persia.

Around 392 BCE, Antalcidas, a Spartan statesman and diplomat, was sent by Sparta on a peacekeeping mission to a governor called Tiribazus. He was the governor (satrap) in charge of Lydia, a Persian province in Asia Minor. When news reached King Artaxerxes II of Persia that Tiribazus was housing a Spartan delegate and dealing with the Spartans, he had the governor replaced.

Artaxerxes II then continued his military campaigns against Sparta until he realized that Athenian power was increasing. Athens had begun invading parts of Asia Minor and bringing former city-states back under Athenian control. On top of this, the Athenians were supporting rebellions of other Persian vassals.

In 388 BCE, Tiribazus was replaced, and he and Antalcidas worked together to win Persian support in the war. Although it took some time for Artaxerxes to get on board, Persia and Sparta would become unlikely allies once more. All that was left to do was convince the coalition Greeks to lay down their arms.

Peace by Force

Although the Persians were convinced that peace with Sparta was the way to go, the Athenians were not. They had struggled to come this far against the Spartans, and they were not willing to lose to them again.

Antalcidas, gleaning from the histories of Sparta's warfare against Athens, knew the quickest way to move the Athenians to cooperation. He ordered a ninety-ship fleet to move from Sparta to the Hellespont, blocking supply and trade routes to Athens.

This worked. The Athenians consented to lay down their arms, and the coalition of Corinth, Argos, and Thebes was essentially powerless without their leader. They found themselves at a table with Sparta and Persia, with the terms of the treaty dictated by King Artaxerxes.

The terms were more favorable to Persia than any other state in attendance. Sparta's domain was hardly affected, so the Spartans could care less, but the Ionian Greek city-states that had been liberated by Athens after the Greco-Persian Wars would be reabsorbed into Artaxerxes's empire. The autonomous states would be left to run their own affairs. The alliances forged against Sparta, such as between Corinth and Argos, were dissolved.

The year was 387 BCE, and eight years had passed since the Corinthian War first broke out. And it seems that Sparta was once again victorious. (It should be noted that there was no real winner of the war; however, Sparta suffered the least of the major powers, and it was responsible for keeping the peace.)

Was there really no one up to the task of bringing the mighty Spartans to heel?

Chapter 11 – Sparta's Decline

The Beginning of the End

After the Corinthian War, the broken bridges between Sparta and her allies could never be mended. The Peloponnesian League saw a massive decline in membership, and Sparta struggled to maintain control of what was left of her empire after the scourge of war.

In 385 BCE, two years after the King's Peace was ratified, Sparta laid siege to Mantinea, its former ally that had sided with Athens during the Peloponnesian War. Sparta was joined by Thebes, and together, they pulled down the city of Mantinea as a deterrent to other erring allies.

Sparta went on a rampage of merciless revenge against other weak former allies. Meanwhile, there was a population decline crisis back home. Due to the Greco-Persian Wars, the Peloponnesian War, and the Corinthian War, a good number of Spartans had perished in battle. Foreigners could not become fully-fledged Spartan citizens, which means the number of true Spartans depended on the remaining Spartans' ability to procreate. All the while, the helot population continued to grow.

In time, the weakening Spartiate population affected the size of the average Spartan army. This marked the beginning of the end for the most powerful city-state in classical Greece.

The Age of Thebes

"Brothers In Harm"

The Peace of Antalcidas, which ended the Corinthian War, had removed all of Boeotia from Theban control. It was part of the treaty's conditions that all autonomous Greek states that had been forced to become vassals in the course of the Corinthian War would be freed. Thus, Thebes suffered a two-pronged defeat. Their troops had been humiliated at the Battle of Coronea by the Spartan forces, and at the negotiating table, they were compelled to withdraw from controlling parts of Boeotia.

Five years after the Peace of Antalcidas, Sparta provoked Thebes for daring to hold hands with Athens during the Corinthian War. Thebes imploded with internal war: the pro-Spartan Oligarchs versus pro-Athenian Democrats. A bloody coup ousted many prominent Thebans from their country, and an oligarchy was established. The Cadmeia, Thebes' historic fortress and an important citadel, was garrisoned by Spartan troops in 382 BCE.

This sudden occupation of Thebes was surprising, considering that the two states seemed to get along after the Corinthian War. The Thebans had fought shoulder to shoulder against Mantinea only two years earlier. Epaminondas, an excellent Theban soldier and general, had led his troops on Sparta's side during the Siege of Mantinea. The Thebans were most likely bewildered at Sparta's sudden switch in relations with them, but they had, after all, sided against them during the Corinthian War.

Now fugitives expelled from their own country, the ousted Thebans rode to Athens. They were led by a nobleman warlord and Democrat named Pelopidas. He also had fought with the Spartans at the Battle of Mantinea. Plutarch records that he would have lost his life were it not for the timely intervention of his friend, Epaminondas:

> "Pelopidas, after receiving seven wounds in front, sank down upon a great heap of friends and enemies who lay dead together; but Epaminondas, although he thought him lifeless, stood forth to defend his body and his arms, and fought desperately, single-handed against many, determined to die rather than leave Pelopidas lying there. And now he too was in a sorry plight, having been wounded in the breast with a spear and in the arm with a sword, when Agesipolis the Spartan king came to his aid from the other wing, and when all hope was lost, saved them both."

The oligarchy in Thebes only lasted for three years before it was toppled by the exiled Democrats. Knowing that the Spartans would soon return, they spurred the warriors of Thebes to fight for the sovereignty of their country and take back the Cadmeia. The Thebans marched to the Cadmeia and besieged it.

The fighting was fierce, but the Spartans inside the Cadmeia agreed to surrender if they could leave unharmed. Since the Thebans wanted to avoid Spartan reinforcements, they agreed. It is speculated that if the Thebans had not agreed, they likely would have been beaten. The retreating Spartans met the reinforcement troop on their way home.

The Spartan kings, Agesilaus II and Cleombrotus I, continued pushing into Boeotia and antagonizing Thebes. Athens eventually came on board as an ally of Thebes, and in 378 BCE, the Boeotian War (also known as the Theban War) took center stage.

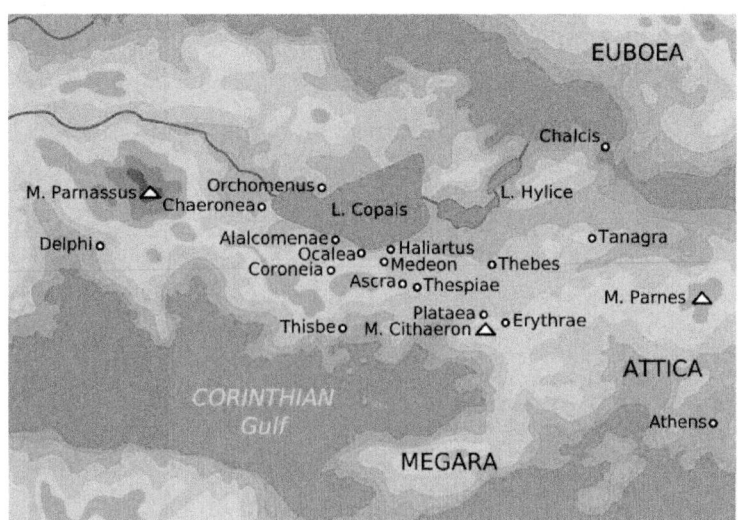

What Boeotia looked like during this time.

Sparta was ready as ever, as it was not the first time that alliances had formed against her. Thebes and Athens had tested the strength of Sparta in the past and bled for it. The Boeotian War could drag on for another fifty years for all the Spartans cared.

They knew they would achieve victory. But did history have something else in mind for them?

The Battle of Leuctra

The year was 371 BCE—seven years into the Boeotian War. Seven years of seemingly endless slaughter. Greece's soil was soaked with blood, yet neither victor nor vanquished had emerged.

The Thebans and Athenians were no longer getting along. The Thebans had taken Plataea in 373, which greatly upset Athens. It was also clear to Athens that Thebes was on a quest to create a Boeotian confederacy and eventually challenge Sparta's political domination, something they were likely eager to avoid.

Although a peace conference was formed, nothing came of it. Epaminondas insisted on signing for all of Boeotia instead of just Thebes. This upset King Agesilaus so much that he took Thebes' name off the treaty altogether. Needless to say, the treaty was not signed. The Thebans and Spartans stormed out of the peace conference with renewed determination to see the war to its end.

King Cleombrotus of Sparta mustered around eleven thousand Spartan hoplites and one thousand cavalrymen. He led the march to a small town in Boeotia located along the Gulf of Corinth. The Thebans didn't anticipate this move, so they hurriedly moved to block the Spartan troops at Leuctra.

Here, unknown to the Thebans or even the Spartans, history would be made.

The Theban general in charge of this fight was none other than Epaminondas, and he had selected an interesting squadron to secure the left wing. It was the Sacred Band of Thebes. The band was comprised of three hundred Theban men. More specifically, the Sacred Band was composed of 150 couples, with one older and one younger. In Plato's philosophical text *Symposium*, he implies that the men in the Sacred Band were the best of warriors because they would fight hard to protect their lovers.

Epaminondas was nothing like the war generals the Spartans had encountered in the past. His strategy was to attack the Spartan king and the strongest men in his army. Leuctra was the perfect place for this, as there were no obstacles of nature or impediments to the execution of his strategy.

The whole of Greece knew that the strength of Sparta was in the phalanx, and the traditional Spartan phalanx had a long wall, ten to twelve files deep. Epaminondas deviated from the norm and ordered a narrower phalanx, one that was fifty files deep. He also set the Sacred Band and light infantry ahead of the phalanx to break the Spartan lines. Puzzled by Epaminondas's tactics, Cleombrotus commanded the Spartan cavalry to come out front, exposing the left wing to attack.

The Thebans would not miss this chance for the world.

The men of the Sacred Band proved their mettle against the Spartan cavalry and sent them retreating to their original position.

This broke the Spartan defensive line, and the Thebans breached it, sending shockwaves to King Cleombrotus's troops.

The twelve-file Spartan phalanx could not hold against Epaminondas's fifty files. Four hundred of Sparta's finest soldiers fell in the battle, including King Cleombrotus.

In total, the Spartans lost between one thousand and four thousand men. The Thebans, on the other hand, lost between less than one hundred to around three hundred men of their original six thousand units. It was a monumental victory for Thebes and the worst defeat that Sparta had ever encountered.

The news spread from the battlefield to the city gates and every street therein. The invincible Sparta, which had just been defeated by the underdog Thebes, might not be so invincible after all.

The Aftermath of the War

Epaminondas and his Theban army had saved Boeotia, but the war was not over yet. Winter came quickly that year, but it was not enough to hold the eager Thebans from marching south. There, they launched coordinated attacks on the Peloponnese, sticking a spear in the very heart of Sparta.

Within the city walls of Sparta, the helots had heard of their masters' defeat and had begun another revolt. For the first time, fate was on their side. They found a savior in Epaminondas, and hundreds of thousands of helots were freed from Spartan oppression. Their ancestral home, Messene, was reestablished, and forts were built to repel future Spartan aggression. Centuries after the First Messenian War, the Messenian helots were no longer slaves. They could live as free men and women in their own land. They did not have to look over their shoulders at night or slave away all day for the Spartiates.

Epaminondas moved on to the parts of Arcadia that had long been under Sparta's feet and declared them independent. Forty of these cities came together and formed a new Arcadian League, and they were committed to keeping the Spartans at bay. These

Arcadians, along with the Thebans, founded a capital called Megalopolis.

Sparta was pretty much done as a superpower in Greece. But compared to its centuries of unmatched power in Greece, the newfound Theban supremacy was laughably short-lived.

Epaminondas and Theban Hegemony

Despite his amazing exploits for Thebes, even a man like Epaminondas had haters back home. After stabilizing the southern Peloponnese in Thebes' favor, he returned home to a trial and an approved petition for his dismissal as Boeotarch, a chief officer of the Boeotian League.

He was accused of neglecting his duties and being obsessed with foreign affairs for his own selfish purposes. This was preposterous, considering that he had been away for the good of his country, but Epaminondas could read between the lines.

Having come from a poor aristocratic family and risen to prominence in Theban politics through blood and sweat, he was no stranger to hardships. He would not go down without a fight.

He endured an arduous trial before the Theban council, and in the end, he was granted his release and reelected as a Boeotarch. In 369 BCE, Epaminondas continued his military missions in the Peloponnese. The following year, he saw his friend Pelopidas released from captivity in Thessaly to the north.

For the next few years, he concentrated on subduing Sparta and gaining more allies. However, he eventually had to address the other major power: Athens. It may be somewhat surprising to hear that Athens supported Sparta, but Thebes was quickly becoming a superpower. This was something that Athens could not ignore.

Epaminondas's main target was Byzantium, and in 364 BCE, he set every corner of the empire ablaze with uprisings against Athens.

The Greek city-states in the Peloponnese that had aligned with Thebes found themselves in the same position as before. Like

Athens and Sparta, Thebes had an agenda to undermine their independence and become a hegemon in Greece. There seemed to be no end to the power lust of any state in its golden age, but the Greek city-states would not have Thebes run amok.

In one of his last acts as king, Agesilaus of Sparta approached a few of his former allies, including Athens, to join him on a quest to keep Thebes in check. Thebes had upset many Greek city-states, and what better place to express their displeasure than on the battlefield?

This one was called the Battle of Mantinea.

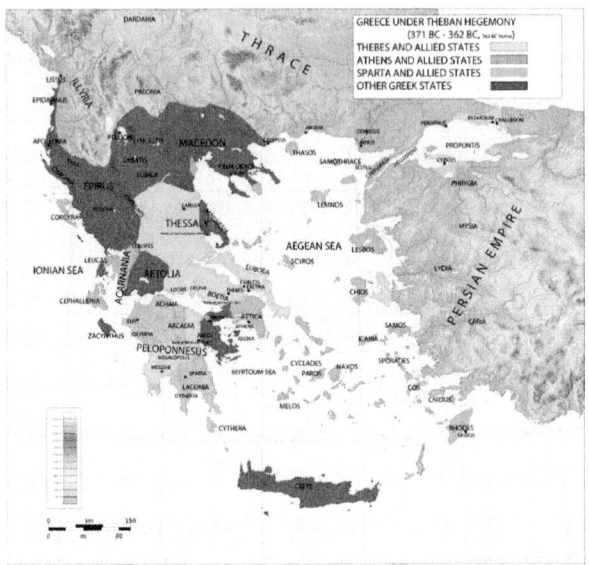

Thebes at the height of its power.

In the summer of 362 BCE, Sparta, Athens, Elis, and Mantinea—a combined force of twenty thousand men—marched against those of the Boeotian League, which was led by Thebes. They had around thirty thousand men altogether.

King Agesilaus II had learned a lot from the defeat and death of his fellow king, Cleombrotus, at the Battle of Leuctra—enough for the Spartans to mortally wound Epaminondas with a spearhead. However, the Spartans lost the battle when the troops of Mantinea fled the scene, leaving them outnumbered and vulnerable.

Epaminondas was quickly moved off the field, but the doctors could not save him. As the life bled out of Epaminondas where he lay, he gave one last admonition to his people: they should make peace with their enemies and focus on developing Thebes.

Epaminondas passed away, and his death was mourned by the warriors of Thebes. Ancient Greek historian Diodorus cites Epaminondas as one of the greatest men in his era:

> "For it seems to me that he surpassed his contemporaries...in skill and experience in the art of war. For among the generation of Epaminondas were famous men: Pelopidas the Theban, Timotheus, and Conon, also Chabrias and Iphicrates...Agesilaus the Spartan, who belonged to a slightly older generation. Still earlier than these, in the times of the Medes and Persians, there were Solon, Themistocles, Miltiades, and Cimon, Myronides, and Pericles and certain others in Athens, and in Sicily Gelon, son of Deinomenes, and still others. All the same, if you should compare the qualities of these with the generalship and reputation of Epaminondas, you would find the qualities possessed by Epaminondas far superior."

Unfortunately, it would seem as though when Epaminondas died, he took the chances at Thebes' successful domination of Greece with him. This was possibly because his successors had also died in the battle, leaving Thebes without anyone at the helm.

Thebes' influence dwindled, and as the Spartans grappled to make a comeback, Athens slowly reemerged to occupy the power seat of Greece. This did not go unopposed by Thebes, but without Epaminondas, things would never be the same for the city-state.

Chaos would swallow Greece whole, and until the death of King Agesilaus, Sparta would remain stuck in the shadows of obscurity.

The Onlooker

All along, a certain royal of a small northern Greek kingdom had been watching the saga unfold. This man was Philip, later known as King Philip II of Macedonia.

Macedonia was no stranger to Athens or Sparta for that matter, and Philip nursed ambitions of holding influence from across the Aegean to the Persian Empire.

While the rest of the world was distracted by the activities of Thebes and Athens, he strengthened his kingdom, which he took over in 359 BCE. After his conquests of parts of Greece, such as Amphipolis, Potidaea, and Methone, one of King Philip's advisors suggested the unification of Greece against Persia, just like old times.

Athens, Corinth, and Thebes vehemently objected to being pawns in King Philip's game of power. Such tropes of a "united Greece" were overplayed by this point in time, and it seems like it never had a happy ending. City-states in Boeotia and the Peloponnese also declined to join Macedonia, but King Philip wasn't asking nicely.

After his landslide victory at the Battle of Chaeronea in August 338 BCE, the Greek city-states that had refused King Philip were forced to agree. That year, he fashioned a brand-new league of Greek city-states under his command: the League of Corinth.

King Philip had chosen the perfect time to emerge as a formidable figure in the politics of Greece, but there was one more state that stood its ground against joining his league. It was none other than Sparta, the wounded lion of Greece.

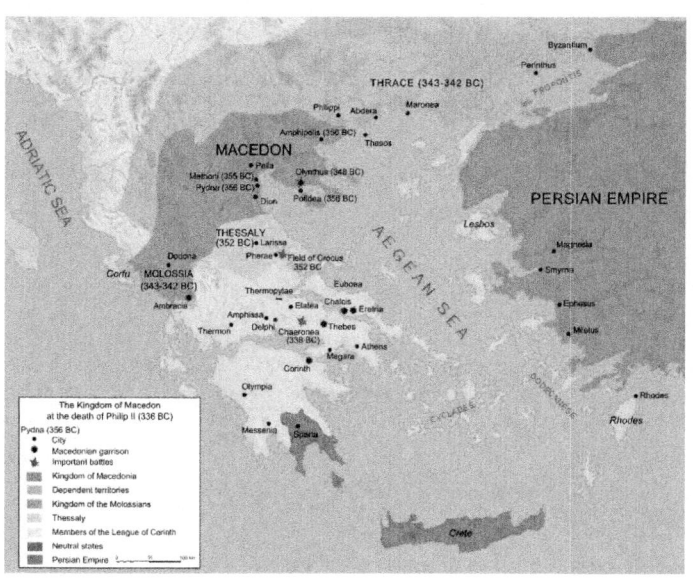

What Macedonia looked like when Philip II died in 336 BCE.
(Credit: https://en.wikipedia.org/wiki/Philip_II_of_Macedon#/media
/File:Map_Macedonia_336_BC-en.svg)

From the Battle of Chaeronea until his assassination in 336 BCE, Philip could not get Sparta to join the League of Corinth. Upon his death, his son, Alexander the Great, took the throne and set out for Asia to continue his father's legacy.

Before his trip, Alexander gave his regent, Antipater, who had also served his father, the charge of dealing with the stubborn Spartans. They had defied his father and defied him by refusing to join the league.

Sparta, now ruled by Agesilaus II's grandson, Agis III, had sought the assistance of Persia to get rid of the Macedonian influence. Although the Persians wanted to help, they couldn't spare much in the way of men since they were dealing with their own Macedonian problems. Sparta also asked Athens for help, but they refused.

Antipater led around forty thousand men from Macedonia to war against Sparta's twenty-two thousand. The armies collided in 331 BCE at Megalopolis. The war actually started on a good note for the Spartans. Midway through, though, the numbers of the Macedonians prevailed, and the Spartans were vanquished.

King Agis ordered his men to pull back, and in the aftermath, Sparta was integrated into the League of Corinth, plunging it further and deeper into political oblivion.

Who could save her?

Chapter 12 – Restoration Attempts and Collapse

After over a decade of being used for his political expansion campaigns, the League of Corinth died in 322 BCE, a year after Alexander the Great perished.

By this time, Sparta had long lost her place as the powerhouse of Greece. Except for maybe Agis III, the reigns of the Eurypontid kings after Agesilaus II were fairly uneventful. Sparta was absent from the frontiers of Greek politics, and the Spartans saw little of the spotlight their ancestors had gloried in.

Perhaps it was for the best. With great power came the heavy burden to keep it—and many times, it was at the expense of peace. Sparta stayed inert, surviving on the glories of the past and dimly hoping that the tables would turn in her favor one day.

This fueled the hopes of a bright-eyed young man who ascended the Spartan throne in 245 BCE.

King Agis IV of Sparta

Plutarch narrates that Agis IV was born into privilege. His mother and grandmother were the wealthiest women in all of Sparta. His father, who had been the king before Agis IV, led an unremarkable reign, although he surely gave his son a decent living and education.

As a boy, Agis IV was fascinated by the works of Lycurgus. The Sparta he had been born into was nothing like Lycurgus's Sparta in the ancient texts. The agoge was very much diminished, and his family hoarded wealth while debt ravaged the working middle class. The Spartiates (citizens of Sparta) comprised a meager seven hundred people, and six hundred of them lived in poverty.

Agis IV became the king at the age of twenty. He had either not undergone the agoge or was still in training, with the former being more likely due to its diminished state. Sparta was drowning in the collective neglect of its many mediocre kings. In his youthful zeal, Agis IV was determined to restore Sparta by reviving the economy and social outlook of Sparta and her people. His agenda was four-pronged, with the end goal of attaining the Sparta Lycurgus wrote about in his accounts.

King Agis IV consulted with his mother, who refused to sponsor his reforms with her wealth—that is, until her brother and the king's uncle, Agesilaus, stepped in. Like the majority of 3rd-century Spartans, Agesilaus, despite having vast estates, was languishing in debt when he heard about the king's reforms.

One of them was debt cancellation.

The Land and Debt Reforms

Only a few months into his reign, the new Spartan king issued a decree that all debts owed by the Spartiates and the non-citizens (the *Perioikoi*) were canceled. This was received with joyful cheer and praises to the king by the impoverished citizens of Sparta.

As part of the reform, King Agis IV, like Lycurgus, proposed the redistribution of land. The land would be divided into equal shares that would be given to the Spartiates, former Spartiates, and the Perioikoi.

Since many Messenian helots were freed after the Battle of Leuctra, the Perioikoi had risen to become the majority in Sparta, yet the average Perioikoi owned no land. All that was about to change.

The Spartan elite grumbled at the news, but when the ephors, led by the king's friend, Lysander (a descendant of the famed Lysander who participated in the Battle of Aegospotami), approved the king's proposal, they could not protest. Also, the king and his family had to let go of their estates as well, leading by example.

Through it all, Leonidas II, the Agiad king of Sparta and Agis IV's co-king, was against the reforms. Leonidas had acquired much wealth for himself, and unlike King Agis IV, he was unwilling to let it go.

Leonidas's attempts at pulling the strings in the Spartan Ephorate against Agis IV backfired, resulting in his banishment from the throne. He was replaced with his son-in-law, Cleombrotus II.

A House of Cards

Canceling debts and reforming land ownership were only some of what Agis had in store for Sparta. He also sought to revive the agoge and the mess halls, the latter of which had helped to put the people on an equal footing. Agis's uncle, Agesilaus, advised him to get the easiest reform done first.

One day, the people of Sparta gathered around a bonfire in the marketplace. There, all records of debt—bonds, securities, and related documents—were burned. The people's debts had been annulled. The king was lauded for fulfilling his promise, and Agis must have looked upon his people happily, knowing he had helped them.

Unfortunately, that was as far as he would ever go. After using his nephew to remove his debts, Agesilaus became a treacherous thorn in King Agis's side.

Once the king was away at war in 241 BCE, Agesilaus puppeteered the Spartan Ephorate to delay the land distribution reform. The masses complained bitterly, but King Agis was at war, having entrusted the affairs of the state to the wrong people.

His friend, Lysander, was no longer an ephor, and there was no one left in the Spartan government willing to uphold the king's reforms. Instead, the banished Leonidas II was reinstated as the Agiad king of Sparta. Cleombrotus, who had been made king with Agis's support, fled Sparta.

King Agis's reforms were thrown out before he returned to Sparta, and upon his arrival, he was arrested and detained. The corrupt ephors and Leonidas quickly pronounced him guilty of tyranny, and he was executed right then and there. His mother and grandmother were also killed at this time.

In the time it took for the people of Sparta to flock to the prison gates, King Agis IV was already dead. The Spartan peasants saw all hopes of land ownership vanish before their eyes. The future of Sparta was dim and bleak once more.

King Agis IV, at the time of his death, had only ruled Sparta for about four years. History would remember him as a round peg in a square hole—a king too soft for the hard times and too trusting to hold the throne of Sparta.

His sadly short life bore proof that it took more than a good nature, regal resplendence, and the noblest intentions to be the king of Sparta.

Cleomenes III of Sparta

Leonidas, the king who had stirred the ephors to murder his equal, King Agis IV, would be rewarded by fate in two ways. First, his son, Cleomenes III, would continue King Agis's legacy to reform Sparta, and second, Cleomenes would be one of the last of Leonidas's lineage (the Agiad line) to sit on the Spartan throne.

After hearing of his father's role in the execution of Agis IV, Cleomenes, then eighteen years old, came home from a hunting trip. His father's actions since before he was exiled and after his reinstatement was despicable, but the young prince was in no position to speak on it.

Cleomenes arrived home and met a rather festive mood. There was food and wine, and servants were preparing the palace for some big event. The curious prince asked his father what the occasion was only to learn that it was a wedding—and not just any wedding but his own.

He was to be wed to Agiatis, the queen of Sparta and Agis's widow. The prince could not fathom his father's cruelty. He feebly protested against the marriage, but by the day's end, he was married.

His marriage was of convenience, as the widowed queen was a wealthy woman. Eventually, though, the couple developed an affection for each other.

Seven years afterward, King Leonidas died mysteriously, and Prince Cleomenes ascended the throne as the Agiad king of Sparta in 235 BCE.

A Clean Sweep

If there was anything that Cleomenes III had learned from the fallen King Agis IV, it was that a king needed power to effect real change. First, he had to address the unchecked power of the Spartan Ephorate. An institution that could so cruelly put a king to death was potentially dangerous to his reign.

In the sixth year of his reign, Cleomenes, fresh from a bloody five-year-long battle, ordered the assassination of the five ephors of Sparta. Four were killed in a surprise attack, and the fifth one fled for his life, never to be heard from again.

With no ephors to challenge his authority, Cleomenes III began his reformation of Sparta, which was unopposed by his co-king from the Eurypontid dynasty.

First, the land redistribution project that Agis IV had begun finally saw its implementation. It was a historic day for the people of Sparta, especially the hardworking Perioikoi. The king awarded citizenship to the most valiant of them, which allowed the citizen population of Sparta to finally increase.

Next, Cleomenes reformed the crippled agoge, which had been the foundation of Sparta's past military reputation. Once again, the citizens would follow the example of their ancestors by sending their young to the agoge. Adults would purge themselves of materialism and return to communal living, eating together in mess halls and making financial contributions to the state.

For the Spartan army, Cleomenes had four thousand Spartan hoplites trained in the old way and ordered the inclusion of the sarissa to Sparta's arsenal. The sarissa was a pike created during the reign of King Philip II. As demonstrated when the Macedonians humiliated Thebes and Athens at the Battle of Chaeronea, the sarissa was more lethal for the phalanxes than the Spartan doru (a type of spear). The Spartan warriors learned how to use the sarissa, and they became the finest troops that Sparta had seen in a long time.

Cleomenes III went a step further to cement his power by deposing the Eurypontid king and replacing him with his brother, Eucleidas. This means there were two Agiad kings on the throne of Sparta, and there were no ephors to stand against it. Unlike all the kings before him, Cleomenes would enjoy the seven years left of his reign unchallenged—at least in Sparta.

The Achaean League

When Cleomenes III rose to the Spartan throne in 235 BCE, a man named Aratus, who came from a tiny city-state called Sicyon, was making political strides in Greece.

Aratus was the leader of the Achaean League, a confederation of Peloponnesian Greek states that came together to stand against the power-thirsty Macedonians. Sparta had aligned with the Achaean League under King Agis IV, but after his tragic death, Aratus was unsure of where Sparta stood.

Cleomenes had no plans to acknowledge Aratus or his Achaean League. Instead, he focused on expanding Sparta's frontiers by invading Arcadia. The Arcadians, alarmed at being targets of Cleomenes's new campaign, turned to the Achaean League for help.

When it became clear that King Cleomenes III wouldn't cooperate with the Achaean League, Aratus declared war on Sparta. This started the Cleomenean War.

What Greece looked like around 228 BCE.
(Credit: MapMaster; Wikimedia Commons)

This war saw Sparta and Elis stand against the Achaean League. Aratus and Cleomenes fought many battles, but Sparta won multiple victories. Tired of being defeated, Aratus appealed to Macedonia for help. The Macedonian king, Antigonus III Doson, agreed to assist Aratus in exchange for a strategic fort in Aratus's control.

It was a heavy price to pay, but Aratus was desperate to beat Cleomenes and the Spartans. So, he agreed.

This pact with Macedonia cost Aratus many allies in the Achaean League. Aratus had let his obsession with winning the war cloud his judgment, but he was well rewarded by Macedonia. In 222 BCE, King Antigonus of Macedonia marched to the pass of Sellasia near Sparta. There, the Macedonians and Achaeans crushed the Spartan army and killed Cleomenes's brother and co-king, Eucleidas.

Cleomenes narrowly escaped and fled to Alexandria in Egypt, where he had an old friend: Ptolemy Euergetes. Unfortunately, when his friend died that same year, the new ruler, Ptolemy Philopator, detained Cleomenes. Cleomenes escaped captivity in 219, but no one in Alexandria supported him. To avoid being captured again, he committed suicide. It was a tragic end to a man who had big dreams for Sparta.

After King Cleomenes's death, Agesipolis III, a grandson of Leonidas II, took the throne. He would be the last Agiad king. A fragile Sparta collapsed in anarchy, and several factions scrambled brutally for the throne of Sparta until a regent named Nabis seized it for himself in 207 BCE.

King Nabis reigned for fifteen years. He was loved by some, as he expelled the greedy aristocrats and redistributed their wealth. He also granted more non-Spartiates citizenship to grow the Spartan population and rebuilt the Spartan navy. To others, he was a land-grabbing tyrant with unrealistic imperialist ambitions.

Sparta no longer had what it took to build an empire, but King Nabis was undeterred in his venture. Like King Cleomenes III, he despised the Achaean League and conflicted with them, although he was often defeated.

King Nabis of Sparta extended a hand of friendship to King Philip V of Macedonia since they had a common enemy: the Achaeans. This genius power play won him the control of Argos, which had been Sparta's enemy for ages. When Macedonia was defeated by Rome in the Macedonian Wars, King Nabis was forced to give up Argos.

He had seen this coming, and he subtly defected to Rome, which helped curtail his losses. His alliance with Rome was short-lived due to his ambitions to expand Spartan power to the Roman territories in Greece.

King Nabis was assassinated within his own city by men he had trusted as allies, and for the first time in history, ancient Sparta became a vassal state. It would never again taste independence.

Part Four: Spartan Life and Social Structure

Chapter 13 – The Agoge

Education formed an integral core of many ancient civilizations, and Sparta was not exempt from this. No one became a true Spartan citizen (Spartiate) merely by birth. Only the toughened and strong earned the right to call themselves Spartans, and by the 7th century BCE, the ultimate determiner of that was the Spartan agoge.

The agoge was the birthplace of Sparta's finest warriors, like the brave three hundred who stood against Xerxes's hundreds of thousands at the Hot Gates of Thermopylae. The agoge was a system of education unlike any other that existed in classical Greece, and while its origins are widely debated, the histories point to one man: Lycurgus.

Origins

You will remember Lycurgus of Sparta as the man who left his country and esteemed political position to absolve himself of suspicions of treason against his young nephew and king-to-be, Charilaus. He traveled the world in search of exposure and knowledge, which he found in abundance, and then returned home.

This knowledge would be the foundation for a brand-new militaristic Spartan society that would pluck the city-state out of obscurity and set it on the center stage of political prominence.

Lycurgus had realized that the first point of change in any given society had to be psychological. How the people perceived themselves and their duty to their country would influence the efforts at sustaining the Sparta he envisioned. And what better time to begin instilling values in a human than childhood?

Lycurgus got to work, and the agoge came into being. It was an educational system that leaned more heavily on physical activity than book-learning education. It would play a large role in Sparta's glorious, war-filled future.

Getting in the Agoge

When a Spartan son was born, the infant would undergo a thorough inspection by the elders. If the infant was sickly or deformed, he would not be admitted into the agoge. Plutarch implies that such infants were discarded or left for dead in a cave or even thrown off a mountain, but this remains to be proven. Killed or not, deformity or ill health disqualified any child from joining the agoge.

If he was healthy, the child would be given back to his mother to be nurtured and raised until he turned seven years old. That age would mark the separation of the boy from his mother and a long, brutal initiation into manhood.

Getting into the agoge was the greatest honor a boy could receive in Sparta, and as hard as it must have been for many mothers, they could not object to having their sons carted away, sometimes never to return.

Exclusivity was an intentional tenet of the agoge, considering that classical Sparta was home to three classes of Greeks. At the top of the social chain were the Spartiates, the citizens of Sparta whose men were warriors. At the bottom were the helots: slaves and serfs to the Spartiates. Neither the helots nor the third class of people called the Perioikoi (non-citizen artisans, merchants, and petty traders) could participate in the agoge, no matter how much they desired to. Only the Spartiates were recognized by Spartan law to join the agoge. On a few occasions, the sons of high-ranking foreigners were accepted into the agoge, with Xenophon of Athens being one.

Survival

No doubt, the first night at the agoge would have been rough for many boys, even those who had long anticipated it. The reality was crueler than any expectation, and for every batch of boys taken away from home, some would not survive. They would fall, either by the whip, starvation, or exhaustion, and then they would be buried and forgotten. There was no room for "weakness" in the agoge—or in Sparta.

Paides

Upon arriving at the agoge, the boys had their heads shaved, and their shoes were taken from them. The agoge was so austere that such things as footwear and hair-grooming were a luxury. The boys' heads and feet would be bare at all times and in all seasons, enduring every discomfort to become both hard and agile.

Next, the boys were split into age groups. The newbies were typically seven years old, although some were as young as five, and they were organized into adult-supervised packs known as the paides.

The paides were between five and twelve years old, and they were educated in basic reading, writing, and possibly arithmetic. Classical Sparta's formal education is often appraised as brief yet meaningful. The boys were tutored in the art of making music with the flute, singing traditional war songs, and an intriguing dance called the Pyrrhichios.

The Pyrrhichios was a war dance, and it was quite popular for festivities in ancient Greece. Spartans used it to train their young for warfare. The boys would dance while bearing heavy Spartan weapons until their minds and bodies became one with their weapons. It is no wonder that the Spartan warriors were famed for wielding their weapons with superior dexterity on the battlefield.

Since physical exercises would make up most of their education in the years to come, the paides performed endurance tasks and athletic competitions in wrestling, war dancing, and running. It was also common practice for the older Spartans to incite fights among the boys. These fights would escalate into ferocious physical combat that made the boys tougher and stronger. From a young age, these future Spartan warriors were taught to eat only as much as they could speak: very little. Thanks to Lycurgus's reforms, Sparta was no place to be gluttonous or talkative. The paides were fed little food to tame their appetites and, interestingly, to encourage food theft. The boys would employ different tactics to steal food for themselves. If they were caught, they were brutally condemned to endure a whipping at the Temple of Artemis Orthia. This punishment stood as a deterrent not for stealing but for being bad enough at it to get caught.

In his work *Moralia*, Plutarch tells a famous folktale about this known as "The Spartan Boy and the Fox."

> "In the case of another boy, when the time had arrived during which it was the custom for the free boys to steal whatever they could, and it was a disgrace not to escape being found out when the boys with him had stolen a young fox alive, and given it to him to keep, and those who had lost the fox came in search for it, the boy happened to have slipped the fox under his garment. The beast, however, became savage and ate through his side to the vitals; but the boy did not move or cry out, so as to avoid being exposed, and left, when they had departed, the boys saw what had happened, and blamed him, saying that it would have been better to let the fox be seen than to hide it even unto death; but the boy said, 'Not so, but better to die without yielding

to the pain than through being detected because of weakness of spirit to gain a life to be lived in disgrace.'"

The paides were taught to choose death before dishonor and to take responsibility for their actions. The agoge was a place where they would be stripped—quite literally—of pride, selfishness, and fear.

Regarding speech, the paides learned that a true Spartan spoke very little. The word "laconic" finds its origin in "Laconia," the birthplace of the Spartans, and its meaning infers concise speaking. The paides were also introduced to the Spartan brand of irreverent, witty humor and how to take it heartily.

By the age of twelve, the boys would be regrouped as the paidiskoi, and their physical training would become much more intense and focused.

Paidiskoi

Joining the paidiskoi entailed more than surviving the first phase of the agoge or merely being old enough. A boy would have to excel in his basic education and physical training as a paide to win the approval of instructors for his promotion.

The paidiskoi phase marked the transition from boy to man, and as part of the welcome, each boy had his pretty clothes exchanged for a single cloak. Come summer, springtime, or the harshest winter, the boys could only be draped in their cloaks. They were not given extras or replacements a year had passed.

At this stage in the agoge, bathing and using body ointments quickly became luxuries, and there was more emphasis on the need to speak less. As expected, physical training for war and combat were taken up several notches, and the punishments for erring went from brutal to fatal. More child soldiers would die during this stage, leaving only the most rugged to proceed.

An important feature of the paidiskoi phase was that it fostered a special relationship between the boys and older Spartan men (young adults). As one of Lycurgus's reforms, a system called the syssitia mandated all Spartan men to eat at public mess halls. The paidiskoi could join young adult Spartan men at the tables, and they were taught to see every older man as their father.

Plutarch infers that these relationships were often sexual, but the Athenian Xenophon, whose sons had also undergone the agoge, denied this. According to Xenophon, the process allowed bonds of brotherhood to form—a bond based on unquenchable love and loyalty to Sparta, as well as to fellow soldiers in battle.

Hebontes

At twenty, the average trainee had endured the most extreme, life-threatening conditions in the agoge. He would have learned how to live without clothes and shoes, how to make his own bed with reeds he'd harvested by hand from the Eurotas River, how to wield a sword and spear, how to never cower in battle, and how to relate with his peers and superiors.

He would have been well on his way to becoming a true warrior of Sparta, but first, he had to serve. To this end, the hebontes were dispatched to different sectors to prove their mettle.

Some were appointed eirens, which were similar to prefects. These eirens were put in charge of the younger boys and carried whips for correctional purposes. This was no small responsibility since the eirens were responsible to their superiors, the Paidomonos, and other elders.

Other hebontes were posted as cadets to the battlefield as reserve troops. For those hebontes who performed outstandingly as paides and paidiskoi, their instructors might recommend them for positions in the Spartan Crypteia.

The Crypteia was another one of Lycurgus's innovations. It was a police system tasked with keeping the massive helot population in check through government-endorsed routine massacres. They would be sent to spy on and kill any helots suspected of inciting revolt. Only young, agile Spartans could join the Crypteia since their activities required stealth, camouflage, and swiftness.

Hebontes posted to the Crypteia could be assigned a few or multiple missions, depending on how well they performed.

As an additional requirement, hebontes were to be part of at least one mess group. Mess groups were social subgroups in Sparta, and each group had financial obligations to the government. Mess groups members were friends who ate, trained, slept, and fought together like brothers. In the previous phase of training (the paidiskoi), the agoge allowed boys to mingle with these groups and determine which ones were best for them.

To be accepted into a mess group, one would have to win the approval of every member. Many mess groups would accept only boys of good pedigree (from wealthy or famous families) and/or boys who stood out from their peers during training.

As an incentive not to become too lax, the Spartan agoge system had the most disgraceful punishment of all. It was not public whipping but rather deselection. If a hebontes was found to be cowardly, weak, or left unpicked by any mess group, he could be expelled from the agoge. In all of Sparta, there was almost no greater dishonor for a young man. Many would rather embrace death than such a life of shame, and so, the hebontes worked hard to earn their place.

For many years, the hebontes would serve in any capacity that Sparta saw fit—until one glorious day when he was thirty years old.

Sports and Other Rites

Sparta did not attain the esteem it did by sheer luck; a lot of hard work was put in to make it an elite society. The Spartans lived out every aspect of their lives per Lycurgus's recommendations for a truly warlike society. They were obsessed with physical appearance and the performance of their warriors, hence the continuance of the ascetic agoge.

The Phouxir

In the Spartans' eyes, a twelve-year-old boy was old enough for an extreme wilderness adventure.

One day, the boy would be handed a blunt spear and tossed into the wild in the most unfavorable climatic conditions to pit his grit and wits against nature. Of course, the boy would wander the wild barefooted and with a flimsy cloak as clothes. If he was unlucky enough to be sent out during winter, the odds were against him, and he would get no special treatment.

This exercise was called the phouxir, and every boy in the agoge, noble or commoner, could not escape it. For several days and nights, he would be left to take care of himself with just his spear and the determination to make it out alive. He would have to hunt or gather his own food. The smarter boys could steal food on their way into the wild, but they could not get caught.

Stealing soon became rampant among the boys of the agoge, and the citizens of Sparta (especially traders, merchants, and wives) had to be on their guard when around them. Often, even their vigilance was no match for the boys' rugged determination. Generation after generation, agoge boys during the phouxir would devise the craftiest means to pull off the perfect theft, and the villagers, once robbed, had to put up with it.

The Episkyros

For recreation, the agoge system featured a ball sport known as episkyros. It was a popular game in ancient Greece, but as expected, the Spartans sprinkled in a little more violence. Tackling to gain possession of the ball would quickly become a staple in Sparta, and many players would get severely wounded.

The essence of this sport was teamwork, a vital basis of the phalanx, Sparta's signature battle formation. As part of their training, agoge boys played this sport during city festivals to showcase their endurance and ability to function as an unstoppable team.

Historians consider this sport to be one of the oldest forms of soccer, but unlike soccer, the ball could be handled with both hands and feet. The episkyros is also said to have borne some semblance to the Japanese ball game cuju.

For a game of episkyros, the boys would be split into two teams of twelve to fourteen players, and each team had two objectives: to get the ball past a white line (the skuros) and score goals against the other team, as well as to defend their side of the line against goals from the other team.

This game was tougher in practice. Getting past the defensive line of the opposing team took a stronger, more organized team. Tackling was allowed to gain or retain possession of the ball, and brute strength was required to excel at it.

Every year, citizens and other inhabitants of Sparta would come to watch this game, cheering on their favorite teams in the arena. Although it was more common among the agoge boys, Spartan girls also played this game.

The Hoplite

From his first night as an inexperienced paide to his eventual emergence as a true hoplite, there was no rest in the agoge. It was a no-brainer that the boys were drilled in the art of wielding weapons.

The Spartan aspis (shield) was large and heavy. It took years to get accustomed to its weight. Spartan spears were also unusually long, which made them excellent for long- and short-distance attacks. The agoge boys were taught to handle these, along with their swords, skillfully.

Coordination, stamina, strength, and endurance were the most tested traits in battle, and a true hoplite could tick every box. He would leave the warmth of home at the age of seven and be trained to show no mercy in battle.

At the age of thirty, the agoge student could reenter society. He was no longer a boy but a fully-fledged Spartan warrior, broken and forged to perfection in the fires of the most arduous educational system in the world: the agoge.

Chapter 14 – The Spartan Government

Leadership

Sparta's rise to political prestige was one thing; staying relevant as a Peloponnesian superpower was another. It would take a superior government to ensure Sparta's place in Greece. Lycurgus was the genius statesman and creator of the Great Rhetra, a constitution that guided Sparta out of the Greek Dark Ages.

During his voyage to Crete, Lycurgus observed how King Minos ruled his people. He longed for Sparta to have a similar model of governance. Upon his celebrated return to Sparta, Lycurgus confirmed his mandate to transform the political structure of Sparta from the Oracle of Delphi. Then, he rolled up his sleeves and got to work.

Lycurgus's efforts would see Sparta restructured into an oligarchy, although it would consist of multiple decision-making bodies to lower the risks of tyranny and dictatorship. Sparta was not for one man or king. Lycurgus's model of governance would outlive him for four centuries.

Gerousia: A Transition to Power

Elders were revered in antiquity as custodians of wisdom, and this was especially so in Sparta. Having lived out their youth in service to Sparta on the battlefield, older men were eligible to join the council of elders as drafted by Lycurgus. Not just any older man could join; they had to have proven themselves as war heroes and champions.

This council of elders, called the Gerousia, held the highest authority in the Spartan government. This institution was first referenced in Plutarch's piece titled "Life of Lycurgus," and it acted as a supreme court of sorts, as the Gerousia was empowered to make the most crucial decisions affecting the state.

A man had to be at least sixty years old to join the Gerousia, and the council of elders had only thirty members, which included the two kings of Sparta. While positions in the Gerousia were open to any elder Spartiate who met the age and war experience requirements, it was easier for men from affluent, aristocratic families to actually secure positions. The poorer, unpopular Spartiates often lacked the resources and influence to garner votes from the people, so they often took a back seat during the elections.

The twenty-eight members of the Gerousia, apart from the two kings of Sparta, were called gerontes, and their position was lifelong, just as the kingship was. Every time a geronte passed away, a spot would open up. Elections would be held in the city hall. The men of Sparta would gather and vote for the most qualified (and their preferred) man to fill the position.

For this, Sparta made use of a simple and direct voting system: voice voting. Well, to be frank, they simply shouted. There were no modern voting devices or methods in use at the time, but it did not stop the Spartans from getting things done. The elections were presided over by an assembly of incumbent gerontes, and they would select a few trusted men. These men would then be confined to an empty room near the hall. These men would decide the winner of the elections; therefore, they were not permitted to see the candidate being voted for at any given time. That way, they would make a decision based on the name being shouted the loudest. While this voting method had many flaws, it was in use for a long time.

For a people as aggressive as the Spartans, you can expect that their elections were loudly conducted. In Plutarch's words, they were "most hotly disputed."

Once the new geronte was elected, the Gerousia would have to get to work. Every elected geronte would be thoroughly trained to understand his functions and constitutional limits.

The Gerousia's first responsibility, in accordance with the Great Rhetra, was to make laws. This was typical for any legislature, and the Gerousia was tasked with policymaking in order to further expand Sparta.

The council of elders was also responsible for going through what would be discussed at the Apella (citizens' assembly). This was another reason the Gerousia was regarded as the supreme legislative body in Sparta. If the Gerousia deemed a matter too sensitive or unnecessary, it could never be spoken of at the Apella. Ultimately, the Gerousia drafted the agenda for every Apella meeting.

During a meeting of the Apella, the citizens were afforded constitutional rights to make some decisions. In time, however, such resolutions could be overruled by the Gerousia. All the elders had to do to declare their disapproval was walk away from the Apella meeting, and the decision in question would be nullified.

The powers of the Gerousia were not only legislative. The council was also endowed by the Great Rhetra with judicial powers. If any Spartan was accused of grave crimes, such as treason or murder, only the Gerousia could conduct a trial. If found guilty, the Gerousia could mete out punishment to the criminal, which could range from fines to exile or execution. If a king disregarded the customs and rules of Sparta, the Gerousia, with support from the Ephorate, could strip him of his crown and have him expelled.

Such power and responsibility made a position in the Gerousia highly coveted by the men of Sparta, inspiring the younger men to work hard to earn it.

Apella: The People's Mandate

Citizenship in Sparta came with many perks, especially for the males. The Apella was one. This was an assembly of male Spartiates who met every full moon to deliberate on matters affecting the future of Sparta.

To become a true citizen, each man must have been trained in the agoge and succeeded in all his tasks. Most Spartan men in the classical era would have fought in at least one battle. This alone qualified almost every Spartan man to be part of the Apella.

The age of admittance was thirty (the same age for graduating from the agoge). Initially, the Apella would gather in someplace called the agora, which was an open public space. This was Lycurgus's idea, as it would keep the citizens concentrated on the proceedings of the Apella rather than getting distracted by decorative statues or paintings, which were often found in city halls.

The list of topics to be discussed during a meeting of the Apella would have been drawn up by the council of elders (Gerousia), and a meeting could take many hours. Heated arguments were a common occurrence, but a consensus had to be reached on every matter.

Initially, the Apella could make decisions unopposed, but around the 7th century, the kings of Sparta noted how easily resolutions could be made by the people. To cushion the dangers of such freedoms, the Great Rhetra was amended to give veto powers to the Gerousia. Thenceforth, the council of elders could reject a decision made by the Apella if they, in their wisdom and military experience, deemed it unseemly. Also, the ephors and gerontes moderated every meeting of the Apella.

In line with the Spartan constitution, the citizens in attendance of the Apella could deliberate on kingship, succession, foreign policy, war, peace treaties, the military, and legislation. The most significant function of the Apella was the election of ephors and gerontes by voice voting. New ephors were elected every year, but, as you read above, this was not the case for the gerontes since it was a lifetime position.

Lycurgus's vision for the Apella was for Spartan citizens to be a part of the government and for their voices to be heard—very much literally.

The Ephorate: Political Divinity

It is impossible to talk about Sparta's history without coming across a certain institution of five men who shared powers with the kings of Sparta themselves: the ephors.

The historians Plutarch and Herodotus did not agree on the origin of the ephors, which was perhaps the most powerful arm of Sparta, so there are two versions of their origin.

According to Plutarch's account, the ephors came to be at a time when Sparta was engrossed in the Messenian Wars. The two kings of Sparta were away from their thrones for many years, leaving a void in the leadership. A permanent solution was found by electing a committee of men to rule Sparta while the kings were at war.

Herodotus vehemently disagrees with this and claims that the ephors existed long before the Messenian Wars. According to him, the Ephorate was another political brainchild of the great Lycurgus. This institution was an idea inspired by the Oracle when Lycurgus made his famous consultation at Delphi.

Fortunately, these contrasting stories of the Ephorate's origin do not take away from what is known about its functions and powers.

In regards to membership, the Ephorate was for Spartiate men only, as were the other arms of the Spartan government. Five men between the ages of thirty and sixty could be elected as ephors. It is not known why they had to be exactly five in number, but a few historical accounts suggest that Sparta may have been home to five towns and that an ephor came from each one. If this were the case, equal representation would ensure unity among the smaller towns.

A 19ᵗʰ-century drawing of the ephors.

The Ephorate had the highest political authority in the Spartan state, even more so than the Gerousia. They were revered for their political and spiritual eminence, so much that ephors were exempt from bowing to the kings.

It is reasonable to consider that the institution of the Ephorate was seen as a far-reaching opportunity for Spartiate men to taste political power. While the positions in the Gerousia were reserved for noblemen and remained theirs until their death, the Ephorate could be occupied by the poor. Each ephor could serve for only a year, and they could never be reelected, no matter how excellently they performed.

This inclusiveness may have been designed by Lycurgus in good faith, but it has since been criticized as a flaw. These men knew that they only had a year in power and that they were immune to prosecution while it lasted. Thus, there were many instances of ephors being corrupt, demanding, and taking bribes for themselves to grow their wealth.

On the flip side, when their tenure was up, ephors could be prosecuted by their successors. An example was made out of an ephor named Cleandridas, who was found guilty of accepting bribes from the Athenians. He was banned, along with the incumbent King Pleistoanax, who was also found guilty.

The duties of the Ephorate were vast, so it is understandable why a Spartan man could only possess such power for a year in his lifetime. First off, ephors were advisors to the kings of Sparta. Every month, ephors would exchange oaths with the kings, a sacred rite that would be sealed by the Oracle. Since ephors were guardians of the law, the kings could not reject their counsel. They would consult with the ephors on every matter that affected the future of Sparta. At the time, it was very rare for the kings of Sparta to cooperate on every matter, so the ephors served as mediators too.

In times of war, a Spartan king could only declare war or move out troops after the ephors consented to it. Two of the five ephors would go along with the kings to the battlefield to ensure that warfare was conducted according to Spartan customs. Although the kings were the commanders, the ephors exercised authority behind the scenes.

In foreign relations, the ephors stood as representatives of the people of Sparta. They could be sent as emissaries on diplomatic missions, and they could receive foreign guests on behalf of Sparta. By extension, ephors could preside over discussions on treaties, war, and peace. This granted them powers to moderate the Gerousia and Apella meetings and make the final decisions when the people were too unorganized to do so.

The judicial functions of the Ephorate were similar to those of the Gerousia. Grave crimes, such as homicide, treason, and negligence of Spartan customs (especially by kings), were brought before the ephors for trial and punishment. Only ephors reserved the right to give the death penalty and depose kings.

By law, ephors could not sit by and watch a Spartan king remain heirless. They could intervene in private conjugal affairs as long as it affected the succession and stability of Sparta.

These powerful men were really only subject to the Oracle. They held a divine status since they were seen as the mouthpiece of the gods and counseled the kings according to the Oracle's decrees. In essence, the ephors were spiritual leaders.

On the grim side, the ephors were so powerful that every year, they could order the indiscriminate killings of helots. The Ephorate had the Crypteia under its firm control, and to ensure the helots did not uprise, the ephors sent trained warriors to take out the troublesome helots. A few times, the Perioikoi (non-citizen inhabitants of Sparta) were victims of these random massacres.

The ephors also interfered in matters of the agoge, ensuring that its standards of harsh discipline did not dwindle. When a Spartan child, male or female, was born, it would be inspected by the ephors for any signs of physical weaknesses. For boys who passed this test and got into the agoge, this bodily inspection would continue every ten days until adulthood. This made the institution of the ephors socially relevant in Sparta for as long as it existed.

Diarchy: A Reign of Two Kings

Sparta was not nearly as large as the Persian Empire, yet two kings ruled at the same time. While this spoke to how much ancient Spartans must have loved order and organization, there were several other fascinating undertones.

In every Spartan household, children grew up around stories that told them they were proud descendants of Heracles, the son of Zeus. Spartan kings were themselves hallowed by Thucydides as the "seeds of the demigod son of Zeus." This was a reference to Heracles, who in Greek mythology fathered celestial twins and was a direct ancestor of Aristodemus, the Heraclid. According to tradition, Aristodemus's twin sons, Eurysthenes and Procles, were the first dual kings of Sparta.

On a less mythological note, the diarchal nature of Sparta's monarchy finds another origin in the quest to foster peace between the two ruling families, as well as to avoid investing such immense powers into a single man.

Herodotus's explanation differs. According to him, the dual kingship of Sparta was established to ensure the compensation of the former ruling class, the Achaeans, who had been usurped during the Dorian invasion. King Cleomenes I did say it aloud at some point in his life that he was an Achaean, not a Dorian.

Whether by celestial twinship or as a means to resolve conflicts between families and tribes, the reign of two kings in Sparta remained in vogue for many centuries.

Sparta's greatness was epitomized in the acts of her kings in battle. In the histories, the Spartan kings were more military commanders than political heads of state. Since they lived most of their lives on the battlefield, they had little time to be involved in Spartan politics. This was, for the most part, left to the Ephorate.

When the kings were not leading Sparta and other parts of Greece to war, they wielded considerable religious and judicial powers. They were permanent members of the Gerousia, and like the rest of the council, they would deliberate on matters affecting Sparta and her people, albeit guided by the Ephorate.

The kings were revered as being favored by the gods, so they were the chief priests of Sparta. They conducted religious rites and ceremonies, and they oversaw the offer of sacrifices to the gods as required by the Oracle. The kings could not make decisions without the Oracle's blessings through the ephors, but they were adored by their people as royalty.

The two kings shared equal power, which bred frequent clashes when a decision had to be made. The ephors would step in to mediate between the two kings and break the deadlock.

Leonidas I, the seventeenth king of the Agiad dynasty and son of King Anaxandridas II, stands as the most famous Spartan king in history—a sharp contrast to his co-king, Leotychidas, whose treachery ended in a disgraceful exile. King Leonidas is best remembered for standing with his three hundred Spartan warriors against Xerxes's enormous army at the pass of Thermopylae.

Social Structure

Anyone who took a walk down the streets of ancient Sparta was bound to quickly notice something—the people were far from equal.

This was because Sparta operated on a rigid, socially regimented system that favored its citizens (Spartiates) above others. Spartan citizenship was different from other societies, and it was harder to attain than to lose. No one, except perhaps the royals, could be citizens merely by birth. There was a lot of work to be done to earn it—hard work that was not for the feeble-minded. Upon becoming a citizen, a Spartiate would spend the rest of their lives protecting their status. Acts of crime, disobedience, or cowardice could strip the guilty of citizenship, which was a fate more embarrassing than death.

While the kings, ephors, and gerontes retained power in the affairs of the state, only the citizens of Sparta enjoyed true freedom. Ironically, these citizens of Sparta did not constitute a majority of the population. They were the minority, but then, wasn't that the entire point of an oligarchy?

Spartiates: The Privileged Few

Sitting atop the social pyramid in classical Sparta were the Spartiates, the recognized citizens of Sparta. For men, citizenship rights were given at the state-sponsored agoge. There, boys were fashioned into strong, loyal, and nearly invincible Spartan men and tested in battle. If they died in battle or returned alive and victorious, they would become true Spartiates and enjoy the unlimited opportunities that came with it.

For non-royals, there were opportunities to serve Sparta in the capacity of ephors and gerontes, if elected. Spartiates did not need to be elected to be part of the Apella, the esteemed people's assembly.

Male citizens could only marry women of the same standing, and for every child born into a Spartiate family, there was a chance to become a true Spartan. Both male and female Spartiates could own land, which the helots would farm.

Another privilege of being a Spartiate was that, male or female, they were not required by law to work for a living. Despite being the only demographic with unlimited legal rights to wealth, freedom, state protection, and education, the Spartiates did not have to engage in commercial or manual labor.

The only full-time occupation of a true Spartan man was being a warrior or training to be one. For the women, there were was only childbirth, physical training, and supervisory duties in the home. The Perioikoi and helots made up the population of manual and menial laborers.

Perioikoi: Somewhere in the Middle

The second social class of Spartan society did not have an incredibly rough life, at least in comparison to the helots. Known as the Perioikoi (or Perioeci), this caste represented the non-citizen inhabitants of Sparta. They constituted a good part of the population in Laconia and Messenia, which were both Spartan vassals.

These people enjoyed some rights. While many Perioikoi were not born Spartans, some were Spartans who had failed to join the agoge or ex-Spartiates who got demoted, possibly for defaulting on their financial obligations to the government.

This demographic oversaw the commercial sector of the Spartan society. They were weapon and armor makers, craftsmen, farmers, traders, and merchants. The bravest among them could participate in Sparta's military expeditions and fight shoulder to shoulder with the hoplites and helots. If they worked hard enough at their businesses or in battle, a Perioikoi could be rewarded with citizenship, but the Spartans rarely let that happen.

The Perioikoi may have enjoyed some rights to land ownership, but they could not vote or hold positions of leadership. From time to time, these people could fall victim to coordinated attacks aimed at the lowest social stratum in classical Sparta: the helots.

Helots: A Mass of Slaves

Sparta was home to the Spartiates and Perioikoi, but there was another class. These people were seen as the dregs of society, and they were sometimes treated worse than animals. They were none other than the helots.

Life as a helot in ancient Sparta was not coveted. While there are multiple accounts of how they came to be, the helots were no doubt state-owned slaves whose freedoms and rights were next to nonexistent.

One could find helots in every Spartan household, and they would perform domestic and menial labor. They would row the warships and serve in battle as military valets. This made it nearly impossible for the helots to do anything throughout their lifetime that was worthy of special recognition or led to citizenship.

An important distinction between the slaves in other parts of the world and the helots in Sparta was that helots were not owned by any individual. The government reserved the authority to assign and reassign them at will, and their labor was rewarded only by food and drink.

Enough historical sources confirm the ill-treatment of helots by their Spartan masters. They were humiliated and harshly punished for wrongdoings or for doing nothing at all; sometimes, the Spartans punished them just to remind them of their place. Spartans were known for getting their helots drunk on wine and watching them ridicule themselves in public for entertainment or having them serve as lessons to their children to avoid drunkenness.

Helots could not dream of attaining political office or any form of influence in Spartan society. Instead, they had to endure the hatred of their masters and look over their shoulders in case the Spartan Crypteia was lurking in the shadows.

The Intersection

On the surface, there was almost no meeting point for the three social classes that thrived in classical Sparta. Nothing could ever bring the Perioikoi and helots on the same level as the free citizens. Geographically, they didn't occupy the same settlements.

Despite working in Spartan households and farmlands, helots would return to their quarters or settlements at the day's end. Perioikoi would retire to their settlements after leaving the markets or other places of business. Since the helots and Perioikoi were free to practice their native religion, spiritual activities and festivals did not even bring these classes together.

Daily contact with one another would not change the fact that these inhabitants of Sparta lived worlds apart—except for one thing, which frequently happened in Sparta: war. As you have read in this book, wars occupied much of Sparta's history. These wars were the only times when every helot, Perioikoi, or Spartiate fought for himself and Sparta. Every Spartan warrior, regardless of caste, would stand side by side as momentary equals for the glory of Sparta.

In Sparta, the only true leveler was warfare.

Chapter 15 – Spartan Warfare

The battlefield was where the finest soldiers in the classical world, such as the mighty Spartans, were tested and proven. Any man who could emerge from the agoge in one piece was worthy of taking his place on the field against the many enemies of Sparta.

When Xerxes unleashed one of the most terrible monsters the world had ever seen—a ferocious beast made of infantrymen and cavalrymen in their hundreds of thousands—the Spartans led the epic defense. Flanked by their Greek allies, the Spartans fought the monster with their swords, shields, spears, and their lives until the victory was Greece's.

Sparta's role in warding off the Persians set a precedence in the art of warfare that no Greek city-state would beat. And such a feat could only be attained by the brute strength of a Spartan warrior, his superior armor, his unquenchable love for Sparta, and the unbreakable bond with his brothers-in-arms, which was nurtured from childhood and flourished until his death.

Despite their usually smaller numbers, the Spartans would prove time and again that "one Spartan was worth several men."

Sparta's Arsenal

No matter how brave or reckless, no soldier marched off to war unarmed against armed troops and lived to tell the tale. Even the mythical Greek gods who resided in Mount Olympus had Hephaestus, the god of blacksmiths, make them weapons.

An integral lesson in the Spartan agoge was the use of weapons and armor. For years, the boys would train their bodies to become used to the weight of Spartan weapons, along with the best way to wield them. Once the boys had mastered this, their movements with weapons would be seamless and natural.

And for a small city-state, Sparta had a very impressive collection of weapons.

The Aspis: Layered Shields

When you take a look at Spartan shields, your first thought is most likely, "Man, those are big!" They were almost three feet in diameter, and they were as large as they were heavy. This design was intentional.

The aspis (also known as the hoplon) was made from fine quality oak wood and topped with a coat of bronze for shine and protection.

An aspis believed to be from the Battle of Pylos in 425 BCE.
(Credit: Giovanni Dall'Orto)

These were the shields that protected the Spartan warriors from the barrage of arrows ordered by the Persians during the Greco-Persian Wars. The Spartans would cluster their shields together to form an impenetrable bronze wall for both offensive and defensive purposes.

The aspis weighed around sixteen pounds, which means it took quite a bit of strength to carry for several hours. Fortunately, the Spartans were made of steel and had been taught how to bear these shields long before they became men.

The size of these shields could cause fatal damage if they were used to bash an enemy, and the Spartans took the liberty of using this to their advantage. They would crush the bodies of their enemies with a single strike and form impenetrable defensive lines with their shields.

The shield reached from a man's shoulders to his knees, covering the entirety of his middle torso. Each shield had an arm grip for easy mobility and maneuvering.

In modern representations of antiquity, Greek shields have blazons inscribed on them, and those of the Spartans bore the Greek letter "lambda," whose symbol was an inverted "V." Lambda is the equivalent of the letter "L," which supposedly stood for "Lacedaemon," a reference to the native home of the Spartans.

However, many historians have criticized these as false representations, arguing that ancient Spartan shields were not properties of the state but individual belongings. So, people designed their shields with or without blazons and could take them to battle as long as the shield met the required dimensions. A few others agree that Sparta hoplites used shields with the lambda blazons but only from the era of the Peloponnesian War onward. Unfortunately, the Spartans who were alive then are not around to clear the air.

Another unique element to Spartan shields was that it was convex, which means they could use it to float on water. Spartans could cross rivers atop their shields without fear of drowning.

Shields stood for the resilience, valor, and courage of an army, and the Spartans took pride in theirs. Fathers would pass their shields to their sons as heirlooms, and they should never be lost, even in death. A Spartan warrior could misplace his spear or even his sword but never his shield. It would be a huge disgrace.

So, every Spartan man on his way to war would take one look at his shield and remember the words of his wife or mother: "Come back home with your shield or on it."

Doru: Piercing Spears and the Javelin

The Spartan spear was another weapon of ruthless destruction on the battlefield. The doru (also known as the dory) was between seven and ten feet long, so it had to have been incredibly hefty. Nonetheless, Spartan soldiers would hold it in one hand and carry their shields with the other.

Spartan spears were crafted using wood for the handle and heavy iron for the flat spearhead, which was shaped like a leaf. The tip of the spearhead was fatal if thrust in the right part of the body, and its aerodynamic shape allowed the spear to be used for longer distances than other spears.

What made the Spartan doru truly unique was its rear-end thick bronzed spike. This spike served two major purposes: to stabilize the weight of the spear and to be used as a secondary weapon. If the tip of their sword ever got broken or cut off during battle, the Spartans could use the rear end of their spears to deliver considerable damage. After a battle had concluded, you could find the Spartans finishing off the wounded enemy using either side of their spears.

Most importantly, Spartan spears were used in the phalanx formations to keep enemy soldiers at a distance. The added length of the doru gave Spartans an extra advantage, and for any soldiers who came too close, the hoplites could potentially kill them.

The Greco-Persian Wars saw the superiority of Spartan spears on full display. The Persians had shorter, weaker spears against the formidable Spartan dorus.

In instances of long-distance hurls, the Spartan doru could only do so much, which was why the Spartans also had javelins with them. Since war was their full-time occupation, Spartans were extremely good at practically anything to do with warfare. They would never march into battle with poorly made or insufficient weapons. For every doru, there was an accompanying javelin. Javelins could go the farthest; they could break enemy lines and disrupt enemy formations.

Xiphos and Kopis: Lethal Blades

The Spartan phalanx could not keep the enemy at a distance forever, especially if they were counter-attacking with a phalanx. In this situation, the shield walls of the warring armies could collide, bringing the enemy troops too close for spears or javelins to be used effectively.

In other instances, the firm Spartan lines could be broken by a charging cavalry or formidable infantry, with the enemy then bearing down on the warriors of Sparta, slaying them without mercy.

Therefore, close-range combat required another type of weapon, something that was shorter, more precise, and just as lethal. This was the xiphos, a double-edged sword that dates to the Iron Age. The Spartans, who were unafraid of battling their enemies at any range, fashioned their xiphe (plural of xiphos) to be twelve inches long, which was shorter than the standard twenty-inch Greek model. On their way to battle, the Spartan soldier would sheathe his xiphos and let it hang from his shoulder belt (the baldric).

Modern reconstruction of a xiphos.
(Credit: Phokion; Wikimedia Commons)

On the flip side, for combat against enemy soldiers on horseback, the Spartans used a longer, single-edged sword called the kopis. Its thick, curved upper blade gave it the crushing momentum of an ax, and this was useful for knocking enemy riders off their horses.

Modern reconstruction of a kopis.
(Credit: Phokion; Wikimedia Commons)

Swords may have been secondary weapons, but the warring Spartans would master their use as well. The agoge created the best of the best.

Spartan Armor and Military Tactics

Sparta's army was the centerpiece of her existence. And for a city-state that soon extended its power to the entire Peloponnese, wars were inevitable. The Spartans soon earned the fear and respect of their neighbors as war machines who would choose death over defeat. From the 7th to 4th centuries BCE, Sparta flourished, and from the time of the great Lycurgus, the quality of men in Sparta's military ranks would never be questioned.

The Spartans would don their long crimson cloaks, horse-haired bronze helmets fashioned in the Corinthian style, leather bracers, and metal greaves. They bore their shields and various weapons. Essentially, the Spartan soldiers were intent on looking menacing to their enemy.

Beyond the physical, however, the Spartans fought as a single, powerful unit. While they were prepared to die for Sparta, they took an oath to protect one another on the battlefield—this was the entire purpose of the phalanx.

The Phalanx

The phalanx was a common defense battle formation in ancient Greece, but the Spartans were in a class of their own. Having undergone the most extreme form of training known to man at the time, the Spartans were reputed for their ability to hold a solid shield wall for longer than most. This was probably owing to the Spartan code of honor.

This sacred code recognized all soldiers as being equal, and it forbade the reckless breaking of ranks and suicide. No soldier was permitted to die in a fit of careless rage or desert his brothers in battle. They could not drop or lose his shield, as this would be greatly dishonorable. But most importantly, no soldier could break formation. The survival of the entire Spartan army depended on it.

The phalanx formation was simple in theory. A contingent of Spartans would lock their large shields together to form a dense wall, and another contingent would stick out long spears through small openings of the shield wall. This formation was used for defense, and breaking Spartan lines was often difficult for enemy troops.

To strengthen the wall, Spartan soldiers would cohesively stand shoulder to shoulder several files deep, with the next man ready to replace the one in front of him if he got killed. If the phalanx was attacked by a barrage of arrows, the Spartans would swiftly put down their spears and form a shield wall in defense.

In battle, the typical Spartan phalanx would be eight files deep at least. Using the phalanx for offense was more difficult, as the men would have to advance at the same pace without disrupting the shield wall. Such flawless coordination and teamwork could be found almost only among the warriors of Sparta.

The phalanx.

As thrilling as it must have been for the Spartans to fall into formation to conquer their enemies, the phalanx had its limitations. Since each Spartan would hold their spears with his right hand and the shield with his left, the left wing was more prone to attack.

Another flaw of the Spartan phalanx was that it could never be effective in broken or hilly terrain. The hoplites needed flatland for their formation to stay impenetrable, so, as part of Sparta's classic war tactics, they lured the enemy to where they would have the terrain advantage.

Finally, in instances of prolonged battles, the front rank could be compromised. Only the strongest among the Spartan troops held the front lines, but even they could get exhausted or killed. The middle ranks were often weaker and unable to sustain an onslaught for too long. This is why Spartan soldiers could not remain in positions of defense for too long. They would push back the raging enemy troops, striking them with their spears and short swords while slowly advancing behind their shield walls. If the front rank fell, it usually ended in a Spartan defeat.

But the Spartans were men of war, and their repute throughout Greece and beyond was of men whose defenses would never falter.

Rituals of Battle

Prior to leaving home for war, the kings of Sparta would offer burned sacrifices of sheep and goats to Zeus, inquiring if the battle was theirs to fight. If the Oracle assented to it, the animals slaughtered for sacrifice would be fed to the soldiers.

While others marched into battle with the sound of splitting war drums, the heroes of Sparta would serenade themselves with sweet and soft melodies of the flute. They would sing songs that reminded them of their love and pride for Sparta.

After a long bloody day, the Spartans would gather their dead and move them on their shields to be buried. For warriors like Leonidas, whose bravery was outstanding and uncommon, they would build national monuments of stone and iron. Hero cults were also common at the time, and they were committed to preserving and revering the memories of extraordinary Spartan warriors for generations.

For their brothers-in-arms who fell in battle, the surviving Spartans soldiers would grieve and send them off with rituals. If they were victorious afterward, they would celebrate.

Crypteia: National Assassins

In many ancient stories, Sparta was a hero, the savior of Greece, and the pride of the Peloponnese.

In this particular story, however, Sparta was a horrific villain—a villain whose monstrous appetite could never be satisfied, no matter how many slaves it devoured. This grim, dark tale is about a ruthless band of Spartan guerillas who were dispatched to the countryside of Laconia every autumn night.

Plutarch says that they were young, able-bodied men, fresh from the agoge. However, no one truly knows when the Crypteia was established. A few ancient sources credit its establishment to the era of Lycurgus's reforms in the 7th century BCE. However, historians like Plutarch find it hard to believe that Lycurgus was the brain behind such an institution, saying, "I certainly cannot ascribe to Lycurgus so abominable a measure as the 'krypteia,' judging from his mildness and justice in all other instances."

Plutarch's position is logical, considering that the nature of the Crypteia was in sharp contrast to what the Spartan military represented. Unlike the mainstream Spartan army, whose hallmark was organization and teamwork, the Crypteia taught its young Spartiate members independence, self-sufficiency, and stealth.

Young men assigned to the Crypteia were the finest among their peers and vicious masters of disguise. They would be sent out with daggers and some food. They were like predators who had only one kind of prey: unsuspecting helots.

During the day, the men from the Crypteia spied on the helots, sometimes marking out the errant and insubordinate among them—in other words, those most likely to incite revolts against Sparta. When the sun fell, these Spartan spies would execute the helots in the most brutal of ways, typically stabbing them to death with their daggers. Other helots who roamed the streets or worked late on farmlands during state-imposed curfews were also mercilessly killed.

These gruesome murders were not only sanctioned by the Spartan state through the Ephorate, but they would also go unpunished. The first few massacres by this "secret police" went unnoticed by the helots, but in time, it was clear that the state of Sparta was at war with them.

For generations, the Spartans had feared that the helots would one day take advantage of their large numbers and rise against them, which would, of course, pose a major threat to national security. To be a step ahead of this, the Spartan government tasked the Crypteia with the indiscriminate decimation of the helot population. It was a brutal way to remind the helots of their place: under Sparta's feet.

In the *History of the Peloponnesian War,* Thucydides tells a chilling story of two thousand helots who were invited to the city one day in 424 BCE. It was a very unusual day; the helots had received news that their Spartan masters were pleased with them for all their hard work over the decades and wished to reward them. The helots were requested to send their best men as representatives to receive their reward.

The helots could not believe their good fortune. In celebration of what seemed like an end to the fractious relationship with the Spartans, they sent two thousand of their best. The Spartans welcomed them and invited them to the temple for worship. The helots were decorated with garlands and assured freedom from their slave status. Overjoyed, the helots moved freely around the temple grounds, relishing the new, sweet air of freedom—until it became a dreadful mirage.

One after the other, the two thousand helots died mysteriously, and their killers, the Spartans, were neither investigated nor punished. This story exemplifies the horror the helots faced at the hands of the Spartans and the Crypteia.

Other historical accounts present the Crypteia as a rite of passage for young men who had just completed their training in the agoge. Nonetheless, countless helots were murdered by these young Spartans in service to the state.

The Spartans were able to subdue the helots into submission like they desired, but they could only stay shackled for so long. With the emergence of a younger generation of courageous and rebellious helots came a civil war. It was a war that would nearly consume mighty Sparta.

Chapter 16 – Women in Sparta

As history tells, the plight of women in ancient history was hardly palatable. In a typical ancient society, women were not equal to men. At best, they were housewives, mothers of children, slaves, or spoils of war. They could not own land or property; instead, they were properties of their fathers and later their husbands.

Despite this, women were seen as essential parts of society, and it is believed they embraced their roles. However, the fact that women were typically seen as insignificant in matters of culture, the military, and politics cannot be ignored.

There are some ancient societies that went against the norm, and one of those was a small Greek city-state in the Peloponnesian Peninsula. Spartan women were free to participate in many aspects of their society. These benefits are credited to the genius reforms of Lycurgus. He held the firm belief that women were the bedrock of society and that for Sparta's line of strong, courageous men to endure, the women who gave birth to them had to be strong as well.

With the acceptance of his political ideas in the 7th century BCE, Spartan women were ushered into a new way of life that would last for multiple generations. Unlike their sisters in Athens and other parts of Greece, the women of Sparta held considerable cultural power. Their fierceness quickly earned them repute in ancient Greece and a place in history.

Growing Up

When a Spartan girl was born, she would be inspected by the ephors for any deformities or illnesses. There are no records to prove that imperfect Spartan baby girls, like boys, were abandoned to die, but for the healthy, years of education awaited.

Spartan girls did not undergo the agoge. Instead, they would be formally educated at home by their mothers. They would learn to read and write and take classes in the arts and music. An emphasis was placed on poetry, dancing, singing, and learning how to play a wide range of musical instruments. During Spartan festivals, the girls would compete with their male counterparts in traditional dances and other activities for prizes and fame. The girls were also educated in philosophy to make them incredibly witty and sharp-minded.

It seems that the education of Spartan girls from aristocratic families was more sophisticated than those of the lower classes, but the basics were accessible to every Spartan girl.

Another fascinating detail in Spartan girls' childhoods was that they were fed the same rations as the boys. Spartans instilled the belief of minimalistic eating in their children at a very early age. So, in line with social norms, food rations were not gender-based. As adults, Spartan girls would also dine in public mess halls.

The similarities between Spartan girls and boys do not end there. Although Spartan boys could be found grunting and sweating through arduous physical training in the agoge, a Spartan girl would be doing just the same at home. Girls were not exempted from physical training in ancient Sparta. The routines were essentially the same irrespective of gender differences or individual weaknesses. The only difference to their training in comparison to those of Spartan boys was their purpose. Spartan women trained not for war but to keep their bodies fit and healthy for children.

Lycurgus believed that healthy Spartan men and women could only come from women with healthy bodies. Physical exercise was the means to that end. Thus, Spartan girls would participate in the same routines as boys: wrestling, foot races, javelin and discus throwing, boxing, and horseback riding.

Let us focus on the Olympics Games in ancient Greece for a moment, as it was a very significant event. The Greeks called it sacred, and as such, the arena was no place for married women, not even as spectators. Only unmarried women could watch the games; any married woman caught in the arena was put to a cruel death.

Pausanias tells the story of a noblewoman of Rhodes named Kallipateira. In defiance of the Olympic laws, she disguised herself as a male trainer just to watch her son wrestle. She was discovered and only escaped the death penalty because of her status. That incident led to the enforcement of stricter laws for subsequent Olympic events. Thenceforth, male trainers would be required to strip their clothes and be thoroughly checked before entering the arena.

Be that as it might, another woman would defy this. Cynisca was ready to challenge anything that stood in the way of her freedom. She was a Spartan royal and the daughter of King Archidamus II. She owned racehorses, which was a rarity even in Sparta, but the princess was very wealthy. Leveraging on her status and access to racehorses, Cynisca entered the Olympics and won two chariot races, bringing the freedom of Spartan women into the spotlight. It should be noted that she did not physically participate in the games herself, but since she owned the horses that won, the victory belonged to her.

The Freest of Women

Spartan girls were well-versed in Greek texts, the art of war, and how to tease agoge boys who performed poorly in physical training and competitions. This was aimed at spurring the boys to do better and to foster intimate relations with the opposite sex. It is little wonder that Spartan girls were sexually liberated so early in life.

In other parts of Greece, women would be given away in marriage long before they became adults. This was done to preserve the women's virtue for their husbands. In Sparta, however, women typically married when they were between eighteen and twenty years old. Traditionally, a Spartan man could not be truly married until he completed his training at the age of thirty. In effect, the age gaps between Spartan women and men were not as wide as those of other Greeks.

This afforded the women of Sparta time to freely explore their sexuality. While the men were away, Spartan women could befriend one another and engage in platonic and/or erotic relationships if they so wished. They could also have as many male lovers as they desired before marriage. A Spartan woman's pride wasn't in celibacy; it was in the strength of her body and mind.

Frequent physical training and exercise required comfortable, minimal clothing, which was another freedom that Spartan girls enjoyed. In many neighboring Greek city-states like Athens, women and girls were strictly conditioned to dress modestly. Long dresses symbolized the modesty and virtue of women, so they were not permitted to wear revealing clothes, much less bare their bodies.

This was not the case in Sparta. Even in childhood, Spartan girls would wear clothing that would seem scandalous to other Greek societies, and on special occasions, such as the Gymnopaedia, they could wear much less.

The Gymnopaedia was an annual Spartan festival held in honor of Apollo, Artemis, and Leto. Every summer, the Spartans would converge in public squares to celebrate the coming of age of young Spartans and the collective heritage of Spartans. This festival would go on for many days, with young Spartan men and women trooping out in groups to dance naked and sing traditional songs and epic poems. Stark nudity was a major highlight of ancient Sparta's culture, so Spartan women could not be disparaged for being a part of it.

A conversation about the freedoms women had in Sparta would not be complete without mentioning their wealth. They were the richest women in the Peloponnese and perhaps in the whole of Greece because they could own property and land. At the time, land ownership was a privilege afforded to only male citizens in other city-states, but Spartan women could own vast expanses of land as long as they could afford it. In the 5th century BCE, it is believed that one-third of Sparta's landmass was owned by women.

This is to be expected, though, given their thorough exposure to the economy through formal education. However, a more significant factor to their ability to amass wealth was their non-involvement in domestic chores. In Athens, girls were raised to keep the house orderly. As women, they would be in charge of it. They would cook, clean, weave clothing, and raise children.

The women of Sparta were different. They had helots to do all the domestic chores while they took on supervisory and administrative duties. A Spartan woman would never get her hands dirty doing menial chores, and she wasn't expected to. Consequently, Spartan women could focus more on their children, as well as the management of their prosperous estates. With this wealth at their disposal, the powerful women of Sparta could influence the course of the economy and politics.

Wives and Mothers

For a woman about to wed in ancient Sparta, love was very likely the least of her concerns. There were strong, handsome men everywhere she turned. She had to base her marriage on more than feelings. A core duty of any Spartan woman was to bear strong children and succeed financially.

Having been raised as independent and psychologically liberated, Spartan women had to be compatible with their husbands socially and sexually for a marriage to succeed. If it turned out that a union would not produce healthy children or any children at all, divorce was encouraged.

A Spartan woman was not obligated to be a virgin or celibate. As a matter of fact, Herodotus tells of the prevalence of polyandry. This kind of freedom allowed for the most outlandish family structures that ancient Greece witnessed. For instance, a man, after having his children, could have his wife move on to another man to give him more children. That way, women could birth more children, preferably males, to increase the military population of Sparta.

But before this happened, a marriage had to occur. In the classical era, many brides would fuss over what clothes to wear and how their hair looked on their wedding day. Even Viking brides obsessed over wearing their hair long and pretty for an elaborate ceremony. Athenians celebrated marriages with songs and dancing to bless the new couple, and the brides were expected to look their best.

The Spartans could care less for any of that.

Typically, the bride-to-be was no stranger to her groom. She would have known him by name and pedigree since she would have trained with him in childhood, jeered at him when he fell short of the standard, and danced with him at the Gymnopaedia. There was no need for elaborate introductions or prolonged betrothals.

It was also customary for Spartan women to give their consent to a suitor before marriage. If her father brought forward a suitor she did not desire, the woman, supported by her mother, could reject him for a more preferred man.

On the wedding day, there might have been a loud party. But the most important ceremony took place that night. On her wedding night, the newly-wed bride would shave her head and put on the clothes and shoes of a man. Then, patiently, she would lie in a dark room where her husband would come to her. After a brief, intense ritual tussle, her husband would whisk her away to their new home.

If her husband was still in the agoge, he could only sneak out at night to meet with her until he completed his training.

Men of Sparta were hardly ever home throughout their lives, so their wives held the fort as heads of the household. Historians like the Athenian Aristotle criticized how much power these matriarchs wielded in society, but it would remain the norm for as long as ancient Sparta existed.

While a Spartan woman spent her childhood and spinsterhood reveling in the rare freedoms and privileges she enjoyed as a citizen, motherhood called for a brand-new focus: ruthless courage in service to Sparta.

It was common knowledge that birthing children unfit to join Spartan society was a great dishonor. This propelled Spartan women to endure every physical training necessary to fortify their bodies against weak children.

After their children were born, the boys would be raised at home until they were seven years old and sent to the agoge. Female children would be around for much longer, typically until they were old enough to be married.

The joy of every Spartan mother was knowing her son was performing admirably on the battlefield. If he died in battle, his mother would, of course, grieve his passing, but she would be very proud that he had died as a brave warrior. She would brag about her son's sacrifice for Sparta to the envy of other women. This also applied to the honorable death of a husband.

A Spartan mother's duty did not end at celebrating the heroic deeds of her children; it also extended to meting out cruel punishments to errant sons. Any woman whose son betrayed or deserted his brothers-in-arms was a disgrace. Such cowardly men were never to be protected, and so, their mothers would often kill them if they returned home.

Cults of Women

Religion was an important aspect of ancient Sparta's society, and women featured heavily in it. The most prominent religious cults in Sparta were the cults of Artemis, Helen, and Eileithyia.

Artemis was the revered Greek goddess of fertility and the hunt, and she was seen as the protector of mothers and their children. The cult of Artemis erected a site for worship on the border of Messenia and Laconia. Spartan girls and women led their men in erotic dances. They wore face masks and sang hymns to honor the goddess of fertility. In the religious realm of ancient Sparta, the priestesses of Artemis were seen as considerably powerful.

The cult of Helen was another popular cult. There were many worship centers where Spartan women danced and sang in celebration of Helen's union with King Menelaus of Mycenae (pre-Dorian Sparta). Despite Helen's scandal with the prince of Troy, which led to the famous Trojan War, she was adored by many Spartan women upon her return to Sparta and posthumously. This confirms that the Spartan society was not averse to adultery, especially not when it was done by a daughter of Zeus.

At Helen's biggest shrine in Therapne, located near the Eurotas River, there were annual celebrations where the maidens of Sparta would sing and dance to worship their "pure and proper" heroine. There would also be physical bouts among the women to show their strength and for entertainment.

The cult of Eileithyia was another prominent cult among the women of Sparta. Eileithyia, the daughter of Zeus and Hera, was the goddess of childbirth, and she was revered by Spartan midwives, mothers, and pregnant women. When a Spartan woman was in labor, Eileithyia would be invoked to soothe her pain and grant an easy delivery.

A shrine for Eileithyia was built near the Temple of Artemis in Sparta. There, Spartan women would give offerings and make requests for fertility and healthy children.

Cults existed for Hera, Athena, and Aphrodite as well, among others. Spartan women would also hold memorial ceremonies for their fellow women who died during childbirth and erect specially-named gravestones for those who died while holding a religious position. Prayers, votive offerings, and sacrifices to Apollo for the victory of their men at war were also common among the women of Sparta.

Non-Spartan Women

The privileges mentioned above were, for the most part, enjoyed by the Spartiates, but there were also women from other classes who lived in Sparta. Female helots acted as domestic servants to Spartan mistresses, and you would find them in the kitchen as cooks or as maids. Some worked the farms, while others were fabric weavers.

Helot women, unlike the Perioikoi, were never paid for their labor. They were at the mercy of their Spartan mistresses and were natural targets of the Crypteia. There were instances of helot women having children for Spartan men. This brought about another class in Sparta called mothakes. It has been suggested that female mothakes were killed off at birth and that the males were allowed to live and join Sparta's army. However, there is not enough evidence to support this theory, as the information on the lower classes is lacking in comparison to the Spartiates in general.

In what may be considered a small form of freedom, helot women were allowed to choose husbands for themselves and live with their families. Unlike other Greek city-states, which instituted separate quarters for male and female servants, helots in Sparta lived together whether they were married or unmarried.

The Perioikoi women in Sparta could be found in the marketplace as traders and weavers. They earned their living through small- to medium-scale businesses and, like the helots, were permitted to live with their families. Another famous occupation for Perioikoi women was nursing. Non-citizen Spartans were hired by elite families within and outside Sparta for nursing services. This was the most prestigious occupation that Perioikoi women could find for themselves.

When Lycurgus's laws about prostitution began to lax, a few non-Spartiate women took up the occupation, and brothels became fairly common.

Dressing and Style

A woman in ancient Sparta could wear different clothes for different occasions.

The early stages of her life would have been taken over by physical training, and for this, she would wear short clothes. On special occasions, such as festivals or rites of passage, Spartan women might walk around naked, even around the men.

As one of Lycurgus's reforms, Spartans were not allowed to wear or spend gold and silver. This was to curb greed and encourage contentment. This law may have been binding during his time and for a few decades after, but eventually, wealthy Spartan women would own and adorn themselves with precious metals. They also wore scented oils as perfume and lined their eyes with charcoal to enhance their beauty.

The peplos, a full-length dress, was worn by women in ancient Greece. It was made from fine wool. Wealthier women wore peplos made from silk or linen, and Spartan women based theirs off the Doric chiton, as it was open on one side. Unlike their sisters in Athens, Spartan women could wear much shorter forms of the peplos or show off their thighs with high side slits. The Spartan peplos was held in place at the wearer's shoulders using ornamental pins called fibulae.

An example of a peplos.

Married women in Sparta preferred to cover their short hair with veils, but the younger, more spirited women flaunted their long hair uncovered. The only time Spartan women would weave fabric themselves was for religious festivities. Personal wardrobes were tended by the helots.

Spartan women had a unique style and were reputed to be beautiful and physically stronger than most. Such pride in their beauty, social status, and motherhood must have led a certain perplexed Attican to ask, "Why are you Spartan women the only ones who can rule men?"

Queen Gorgo's famous reply on behalf of the women of Sparta would resound through the ages: "Because we are also the only ones who give birth to [real] men."

Chapter 17 – Laconizein: The Art of Minimalism

In Eating

In many ancient civilizations, warriors ate in cycles; there would be extended times of minimal food consumption and brief windows of overeating. The Spartans, however, preferred a more consistent pattern. Young or old, no one was permitted to eat in large quantities, not even in celebration. Drunkenness was equally condemned as humiliating and despicable.

Spartan minimalism wasn't only in speech; a true Spartan was not a lover of food. He ate only to survive. Over-indulgence in food or obesity would make anyone subject to public ridicule, so Spartans trained hard and ate less to stay lean and in shape throughout their lives.

The Spartan diet was neither elaborate nor exquisite, even among the aristocrats. For the most part, everyone ate at public mess halls, leaving no room for pubs or *thermopolia* (public eateries in ancient Greece). Importation of food items was prohibited, so the Spartan populace could only eat the food that was grown on the farmlands tended by the helots. Pigs, goats, and sheep were slaughtered for food, and fish was commonly consumed.

Age groups dined differently from one another. While toddlers and children were given small rations of barley cakes, cheese, and goat milk, younger adults and the elders ate olives, figs, and the famous melas zomos: black soup.

Black Soup

For athletes and trainees in the agoge, there was much less food, and the quality was poorer. This was intentional, as it was believed it would instill endurance and restraint in young Spartans.

The agoge was no place for comfort, no matter one's social status. There were no servants to serve the trainees food or pour them wine. So, for the majority of their formative years in the agoge, the boys' stomachs would quickly get acquainted with a rather dreary dish: black soup (melas zomos).

No original recipe for black soup survived the classical times, but there is proof that raw pork was boiled in pig's blood and garnished with onions, salt, and vinegar to make it. Spartan cooks could only use salt and vinegar as seasoning, no matter the diet. Salt was used for taste, and vinegar, if used, was for preserving the animal's blood.

In a comical story by Herodotus, a certain tyrant from Sicily named Dionysus heard of the Spartan black soup and ordered that it be made for him. One taste of it repulsed him so terribly that he remarked, "It is no wonder that Spartans are the bravest men in the world; for anyone in his right mind would prefer to die ten thousand times rather than share in such poor living."

Back soup was a staple meal, not only among agoge trainees but also for the adults and elders. Elders were noted for preferring black soup over goat meat or dairy products.

Plutarch recounts that in Spartan mess halls, each group was mandated to make financial contributions for the purchase of piglets for this dish. The animal would be sacrificed to the gods, and every part of it would be cooked and eaten by the people. Black soup could have been eaten with wheat or barley bread, legumes, and dates.

Other "Delicacies"

Men in the agoge indulged in moderation in regards to wine. Getting drunk was met with harsh whiplashing and starvation for many days. When wine was consumed in large quantities, especially during ceremonies and feasts, Spartans, like other Greeks, would dilute their wine with water.

For the peasant Spartans who could not afford meat, pea soup, raw greens, and dry beans were staples. As a rule of thumb in ancient Sparta, carbohydrates formed most of their diet to supply energy for the day's hard work.

In Speech

The English word "laconic" comes to us from one of the core tenets of ancient Sparta's society: minimalism. The word "laconic" is synonymous with pithiness and conciseness.

As a militaristic people, Spartans made the most contact with the outside world on the fields of battle. They were blatantly uninterested in trade or friendly foreign relations (at least for the most part), and they were certainly not interested in a partnership where they would be the lesser power.

Lycurgus, who laid the foundations for the classical Spartan society, was emphatic on developing the country without foreign support. So, he banned the use of gold and silver and replaced them with worthless metal rounds to dissuade foreign trade relations. For quite a while, Sparta focused on growing her economy independently.

When Sparta sought to expand, it would interact with its neighbors and other countries through an endless series of wars. While the women and children remained mostly uninvolved in foreign relations, the men of Sparta were known to be abrasive and violent on the battlefield. Their festivals, as would be discovered by conquered city-states, were characterized by loud merrymaking. It became clear to others that the Spartans were not very great at etiquette.

Their fellow Greeks would dismiss them as a bunch of lewd, primitive, and illiterate people with a simplistic and myopic outlook on life. Conversely, the Spartans did next to nothing to change this perception. If they were feared as ruthless savages, their enemies would not dare undermine them in battle.

In time, a few foreign intellectuals saw through the smokescreen. The Spartans were not savages but smart and witty people. True, they were not lovers of all things artsy and sophisticatedly poetic like the Athenians, but they found delight in simple, non-luxurious living.

Most significantly, the Spartans could not stand chatty people who talked just to hear the sound of their own voice. Even when provoked to anger, a true Spartan let his actions speak in place of his words. This may have come from a lack of eloquence or an inability to articulate. A Spartan would respond bluntly to every matter and use few words. A Spartan was not given to flattery or flowery speeches but would show love and affection through their actions.

Plutarch fondly documents some laconic phrases from famous Spartans in a chapter of his work *Moralia* titled "Apophthegmata Laconica."

Labotas

"Labotas, when someone spoke at very great length, said, 'Why, pray, such a big introduction to a small subject? For proportionate to the topic should be the words you use.'"

Leonidas, Son of Anaxandridas

"Leonidas, the son of Anaxandridas and the brother of Cleomenes, in answer to a man who remarked, 'Except for your

being king, you are no different from the rest of us,' said, 'But if I were no better than you others, I should not be king.'"

"His wife Gorgo inquired, at the time when he was setting forth to Thermopylae to fight the Persian, if he had any instructions to give her, and he said, 'To marry good men and bear good children.'"

"Xerxes wrote to him, 'It is possible for you, by not fighting against God but by ranging yourself on my side, to be the sole ruler of Greece.' But he wrote in reply, 'If you had any knowledge of the noble things of life, you would refrain from coveting others' possessions; but for me to die for Greece is better than to be the sole ruler over the people of my race.'"

"When Xerxes wrote again, 'Hand over your arms,' he wrote in reply, 'Come and take them.'"

Alcamenes, Son of Teleclus

"Alcamenes, the son of Teleclus, when somebody inquired how a man could best keep a kingdom secure, said, 'If he should not hold his own advantage too high.'"

"When another person sought to know the reason why he did not accept gifts from the Messenians, he said, 'Because if I took gifts, it would be impossible to maintain peace with impartial regard for the laws.'"

Lycurgus

"He set limits to the time of marriage for both men and women, and, in answer to the man who inquired about this, he said, 'So that the offspring may be sturdy by being sprung from mature parents.'"

Anaxander, Son of Eurycrates

"Anaxander, the son of Eurycrates, when someone inquired why the Spartans did not amass money in the public treasury, said, 'So that those made the guardians of it may not become corrupt.'"

Archidamus, Son of Agesilaus

"Archidamus, the son of Agesilaus, when Philip, after the battle of Chaeronea, wrote him a somewhat haughty letter, wrote in reply, 'If you should measure your own shadow, you would not find that it has become any greater than before you were victorious.'"

"Being asked how much land the Spartans controlled, he said, 'As much as they can reach with the spear.'"

"Periander, the physician, was distinguished in his profession and commended very highly, but was a writer of wretched verses. 'Why in the world, Periander,' said Archidamus, 'do you yearn to be called a bad poet instead of a skillful physician?'"

Bias

"Bias, caught in an ambush by Iphicrates the Athenian general, and asked by his soldiers what was to be done, said, 'What else except for you to save your lives and for me to die fighting?'"

Damindas

"When Philip invaded the Peloponnesus, and someone said, 'There is danger that the Spartans may meet a dire fate if they do not make terms with the invader,' Damindas exclaimed, 'You poor womanish thing! What dire fate could be ours if we have no fear of death?'"

Anaxandridas

"Anaxandridas, the son of Leo, in answer to a man who took much to heart the sentence imposed upon him of exile from the country, said, 'My good sir, be not downcast at being an exile from your country but at being an exile from justice.'"

"To a man who told the Ephors of things that were needful, but spoke at greater length than would have sufficed, he said, 'My friend, in needless time you dwell upon the need!'"

"When someone inquired why they put their fields in the hands of the Helots, and did not take care of them themselves, he said, 'It was by not taking care of the fields, but of ourselves, that we acquired those fields.'"

"When someone else said that high repute works injury to men and that he who is freed from this will be happy, he retorted, 'Then those who commit crimes would, according to your reasoning, be happy. For how could any man, in committing sacrilege or any other crime, be concerned over high repute?'"

"When another person asked why the Spartans, in their wars, ventured boldly into danger, he said, 'Because we train ourselves to have regard for life and not, like others, to be timid about it.'"

"When someone asked him why the elders continue the trials of capital cases over several days, and why, even if the defendant is acquitted, he is none the less still under indictment, he said, 'They take many days to decide, because, if they make an error in a capital case, there can be no reversal of the judgment; and the accused continues, perforce, to be under indictment of the law, because, under this law, it may be possible, by deliberation, to arrive at a better decision.'"

Brasidas

"Brasidas caught a mouse among some figs, and, when he got bitten, let it go. Then, turning to those who were present, he said, 'There is nothing so small that it does not save its life if it has the courage to defend itself against those who would lay hand on it.'"

"In a battle he was wounded by a spear which pierced his shield, and, pulling the weapon out of the wound, with this very spear he slew the foe. Asked how he got his wound, he said, 'Twas when my shield turned traitor.'"

"As he was going forth to war he wrote to the Ephors, 'What I wull to dae I'll dae as regards the war or be a deid mon [sic].'"

"When it came to pass that he fell in trying to win independence for the Greeks who were living in the region of Thrace, the committee which was sent to Sparta waited upon his mother Argileonis. Her first question was whether Brasidas had come to his end honorably; and when the Thracians spoke of him in the highest terms, and said that there was no other like him, she said, 'You have no knowledge of that, sirs, being from abroad; for Brasidas was indeed a good man, but Sparta has many better than he was.'"

Thearidas

"Thearidas, as he was whetting his sword, was asked if it was sharp, and he replied, 'Sharper than slander.'"

Another legendary display of Spartan laconism was in the 3rd century BCE when King Philip II of Macedonia sought to conquer Sparta and annex all of ancient Greece. In an act of war, King Philip sent a message to the Spartans, saying, "You are advised to submit without further delay, for if I bring my army into your land, I will destroy your farms, slay your people and raze your city."

This heavy threat would either cause a nation to surrender or respond with a long string of equally frightening words, but Sparta was no regular city-state. The Spartans sent word back to Philip—literally: "If."

This one word was a declaration of Sparta's readiness to go to war with Macedonia and an expression of the Spartans' confidence in their victory. It was also a stern warning to Philip to save himself and his troops from the wrath of the Spartan warriors. Subsequently, Philip sent another message to Sparta, demanding if Sparta desired they be friends or foes. "Neither" was the response that he received from the proud Spartans. Philip took their cue and suspended his planned campaign against Sparta. His son, Alexander, would not antagonize them either.

For a people who dedicated their lives to wars and violence, the Spartans had an incredible sense of humor. They would swap short, dry, witty jokes. Other Greeks would find these jokes unconventional and sometimes offensive, but Spartan men and women would have a good laugh at them. This further alienated Spartans from the other Greeks, but they could care less. It was all part of their intentional exclusiveness.

Speech minimalism as a cultural value remained with the ancient Spartans for many generations, and its legacy retains relevance in contemporary times. During the Middle Ages, Sparta's Laconian dialect became known as Tsakonian, and it is spoken by thousands of modern Greeks. It is the oldest and only surviving dialect from the western Doric languages.

A quaint Greek village named Pera Melana, located in the mountains of the southern Peloponnese, is home to a Tsakonian-speaking people, and they see themselves as proud descendants of ancient Sparta. Despite the many threats to its extinction, the dialect has thrived for generations and is being taught in rural schools.

Today, if you walked into a house or pub in Pera Melana, you would hear the elders having full-on conversations in Tsakonian. The bold fight to keep this language alive is proof that the descendants of the ancient Spartans inherited the bravery and resilience of their ancestors after all!

Conclusion

It took one man to lay the foundations for the solid structure that was ancient Sparta, but it took generations to build it into the city-state that we remember today.

There were men like Leonidas, who showed the world at Thermopylae that numbers meant nothing as long as men died fighting for the country they loved. Of course, there were also people in Sparta's history who would try to bring it down, such as the traitor Ephialtes of Trachis, whose actions determined the fate of nations in the years that followed.

Through it all, Sparta would endure. For a people so few, the Spartans took the entire world by storm with their displays of bravery, resilience, sacrifice, and discipline. And perhaps it is no wonder that the people were so mighty, especially in the eyes of the people living back then. After all, they could trace their origin to divinity, to Zeus himself. Their culture, though misunderstood even today, was unique, jeweled with values that shone as bright as their shields on the battlefields.

This book has taken you on a journey through the ups and downs of a sophisticated military society in antiquity and its legacy in the world as we know it. We began with the founding of Sparta to when the Dorians occupied Greece in the 7th century BCE.

Sparta's intriguing roots foreshadowed a prominent future. Lycurgus, the political genius who helped guide Sparta out of the Greek Dark Ages, set the perfect stage on which the city-state announced her supremacy to all of Europe and Asia.

Generation after another, from the Mycenean to the Hellenistic era, Sparta stayed relevant in Greek politics and culture. The Peloponnese benefited immensely from Sparta's protection while it lasted. Athens, which is famous for being the birthplace of democracy and is renowned for its philosophy, literature, and the arts, was able to survive the Greco-Persian Wars largely because Spartan men showed exemplary courage, bravery, and discipline when faced against insurmountable odds.

The influence of ancient Sparta would transcend the ages and come alive again in popular culture. Today, we remember their stories through new tales in all sorts of mediums. And it should come as no surprise that they are remembered so fondly today. Their exploits on the battlefield remain legendary, their political structure ensured there were checks and balances, and they recognized a more advanced form of gender equality than the other Greek city-states. They were proud to call themselves Spartans.

Although Sparta declined around 2,500 years ago, it is not dead. It exists as the picturesque capital of Laconia in the country of Greece. The ruins of ancient Sparta are an important tourist attraction, and it is located north of the city of Sparta. The people of Sparta believe that this site immortalizes the lives of their ancestors. You will also find thousands of artifacts from ancient Sparta housed in the Archaeological Museum of Sparta. There are also monuments like the Tomb of Leonidas, whose bravery at Thermopylae will be forever told.

Every year, a marathon race is held in honor of Pheidippides, the Athenian athlete who ran for two days from Athens to Sparta to gain the assistance of the Spartans in the Battle of Marathon.

At its peak of prominence, the ancient city of Sparta was the powerhouse of Greece, and no one in the world could wear the title more proudly than the fearless Spartans!

Part 2: The Trojan War

An Enthralling Overview of a Legendary Conflict of Ancient Greece and Its Role in History and Greek Mythology

Introduction

The Trojan War: epic story or historical fact? Historians disagree.

Sometime around the year 1200 BCE, a decade-long war raged between the ancient Greeks and their rivals in Troy across the Aegean Sea. The story is among the oldest in the world, and the account written by a Greek poet named Homer still makes it into many high school and university curricula. Who were these Greeks, and what drove them to fight for so long, so far from home? Who were the Trojans, and how were they able to fend off the mighty Greeks for ten long years? Perhaps even more important, what has caused us to tell and retell this story for thousands of years?

Up until the mid-18th century, it was widely held that the Trojan War was a pure myth, but there have always been a few who held that the human side of the story was true. Archeologists have discovered the remains of a city they believe to be Troy's Ancient Bronze Age city, dating back to the 12th century BCE. Evidence includes scattered skeletons and charred debris, indicating the city was destroyed during wartime. Excavations in 1988 revealed a large city (75 acres worth!) surrounded by wheat fields – a city apparently in its heyday. But was this Homer's "Troy"?

Hittite texts close to the period show that the city Homer called Troy was referred to as "Wilusa" – which is rendered "Ilion" in

Greek – the language in which Homer wrote. This points to a connection between "Ilion" and the *Iliad.*

There is little doubt that Homer's story is full of mythological gods who could not have possibly engaged in an *actual* battle, but the fly in the ointment does not render the ointment imaginary; it simply *enhances* it. To understand the *Iliad,* we must consider the time in which it was written.

In the middle of the 8th century BCE, Greece was just coming out of its Dark Ages and saw the reintroduction of written language – something that had been lost. People believed that gods and goddesses played a part in their daily lives and that judgment and fate depended on their worthiness in these gods' eyes. As city-states were on the rise and colonies were being founded within – and outside of – the usual Grecian boundaries, the first notions of classical philosophy were taking hold. These, among other developments, led to a more thoughtful sort of nationalism, and Homer's story was thought to have united weary citizens in a frenzy of patriotism that had been all but lost to the prior centuries.

Great timing for Homer! Dictating the *Iliad* (Homer was blind), he wove mythology in with history, calling his listeners and readers to consider one's morals and choices rather than only victories and losses. Plato would later proclaim that Homer was "the educator of all Greece" for the impact Homer's works had on Greece at that time. And surely, this formative text for the ancient Greeks has had a longstanding effect even dozens of centuries after it was written.

Join us as we look at the background and setting for the Trojan War of Homer's *Iliad* and learn yet another lesson of the futility and folly of warfare. Why did it start? Why did it escalate? What can we learn from this war – mythical or not – today? Much like the historical and mythological source material, the answers to those questions will be interwoven with the actions and politics of the Greek gods. Read on...

PART ONE: BEFORE THE WAR

Chapter 1: Who Were the Trojans?

The city of Troy is found in Turkey, called *Anatolia* in the time of the Trojans of yore. For modern reference, the ruins of the ancient city are located near the city of Gallipoli.

Approximate location of Troy. Credit:
https://www.google.com/maps/place/Gallipoli+Peninsula/@42.7867119,22.06860
44,5z/)

There has been much debate about the heritage of the Trojans. While the invading Greeks were a group from the mainland called the Achaeans, there were plenty of Greek city-states on the other side of the Aegean as well. Given that most stories of the war told by the Greeks paint the Trojans in an equal or even superior light to that of the Achaeans, it was long believed that they were Greek themselves.

However, recent excavations have changed most archaeologists' minds and vindicated the account of Homer and other early Greek historians. Troy's original identification and excavation took place between 1863 and 1890 when Frank Calvert and Heinrich Schliemann uncovered a much less impressive site than scholars were hoping for. A small citadel of about an acre was unearthed, leading to the opinion that Troy must have been far past its prime when the Achaeans invaded and defeated them.

But recent excavations led by Manfred Osman Korfmann have benefitted from both a century of scrutiny and new technologies that have allowed his team to reveal a Troy worthy of the epic story we have come to know. Instead of less than one acre, Troy was a sprawling and fortified seventy-five acres that would have been in the glittering prime of its influence and culture, just as Homer described it. Well, maybe not just as described by Homer, given his penchant for weaving in the interfering nature of the Greek gods and goddesses, but much closer than archaeologists had formerly believed.

These excavations have revealed not only the power and wealth of the Trojans at the time of the war with the Achaeans and their Anatolian heritage. The city planning, buildings, and art were all more consistent with those of southwestern Asia than southeastern Europe. Documents were discovered that linked their language to that of the Hittites of Palestine and provided evidence that they were an ally of Troy. While plenty of Greek influence was found, it was not dominant, and it was much more likely to have been the result of trade and cultural interaction rather than cultural relation.

Given that recent excavations have corroborated much of what Homer and Greek historians have claimed, perhaps more credence can be given to the description of the Trojans provided by their stories. Even Homer's descriptions of the gods and goddesses, once seen at best as pure entertainment and at worst a blight on an otherwise historical record, have begun to receive more attention. That is because once we accept the significant archaeological evidence indicating that Troy was not a Greek city, we are left with the uncomfortable situation of the Trojans worshiping and being aided by certain Greek deities.

Did the Greeks import their gods from the Near East, much like the Romans reappropriated and renamed them centuries later? Or, perhaps, there was simply some overlap. The biggest mystery centers around the role of Apollo, who is credited with building Troy's famous walls that kept the Greeks out for so long. As a character in Homer's tale, he takes the side of the Trojans at key points, beginning with a plague he set loose in the Greek encampment and by guiding the poisoned arrow that ultimately killed the seemingly invulnerable Greek warrior, Achilles.

What is more, Princess Cassandra of Troy was a priestess of Apollo, and her brother Hector, the chief Trojan hero of the tale, was rumored to have been fathered by Apollo. So, if the Trojans were not Greek, what is a Greek god doing so entwined in their culture?

The Significance of Apollo

According to Greek mythology, Apollo was the son of Zeus and Leto, who was a daughter of the Titans that Zeus and his sibling gods overthrew. The fact that there exists an old set of gods that were ousted has long been interpreted to indicate an early struggle of the Greeks against non-Greek leaders for autonomy.

After trapping most of the Titans in Tartarus, Zeus took Hera as his wife, but Leto was the daughter of his former enemies. Even the name Leto has Lydian origins rather than Greek origins, and many temples in her honor have been found across Anatolia. Further, it is important to note that the *Iliad* was written by Homer about four hundred years after the events of the Trojan War, which would have been more than enough time for Leto, Apollo, and his twin sister Artemis to be incorporated into the Greek pantheon. Due to the significance of the war and the Greek victory, Apollo and Artemis were promoted to Mt. Olympus, making them among the most important of their deities.

More evidence of the adoption of Apollo by the Greeks only after the war includes the sheer variety of his powers and gifts. He is the god of the sun, even though the Greeks already had the Titan Helios filling that role. Apollo would drive a ball of fire around the sky each day behind his chariot. He is also the god of light, art, archery, music, plagues, healing, prophecy, and truth, to name just a few. These are arguably more impressive than Zeus himself and are the hallmarks of a more significant deity than his supporting roles in Greek mythology would indicate.

The Royal Family of Troy

The Trojans involved in the tale were mostly the members of the royal family. Like their Greek opponents, Troy governed through a monarchy, at the head of which stood King Priam when the Achaeans stormed across the Aegean Sea to lay siege to their gates for the second time. Yes, *the second time.*

The first time was during the reign of Priam's father, Laomedon. Laomedon made two very famous mistakes for which his people and family would pay dearly. First, he refused payment to Apollo and Poseidon after they had helped to build his city's walls. As punishment, the former unleashed a pestilence upon the city, and the latter set loose a monster called a Cetus to attack it from the sea. It took the efforts of the famous Greek demi-god Heracles to slay the beast and end the plague, but Laomedon made his second and last mistake of refusing to give Heracles the horses that he was promised in exchange for his aid.

Unlike the ten-year campaign that came later, Heracles and his companion, Telamon, made short work of the siege. Telamon's father had helped to construct a part of the wall, and unlike the portions made by Apollo and Poseidon, this part had a weakness. The warriors exploited this secret knowledge to enter the city and kill King Laomedon. As part of their revenge for the dead king's treachery, they set themselves to murdering his sons one by one until they reached young Priam. His sister, Hesione, offered herself as ransom to Telamon, who took her as his wife in return for sparing Priam. In fact, Priam means "the ransomed" (and prior to these events, he had been known as *Podarces*).

Priam ascended to the Trojan throne, and by all accounts, he was a fair and wise leader. Troy prospered under his rule, and he is said to have fathered as many as eighty-six children. In keeping with Trojan custom for aristocratic men, he had many wives – the primary of whom was Hecuba. Hecuba herself gave birth to a staggering nineteen children, among whom were Hector, Paris, and Cassandra, all of whom played significant roles in the Trojan War. Hector was the heir apparent to the throne and the strongest of all the Trojan warriors, even more than his father Priam. Hector was seen as the best that Troy had to offer. Even the Greeks (who were responsible for telling the story) portrayed him as the most heroic of all its characters. Homer's *Iliad* is as much about the tragedy of Hector as it is about the rage of Achilles. Through Homer's work, Hector and his wife Andromache represent both Trojan and Greek ideals for men and women in their societies.

Paris, Hector's brother, is a different story, though, and in some accounts, he is thought to be the son of the god Apollo. While Hector is seen as Troy's greatest defender, Paris is responsible for putting the city in danger. Throughout the story, the contrast between the two brothers is continually highlighted. Where Hector is skilled in the arts of warfare, Paris admits his shortcomings and primarily uses a bow and arrow to avoid close combat. When challenged by the Spartan King Menelaus to single combat to end the war, Paris flees rather than accept his defeat, leading to the deaths of many more Trojans and Greeks. In contrast, Hector is willing to die in defense of the city and his family's honor, which he demonstrates many times over.

Cassandra, daughter of Priam and Hecuba, is another important figure in the events of the Trojan War. As a priestess of Apollo, the god came to her and offered her the gift of prophecy. When she later refused to father his children, Apollo cursed her, telling her that all of her accurate prophecies would always be met with utter disbelief. As a result, she predicted the fall of Troy to the Achaeans, but *no one listened.* This bit of story adds more to the confusion surrounding the role of Apollo, who alternatingly supported and cursed the Trojans. The "Cassandra Syndrome" has made its way into popular culture, referring to anyone who makes valid and prudent warnings that go ignored.

Finally, there is the character Aeneas, who plays only a minor role in the Trojan War but a far greater one in the events that followed. He was the son of a Trojan prince and the goddess Aphrodite, and he is one of the few Trojans to escape slavery or death after the burning of the city by the victorious Greeks. The gods commanded him to flee along with his father, son, and several companions. His story is described by Virgil (a popular Roman poet) in the *Aeneid*, which details his adventures leading up to his relocation to Italy and his connection to Romulus and Remus, the first kings of Rome. In many ways, his tale mirrors that of Odysseus – Ithaca's king and the central figure in the *Odyssey* – and the Greeks attempting to return to Ithaca following the long war.

Chapter 2: Who Were the Achaeans?

The Greeks involved in the Trojan War were part of *Mycenaean Greece*, which lasted from about 1750 BCE until 1050 BCE.

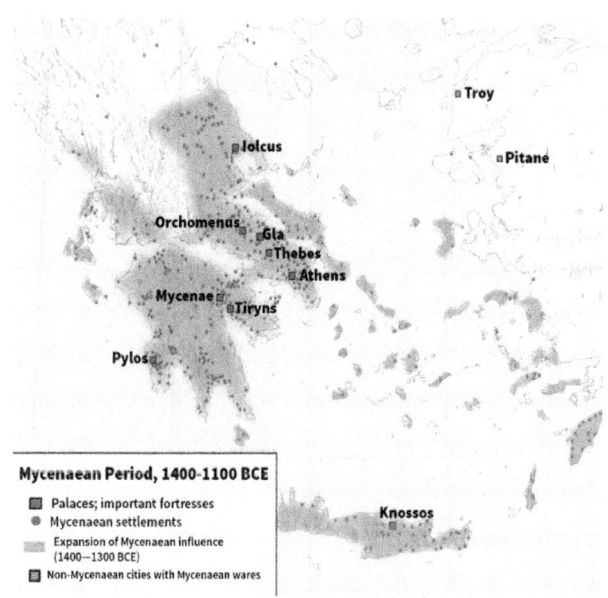

Mycenaean Greece.
Credit: https://en.wikipedia.org/wiki/File:Mycenaean_World_en.png.

Homer refers to these Greeks most commonly as the "Achaeans" in the *Iliad*, and the same convention will be repeated here. However, it should be noted that this is somewhat confusing since the term technically refers to people from the area called Achaea in the northern Peloponnesian Peninsula, and the Achaean League was formed in the third century BCE among the city-states of the region. Homer's Achaeans were not restricted to this region and instead came from kingdoms across the Greek mainland. Homer also refers to the Greek forces as Danaans, Argives, Panhellenes, and Hellenes in the *Iliad*. Again, for the purposes of our discussion, we will use the collective name for these people: "Achaeans."

In many ways, these Achaeans were the Vikings of the Mediterranean during the Bronze Age. They had not yet matured into the classical civilization of Athens during its Golden Age – nor even the structured warrior society of Sparta during the Persian Wars. These Greek civilizations were less powerful but perhaps more menacing than their descendants would be.

In some of the first warships ever built, they fanned out through the islands of the Aegean Sea and took what they could, spreading their culture, goods, language, and a fair amount of death as they went. Still, they were not mere brutes, and their shipbuilding was also used to bolster their economy through trade with neighbors such as Egypt and Assyria. Linguistic analyses, archaeological evidence, and genetic studies indicate that the Achaeans themselves were probably descendants of indigenous Greeks, Minoans from Crete, and one or several Indo-European tribes that settled the area after migrating through the Caucasus.

Agamemnon and Menelaus

Like their Trojan rivals, powerful Achaean city-states were protected by walls since they often warred with one another, and the Greek habit of building citadels upon a hilltop called an acropolis can be traced back to this time period.

Depiction of an acropolis. Credit: Wikimedia Commons.

The largest of these city-states was called *Mycenae* in northeastern Peloponnese near modern-day Mykines. At its peak around 1350 BCE, it had a population of about 30,000 people and was nearly three times larger than its closest Greek rivals and erstwhile allies. Before the Trojan War, the leader of Mycenae was King Atreus. He and his wife, Aerope, had two sons, Agamemnon and Menelaus.

Agamemnon was the heir to the throne, but the family was thrown into chaos when Atreus discovered that Aerope had committed adultery with his brother, Thyestes. Enraged, Atreus not only killed the sons of Thyestes but forced him to eat them. Afterward, Thyestes fathered a new son named Aegisthus through incest with his daughter, Pelopia. Aegisthus grew to adulthood and took revenge for his father, murdering Atreus and installing Thyestes to the throne of Mycenae.

Since the throne had been taken from Agamemnon, he and Menelaus fled. They were given refuge in Sparta by King Tyndareus, who saw the two as innocent amidst all the madness of their family. There, they met Tyndareus's daughter, Helen. News of Helen's beauty had already spread throughout all of the kingdoms, and powerful suitors came from all across Greece with lavish gifts to compete for her hand in marriage. As a woman in her time, place, and social standing, Helen had no choice in the matter of marriage; that job fell to her father, but he feared that doing so would start a war.

Odysseus (one of the suitors) had a clever idea for the king: require all suitors to swear an oath to uphold the final decision *before it was made*. Each quickly agreed since this would ensure the people's support if they were the one selected to marry Helen. Tyndareus selected Menelaus, and all of the suitors left peacefully, except for Odysseus. He had not given his advice for free; in exchange, he requested Tyndareus's support in his courtship of Helen's cousin Penelope, with whom he had fallen in love during his visit.

Agamemnon also married a daughter of Tyndareus named Clytemnestra, but it was Menelaus who ascended the throne upon the king's death because of his marriage to Helen, as he was the elder of the two. Agamemnon's ambition had led him to seek Helen's hand, but he was bound now by his oath to support both his brother's marriage and his new throne. Still seeing an opportunity, he convinced Menelaus to help him take back Mycenae from Thyestes. They marched north and surprised their uncle, chasing him and his son from the city and installing Agamemnon as the most powerful man in Achaean Greece.

Achaean Heroes of the Trojan War

Agamemnon, Menelaus, and Odysseus would all take part in the Trojan War, leading their kingdoms into battle. After departing from Sparta with Penelope, Odysseus soon took the throne from his father, becoming the king of Ithaca. His plan to gain Tyndareus's support for marrying Penelope was no fluke; the idea was carefully crafted. Odysseus is regarded as one of the cleverest protagonists in Greek history and mythology, preferring to outwit his opponents rather than overpower them. This characteristic lies in stark contrast to the Achaean warrior Achilles, who was brash, hot-tempered, and depended on his world-famous prowess in battle to settle disputes.

Odysseus and Nestor (the king of Pylos) became primarily responsible for recruiting and uniting the Achaean kingdoms against Troy in an effort to begin the war. Like Priam, all of Nestor's brothers were killed by Heracles, a Greek demi-god. By the time of the Trojan War, Nestor was an old man – about 70 years old – with a penchant for inspiring others through tales of his heroic youth.

One person that required very little persuasion was Diomedes, king of Argos. According to legend, he was the son of Ares and a favorite of Athena because of the warrior goddess's respect for his skill in battle. He was considered second only to Achilles among the Achaean forces in this regard and had seen more fighting in his young years than even the elderly Nestor. Among all the Achaean heroes, only he and Odysseus were praised in the *Iliad* for their cunning and strategy, making him the complete package. Diomedes later became the king of Argos and founded several cities in Italy, where he became fully deified and worshiped after his death.

Another demi-god on the Achaeans' roster was Ajax the Great, son of King Telamon of Salamis. Homer and others portray Ajax the Great as a courageous and towering figure for the Greeks. He twice fought Hector to a draw, leading to a budding respect between the opposing heroes. There was another Ajax in their ranks as well, called Ajax the Lesser (or sometimes Locrian Ajax) to better distinguish between the two. Neither were kings, but they led their forces from Salamis and Locris, respectively, in the siege of Troy.

Commanding the Cretan armies (whose archers were considered among the best "light missile" troops in the ancient world) was King Idomeneus, a grandson of King Minos of minotaur fame. Over the course of the war, he became one of Agamemnon's most trusted advisors and was among the Achaean warriors who infiltrated Troy's walls by hiding inside of the giant wooden horse as part of the scheme concocted by Odysseus. Another warrior within the walls of the Trojan horse was the Athenian king, Menestheus. Like Diomedes, he knew much of the tactics in war but was often criticized for being less valiant and skilled when it came to his own fighting.

Nearly all of these Achaean heroes were among the suitors of Helen of Sparta and were bound by the oath they gave to support Menelaus. Odysseus's trick may have allowed for a peaceful resolution to the competition for Helen, but when the young prince of Troy absconded with the queen to name her Helen of Troy, they were all ensnared by their honor.

While some painters believe Helen and Paris were in love, most depict Helen's abduction in a violent manner. This one is aptly named The Abduction of Helen, *and it is by Francesco Primaticcio. Credit: Wikimedia Commons.*

Chapter 3: Causes of the Trojan War

In this chapter, we will talk about the events that led up to the Trojan War, like the Apple of Discord, the Judgement of Paris, and the abduction of Helen. We will not discuss the details of the war just yet, but rather set the foundations for a better understanding of the causes.

Many believe that the Trojan War began when Paris kidnapped Helen of Sparta – or the more romantic view: they fell in love and ran away together. The truth of it may be lost to time, and both versions of the story have their merits. Either way, Menelaus was able to rally many of his fellow kings and warriors to launch a thousand ships (sound familiar?) across the Aegean Sea to lay war at the gates of Troy. But like all tales of the ancient Greeks, it is a little more complicated than that.

The seeds for the conflict were planted in both a prophecy and a contest, each involving the gods and goddesses of Mt. Olympus. The prophecy in question was given to the god Zeus and his brother Poseidon, each who had fallen in love with the beautiful sea-nymph named Thetis. They received a prophecy that Thetis' son would rise up to destroy his father, wielding powers untold if he were to be sired by the likes of Zeus or Poseidon. The pair of gods backed off, and Zeus instead decreed that Thetis must marry the elderly King Peleus of Phthia. Zeus had always feared that he would one day be dethroned by his offspring, much the way that he and his siblings and rebelled to defeat their Titan parents. He began to concoct a plan for a war to depopulate the earth of many of the demi-god children running about.

Sea nymph Thetis as depicted on a black-figure dish. Credit:
https://en.wikipedia.org/wiki/Thetis.

The Judgment of Paris

After the wedding of Thetis and Peleus, Zeus organized a huge feast in celebration, but did not invite Eris, the goddess of strife and discord. To sow her revenge – and live up to her name – she tossed a golden apple amid the revelers, with the inscription "To the fairest" engraved upon it. Hera, Athena, and Aphrodite all claimed the golden apple as *obviously* their own, and to settle the dispute, Zeus sent them to Paris of Troy, naming Paris as the deciding judge.

Golden Apple of Discord *by Jacob Jordaens.*
Credit: Wikimedia Commons.

Each goddess attempted to bribe Paris in accordance with their nature. Hera, Zeus' wife and the Queen of the Gods, offered Paris immense power, promising to make him the king of Europa and Asia. The Goddess of Wisdom and War, Athena, told Paris that she would grant him great wisdom and skill in battle if he selected her. Lastly, Aphrodite, the Goddess of Love and Beauty, told Paris that if he chose her, he would fall in love with the most beautiful woman in the world.

Paris chose Aphrodite, and thus fell prey to Zeus' trap, as Helen of Sparta held the title – as she was already betrothed to King Menelaus.

Paris has often been vilified or deemed a coward for his choices, but in this contest, there was no winning. No matter whom he chose, he was making two powerful enemies for Troy who would end up supporting the Greeks in the war to come.

Regardless, after being shown the likeness of Helen by Aphrodite, Paris set sail to Sparta on a diplomatic mission with the ulterior motive of abducting her. To make good on her word, Aphrodite sent Eros (in Roman mythology, Cupid) to shoot an enchanted arrow at Helen just before greeting Paris. When she looked up to see him, she fell in love and agreed to elope and run away with him to the grand citadel of Troy. Other versions claim that Helen was taken against her will; this version was certainly the angle that Menelaus used to convince his fellow Greeks to go to war.

The Love of Helen and Paris *by Jacques-Louis David.*
Credit: Wikimedia Commons.

The Road to War

When Paris and Helen arrived in Troy, the royal family was furious - especially Priam and Hector, who understood that the Greeks would not simply allow this to go unpunished, and that war with Greece was likely inevitable. Menelaus and Odysseus journeyed to Troy to negotiate Helen's release, but Paris (and quite possibly Helen) would not agree to the queen's return. Bound by their own duty to their son and brother, respectively, King Priam and Prince Hector agreed to let Helen stay in their city, turning the Greek emissaries away.

The next time they would see them, the Greeks would arrive with one of the largest armadas that had ever been assembled. Having turned down Hera, Paris and the Trojans would not see their prosperity last and would not become the lords of Europe and Asia. And having turned down Athena, it would be the Greeks who boasted the bold strategies of Odysseus – and who had the greatest warrior of all in Achilles. For a time, though, Paris had Helen of Troy.

To more completely understand the causes of the Trojan War, it is important to take a step back from the myths and look at the context of the Aegean world in the late Bronze Age. While Troy was a Greek rival, the Hittites of Anatolia were likely a Greek enemy. Troy's fortress protected Hittite affluence, a people who remained independent but were in constant threat of being swallowed up by both of its neighboring powers.

While mentions of the Hittites are frustratingly absent from Homer's account of the war in the *Iliad*, it's theorized that perhaps Homer used an unrecognized name to refer to them when counting the allies of Troy. Knowing the power and influence of the Bronze Age Hittites in Anatolia, this would make more sense than leaving them out altogether, and closer relations between the Trojans and the Hittites would have been enough to make the Greeks start worrying about the safety of their own city states in Anatolia. For as long as Troy remained neutral, they had remained safe. Either through miscalculation, misguided strategies, or personal grudges, the Trojans seemed to be turning away from the Greeks, who may have preferred *no Troy at all* over and *enemy Troy.*

Chapter 4: Gathering of the Achaean Forces

Once diplomacy failed to retrieve Helen, Menelaus began recruiting others to his cause. His first stop was Mycenae and his brother, Agamemnon, who agreed to come – only if he would be the commander-in-chief of all the Greek forces on the expedition. Knowing that he needed the might his brother controlled, Menelaus agreed. Yet, alone, their two kingdoms would not be enough.

Adding to the drama, even before the Greeks could leave Aulis for Troy, the city was hit by a plague and forced to remain in port due to an absence of wind. Per myth, Artemis (Goddess of the Hunt) required a sacrifice be made: Agamemnon's daughter, Iphigenia, must be killed. After much consternation, Agamemnon performed the deed before sailing for Troy, leaving behind an angry wife and family. This was only one of several follies awaiting the Greeks before the battle even began!

Odysseus Feigns Madness

They needed cunning, so they sent for Odysseus, now the King of Ithaca. Odysseus had heard that Agamemnon was assembling a force to invade Troy and retrieve Helen for his brother, but he wanted neither conflict with Troy nor an enemy in Agamemnon. Again, relying on his wits, he began to feign madness.

The oath to honor the winner of the contest for Helen's hand in marriage was merely one of his tricks, so Odysseus did not feel bound by it. When Agamemnon's emissary, Palamedes, arrived, he found Odysseus dressed as a peasant, salting his crops and uttering absurdities. Unconvinced by what was admittedly *not his best ruse*, Palamedes placed the Ithacan king's son, Telemachus, in front of the plow Odysseus was using – a modern-day game of chicken – causing Odysseus to swerve and miss, betraying his own game. Proving himself sane and capable of saving his son, Odysseus was now bound to fight for Agamemnon or risk retaliation. Odysseus was tasked along with Nestor to continue rallying the Achaean kingdoms to their side, reminding them of the oath they had sworn to Menelaus at his betrothal to Helen. Diomedes, Ajax the Great, Ajax the Lesser, Idomeneus, and Menestheus all joined the cause, but they still needed the greatest warrior of all: Achilles.

Achilles and Prophecy

Many years had now passed since the wedding of Thetis and Peleus, and they had given birth to a son they named Achilles. Though Zeus had forced Thetis to marry Peleus, she did not want a mortal son. Secretly, she visited the River Styx at the border of Hades, and once there, she dipped her infant son, holding him upside down by his heel. The river made Achilles invulnerable on all parts of his body submerged in the water, leaving only one point of weakness: the very heel his mother had held him by. Some versions of this myth have Peleus disagreeing with such treatment of his son, leading to the deaths of many of Achilles' would-be older siblings.

Like many characters in the Trojan War, Thetis had also been motivated to such dangerous lengths by a prophecy: that her son would be remembered forever as the world's greatest warrior, but that he would die as a young man. Thus, despite his seeming invulnerability, Thetis tried to hide Achilles from Agamemnon's envoys. Once he was found, she passed on the oracle's warning to Achilles. Now, Achilles would need to decide whether he would live long and be forgotten – or die young and be remembered. Due to arrogance that he could avoid such a fate or accept his heroic nature, he agreed to set sail with Agamemnon and the Greeks and lead his much-feared Myrmidon army against the Trojans.

False Starts

Several years had passed in rousing the scattered and famously uncooperative Greek kingdoms, but the successful recruitment campaign led to an alliance of over one hundred thousand Achaean soldiers. This vast army would require over a thousand ships to ferry them across the sea to Anatolia and the beaches of Troy. They agreed to assemble at Aulis, where a series of follies began.

First, during their sacrifices to the gods to favor their side and maintain their goodwill, a snake slithered from beneath the alter, climbed a tree, ate eight sparrow chicks and their mother – and finally turned to stone. A seer named Calchas was present, who interpreted the strange omen to mean that the Achaean's war would last for *nine years* before they defeated the Trojans in the tenth. The soldiers took this omen with mixed emotions; yes, the war would end in victory for them, but it would last a grueling ten years. They set sail to Troy with hopeful but troubled minds and landed in Anatolia to unleash hell on the shores of the great city.

Unfortunately, the city they found was not Troy but rather Mysia, with Telephus, son of Heracles, as their king. Mysia was one of the Greek colonies in Anatolia, and a great and confusing battle ensued that ended with Telephus chasing the Achaeans off in a storm. Once again, they regrouped in Aulis.

The final folly came when Agamemnon, waiting in Aulis once again set sail to Troy, led a hunting party where he not only boasted that he was as great a hunter as the goddess Artemis but also unwittingly killed one of her sacred deer. In anger and vengeance, Artemis stopped all winds from blowing at Aulis, making it impossible for the Achaeans to depart for Troy. The oracle Calchas said that Artemis would only allow it to blow again once a blood sacrifice of Agamemnon's eldest daughter, Iphigenia, was made in return. Menelaus convinced him to send for her, telling her that she was to be married to the great Achilles.

Iphigenia and her mother, Clytemnestra, arrived only to learn it was a trap when they spoke to Achilles – who knew nothing of the plot. Furious at being made a pawn, Achilles told the armies why the winds had stopped and how Calchas had said they would blow again through the sacrifice of Iphigenia. Agamemnon had been close to changing his mind but was now caught between sacrificing his daughter and the murder of his whole family by the restless soldiers who were threatening to turn on him if he did not appease Artemis.

At this point, Iphigenia volunteered for the sacrifice, knowing that she would die either way and seeing an opportunity to save her mother and father. Because of her heroism, Artemis took pity on Iphigenia and spared her from the sacrifice, though her parents would not learn of her survival until later. With Artemis appeased, the winds returned, and the Achaeans set sail once again.

The Sacrifice of Iphigenia *by François Perrier.*
Credit: Wikimedia Commons

They landed in one more place – still not Troy – and stayed long enough for Achilles to slay a son of Apollo. Also, one of the Achaean warriors came down with a mysterious, festering wound that would not heal.

The island they stopped at was called Tenedos, and they wished to resupply before arriving at Troy and commencing the war. The chief god of the island was Apollo, and King Tenes was his son. Achilles lusted after Tenes' sister, Hemithea, who escaped his advances, but the ordeal angered the king, ready to take arms against the great warrior. Thetis appeared and warned Achilles not to harm Tenes, as it would anger Apollo.

However, Achilles would not back down from the challenge, and the fight ended with Achilles driving his sword through the king's chest. As predicted by Thetis, Apollo swore revenge, sealing the fate of Achilles to die in the Trojan War. The Achaeans scrambled to make a sacrifice to appease Apollo, but again, a venomous snake slithered from the altar and bit Philoctetes of Meliboea on his foot. The wound would not heal and was so pungent that his confused and alarmed companions took him to the nearby island of Lemnos, where Philoctetes could heal until they returned for him. Now fully provisioned – but with a powerful enemy in Apollo –the Achaeans finished their journey to Troy.

PART TWO: THE TROJAN WAR

Chapter 5: The War Begins

Perhaps one of the reasons that the Achaeans were both eager to arrive yet seemingly dragging their feet was yet another prophecy by Calchas. She foretold that the first person to step foot on Trojan land would also be the first to die. Odysseus publicly dismissed the oracle's prediction while inwardly remaining cautious. Being pragmatic and knowing that someone had to start lest they rot on their ships, he leaped out of his boat but surreptitiously landed on his shield rather than Trojan soil, beginning the cascade of Achaean soldiers onto the beach.

The first to land firmly on the ground was Protesilaus, who promptly met his death at the hands of none other than Prince Hector – who was leading a charge outside of Troy's walls to greet the Achaeans while they were vulnerable and unfortified. The battle ended with the Achaean force depleted and the Trojans returning to safety behind their walls. The Greeks had won the beachhead at a high cost, though the Trojans were also bloodied; Achilles had fought and killed the famed and feared Cycnus, a son of Poseidon defending Troy.

A Greek Envoy

Once the dust settled and the Achaean army was camped firmly within the Trojan territory, tradition called for one final attempt to avoid war. King Menelaus and King Odysseus were selected as the Greek envoy to negotiate for the return of Helen and the restoration of peace between the kingdoms. They were taken into the home of Antenor, a Trojan noble with many Greek connections both in family and in business. Menelaus would have his honor restored; Odysseus had simply been trying to avoid the gravity of the war since before his recruitment. Antenor gave a sympathetic ear to the Achaeans, each of whom would have been happy to return with Helen.

But peace was not truly in the cards, for King Priam was well and thoroughly trapped by this point. He had already welcomed Helen (and the treasure she came with) into his city, and to return her only after an army showed up would have been admitting he was wrong in the first place. His conundrum caught him between admission of wrongdoing or showing cowardice, or perhaps even *both*. The time to send Helen back to Sparta had long passed, and the meeting turned into nothing more than a formality.

What is more, Menelaus and Odysseus may not have known how close they came to their deaths. A Trojan named Antimachus lobbied for the murder of the kings, not only in retaliation for their invasion and bloodshed but to rob the Achaeans of two of its most important leaders. Menelaus was the symbolic cause of the war for the Trojans and Odysseus among the chief Achaean strategists. The Greeks would have been outraged by the murder plot, but likely would have questioned the logic of fighting to return Helen to a dead king. As a bonus, though they could not have known it at the time, the Trojans would have also eliminated the man that would deal them their death blow with the plot of the Trojan horse.

In the end, the two kings were escorted from the city as peacefully as they had been escorted into it, and both sides began preparing their next moves.

A Long Stalemate

Calchas proved to be correct about the length of the war as it dragged on for nine long years. Troy was never fully under siege by the Greeks, despite the Achaeans controlling much of the Aegean shore and the Dardanelles. While they outnumbered the Trojan forces, they still lacked the numbers to completely encircle the city without spreading themselves too thin, becoming vulnerable to concentrated attacks. As a result, the Trojans maintained communication and trade with their allies and thus avoided the problems of starvation and plague that often come from locking a population inside of a citadel.

Breaching the citadel by brute force was another option for the Achaeans, but it was a bad option. Troy was not merely a city with a large wall around it but also a showcase in Bronze Age military technology. Around the outer wall was a wooden palisade and a trench dug eight to ten feet deep into the bedrock, nearly doubling its height and preventing any tunneling campaigns.

The palisade and trench also prevented their enemies from utilizing siege towers, so any attempt to crest the walls would have to be done with ladders or at the gates – which were defended far better. The citadel (fortification) found inside, called Pergamos, was even more impressive. Its thirty-foot walls sat atop a one-hundred-foot hilltop overlooking the surrounding plains. They were sixteen feet thick, mocking any attempts with a battering ram, and its defenders patrolled its 1100-foot perimeter behind parapets encircling the top. Every attempt by the Achaeans to break the defenses was repelled, with battle cries and then corpses filling the trenches.

Yet despite their elite defensive advantage, the Trojans were still far outnumbered and unable to capitalize after each repulsion of the enemy. Defending the mile-long perimeter of their outer walls required most of their forces and attention; sparing too many soldiers for open engagement would leave them exposed. Wary that the Greeks might simply be attempting to lure them away from their defensive posts, the Trojans remained behind their walls.

However, Priam and Hector's strategy is often criticized for not including more ambushes and guerrilla campaigns against the Achaeans. These would have whittled down the invading warriors' numbers and devastated their morale, being so far from home and for so long. This strategy could have been implemented with forces small enough to avoid compromising their defense, and the absence of such attacks is what many non-Homeric sources use as evidence that the Trojans feared the Greeks.

Over time, the forces settled into a stalemate of sorts, with much of the fighting taking place away from the citadel where Troy's neighbors lacked such glorious walls. The Achaeans had no supply line to speak of, so they took over nearby cities and towns, becoming warlords in the countryside in order to farm and sustain themselves. Unsurprisingly, Achilles and Ajax the Greater were the two most active Achaean leaders in their raids. Achilles and his Myrmidons (mercenaries) laid claim to eleven Anatolian cities and twelve nearby islands.

Odysseus, for his part, busied himself with revenge against Palamedes, the man who recruited him for the war, spoiled his ruse, and endangered his infant son. Being discouraged by the length of the war, Palamedes began to encourage the leaders to give up and go home. The irony of it was too much for Odysseus, *who would not have even been there if not for Palamedes' insistence.* He seized the opportunity to frame Palamedes as a traitor by planting a fortune in Palamedes' tent and forging a letter from King Priam to be discovered along with the bribe. Odysseus claimed that Palamedeshe was working for Priam in trying to encourage retreat, resulting in a sentence of death by stoning – a punishment that Odysseus himself took part in. For all his cleverness, his pride was perhaps even larger. Had he merely sided with Palamedes, maybe he could have returned to Ithaca, Penelope, and their son. But he could not abide surrender, and he could not forgive Palamedes' wrongdoing. Besides, the tenth year of the war was approaching, and the oracle Calchas had not been wrong yet.

Chapter 6: The Iliad

The *Iliad* is the "Story of Ilion," which was the Greek name for Troy. However, the events of Homer's *Iliad* all take place near the end of the war, and it centers around the rage of Achilles.

As you will see, revenge is core to the story. Achilles wants revenge on Agamemnon for taking away Briseus and for the death of his best friend, Patroclus (many today believe that the two were lovers, although the *Iliad* does not explicitly say this). This theme resounds throughout Homer's *Iliad* – and through many other ancient Greek poems and stories.

However, forgiveness is another theme, as Achilles' revenge does not bring him peace. Even making sacrifices to the gods (or dragging Hector's dead body by Chariot) does nothing to reduce his pain. Only by providing King Priam with twelve days of peace – enabling the King to mourn his son's death – does Achilles finally find a measure of peace. After all the battles and death, forgiveness is the key to unlocking his soul's reconciliation.

Aside from lessons of forgiveness, the *Iliad* can be viewed as history's first antiwar propaganda due to its perspective on battles and needless death. Its audience will often read of the horrors of war and the overall tragedy of the Trojan War. Descriptions include:

"He was standing on the stern of his deep-bellied ship, watching the grim toil of war and the miserable rout." *(Homer book 11, lines 600-601.*

"Daughter of Zeus the aegis-wearer, look at this! Shall we two give up caring about the Danaans as they die?" *(Homer book 8, lines 352-353)*

"They piled their dead on to a pyre in silence, grieving in their hearts...In the same way, the well-greaved Achaeans on their side piled their dead on to a pyre, grieving in their hearts" *(Homer book 7, lines 427-431)*

Aside from the lessons of war, Homer's book has garnered much historical significance – so much so that Alexander the Great slept with a copy of the *Iliad* every night! As one of the oldest pieces of literature around, this book is still taught in classrooms around the world today. Let us dive in.

The story picks up after Achilles and Agamemnon raided a nearby village and took two women as captives. Agamemnon claimed Chryseis, and Achilles took her sister, Briseis. The women's father, a man named Chryses (who served as a priest of the god Apollo), found Agamemnon and begged him to return his daughters. He offered to pay whatever ransom was required, yet Agamemnon refused.

Chryses did what most people did during those times; he sought the help of a god. He prayed to Apollo, who set loose a plague on the Achaeans camped outside of Troy. After ten days of watching his fellow Greeks drop dead, Achilles called upon Calchas to use his powers of prophecy to figure out what was going on. Calchas revealed that the plague was part of the vengeance of Apollo. As you will recall, Agamemnon had already found himself on the wrong side of Apollo more than once.

Having much arrogance, he could not succumb to complete defeat, so Agamemnon agreed to return Chryseis, but only if Achilles gave up Briseis as his compensation. As the leader of the

Achaeans, Agamemnon believed that he should have the greatest prize – and that he should be able to outwit adversaries.

Achilles, also always proud, was infuriated and threatened to leave Troy and return to Phthia if Agamemnon persisted. When Agamemnon threatened to charge into Achilles' tent to take Briseis on his own, it took the interference of Athena to prevent Achilles from drawing his sword on the Greek commander. Instead, Achilles backed down and let the King of Mycenae have what he wanted.

After returning to his tent, Achilles prayed to his mother, Thetis, to punish Agamemnon and the rest of the Achaeans for not backing him. Thetis agreed to take the matter to Zeus, who owed her a favor. At first, Zeus was reluctant to help since his wife Hera favored the Greeks. But seeing the opportunity to further reduce the potential demigod challengers to his throne, he agreed to honor the favor. Odysseus returned Chryseis to her father, who prayed to Apollo to lift the curse of pestilence spreading among the Achaeans. However, for many of them, their troubles were just beginning.

In a bold yet somewhat uncharacteristic move, Paris challenged any Achaean to single combat and was dismayed when Menelaus stepped forth. Paris lost his nerve and tried to back away through the Trojan ranks. This situation is somewhat surprising, as it is unclear who Paris thought would accept his challenge, and Menelaus was far from the most skilled warrior the Achaeans had to offer. Hector prevented the cowardly retreat by his brother, instead convincing Paris to duel Menelaus, the Spartan king. Paris found his courage again and declared that the winner would be Helen's rightful husband, an outcome that would effectively end the war.

As Paris and Menelaus were readying themselves for combat, Helen lay inside the city, completely unaware of the development. Per the story, Iris (Messenger of the Gods) disguised herself as Hector's sister and tipped Helen off about the fight, sending her to the city gates to watch. This was not to be the first – or last – time that gods intervened in this war.

The duel started with spears and then moved to swords, and Menelaus gained the upper hand when he cracked Paris over the head with his sword and began dragging him around by his helmet. Aphrodite (goddess of love, beauty, pleasure, passion, and procreation), still siding with the Trojans for Paris' judgment, unfastened the helmet's strap so that Paris could break free of the Spartan's grip. This interference only garnered a brief moment for Paris. As Menelaus was sending a fatal blow of his spear to his opponent's chest, Aphrodite interfered again, instantly transporting Paris back to his room in the palace.

Helen found him there, scolded him, and then laid down with him.

There was great confusion outside of the gates, as the Prince of Troy seemed to have magically vanished rather than being run through by the spear! Agamemnon declared Menelaus the victor and demanded the return of Helen. Of course, Paris and Helen refused, and the Trojan royals backed them.

With the hope of ending the war through single combat vanished, the war raged on. Diomedes and the Trojan hero, Pandarus, met on the battlefield, and Diomedes was badly wounded. Diomedes was one of Goddess Athena's favorite warriors, so she healed him and gave him godlike strength. She also gave him the power to see the gods and goddesses on the field of battle, whose actions had been hidden to him and remained hidden to the other soldiers. She told him that he was not to challenge or harm any of the gods, save Aphrodite.

With his new abilities, he once again found Pandarus on the battlefield, whom he skewered brutally on his spear. He also seriously wounded Aeneas and cut his mother's wrist, Aphrodite, when she went to help him. While Athena's rules permitted this, he went too far when Apollo came to the aid of Aeneas and was attacked by Diomedes as well.

With ease, Apollo pushed Diomedes aside and removed Aeneas from the battlefield to be healed. To punish Diomedes, Apollo left the image of Aeneas' body on the ground to rouse anger among the Trojans – and brought Ares (the Greek god of war) to fight by their side.

All the divine intervention led to the Trojans gaining the upper hand, with Hector and Ares forming a fierce tandem. Hera and Athena became fearful that the tide was turning against them and convinced Zeus to allow them to help the Achaeans.

Ever playing both sides, Zeus agreed.

Athena told Diomedes that he could fight anyone he wanted, and he managed to wound Ares by charging him with a chariot, transporting him back to Mt. Olympus and out of the battle. Athena and Hera decided it was safe to leave after Ares had been dispatched, as the Achaeans were the superior force *when no gods were getting in the way.*

To end the day's ferocious battle and prevent a further advance by the Greeks, Hector emerged to challenge any Achaean to single combat. Menelaus was again the first to step forward, but Agamemnon convinced him that while he easily handled the last prince, he was no match for this one. Nine other Achaeans stepped forward and commenced having a lottery among them; Ajax the Great was chosen as the Achaean champion. Ajax had been described as more of a wall than a man, and Hector knew immediately that he had his work cut out for him. After fighting with spears and lances with no apparent victor, they were about to draw swords when Zeus intervened to call off the fight due to nightfall.

A pact of friendship was made between the warriors, and Hector managed to prevent the Greek forces from taking more

Trojan lives. Still, corpses littered the fields, and both sides agreed on a day's truce to tend to their dead.

During the truce, Zeus also forbade the gods from re-entering the war until he decided which side he would favor. At Mt. Ida in Anatolia, he placed the fates of the Achaeans and Trojans in his scales and sided with Troy when the Greek side plunked down.

In a great storm of lightning, Zeus struck out at the Achaean encampment, all of which began to flee in fear. Hector and the Trojans took advantage of the chaos, sensing a turning point and seeing an opportunity to rid themselves of the Achaeans on their shore. They cut down the retreating Greeks who were starting to make for their ships, and as Hera and Athena were about to help them, Zeus warned them again not to intervene. One would hope this would be the end of battling, but pride took the forefront once again. The Achaeans convinced Zeus to give them one more chance, to which he replied that only Achilles could save them.

Meanwhile, night had fallen on the Achaean retreat, and Hector ordered that campfires be lit so that they could not escape in the dark. The Achaeans sat in despair, with Agamemnon weeping at the thought of returning to Greece in disgrace. Diomedes declared that he would continue fighting even if he were the only one left standing; the Achaeans began to take heart once more in the prophecy of Calchas that declared they were destined to win.

Nestor recommended that Agamemnon make amends with Achilles so that he would return and fight with them once more – and Agamemnon agreed. He sent Odysseus and Ajax the Great a great heap of wealth and fortune on the condition that they returned to the war.

Once back at the battlefield, they found Achilles in his tent, relaxed and playing the lyre with his long-time friend and deputy Patroclus. The two had grown up together and shared a bond so close that scholars are left unsure of whether they may have also been lovers, something fairly common among Achaean soldiers.

Upon hearing the offer, Achilles rejected it outright, reciting his plans to return home to Phthia; the Achaean forces returned to their despair.

Hector and Ajax the Great met once again in battle, and once again, they fought to a draw. The Trojans kept pushing them back until - as the story goes - Hector was close enough to touch a ship. Upon seeing this, Patroclus gives in, telling Achilles that he will go and join the fight in an effort to save the ships. As Achilles still refused to join in the battle, Patroclus asked if he could wear his armor; Achilles agreed. Patroclus and the Myrmidons rushed to help push back the Trojan advance, and Achilles prayed for the safety of both the ships and of Patroclus. Homer tells us that Zeus would only grant *one* of those prayers.

At the sight of Achilles' armor, the Trojans (or those who were *able to*) immediately retreated from the Achaean ships. Many had their retreat cut short by the sudden and unexpected entrance of new combatants; Patroclus dispatched them with great prejudice, including Zeus' mortal son Sarpedon. While Zeus accepted his son's death without intervention, he decided that Patroclus had to die in return. Seeing so many retreating Trojans, Patroclus broke his word to Achilles by pursuing Hector's forces.

At the gates of the city, Hector turned to meet the foe that he still believed to be Achilles, and the two engaged in single combat. During the fight, Hector realized that his foe was not actually Achilles; and so he slew Patroclus, taunting with the words:

"Wretch! Achilles, great as he was, could do nothing to help you."

Patroclus' last words to Hector foretold his enemy's pending doom:

"You yourself are not one who shall live long, but now already death and powerful   destiny are standing beside you, to go down under the hands of Peleus' great son, Achilles."

In the immediate aftermath, Trojans and Greeks began to fight over Achilles' armor, but Hector snatches the armor, taking it back to the city.

When Achilles heard of Patroclus's death, he began a violent breakdown. His anguished wails were loud enough that Thetis heard and came to see what troubled him. Knowing that she could no longer sway him against the life of a warrior, she begged him to wait one day before seeking vengeance. This, she argued, would allow time for Hephaestus (Greek god of blacksmiths, metalworking, carpenters, craftsmen, artisans, etc.) to make him a new set of armor, replacing the one taken by Hector.

Each army began constructing new plans and strategies now that Achilles was returning to the battle. The Trojans considered returning to the safety of their walls, but Hector refused, not wanting to cede any of the ground they had gained over the recent weeks.

Thetis returned the next day to give Achilles his new body armor, promising to look after Patroclus' body. Donning his new armor and attending the Achaean assembly, Achilles formally reconciled with Agamemnon, who made good on his promise of gifts - and Briseus - in exchange for him resuming the battle. Achilles vowed to do nothing, *not even eat*, until Hector was dead by his hand. Achilles' seething wrath was so great that Zeus feared that he might tear down the entire Trojan civilization before it was time. The rest of the gods had no longer wanted to interfere but rather took up seats to watch how the end would play out with the mortals on their own - and Achilles in a far more murderous temper than usual.

Achilles charged the Trojans near the Scamander River, killing so many of them that the river became clogged and dammed with bodies. The river gods were overwhelmed by what was happening and called on the gods of Mt. Olympus for help. Hearing the plea, Achilles was attacked by the river and dragged downstream until the Hephaestus (the god of blacksmiths) boiled the water out of the river until it released Achilles. During this melee, most of the gods and goddesses watching the unfolding events had whipped themselves into such a frenzy that they began fighting each other.

Meanwhile, King Priam opened the gates of Troy to allow his soldiers to retreat and escape Achilles' pursuit and was barely able to shut them in time before Achilles could enter from behind. Hector, alone, remained outside of the gates, ashamed of his decision not to retreat – a decision that had gotten so many Trojans killed. Zeus once again went to Mt. Ida to judge fates, this time that of Achilles and Hector, now facing each other for the first time in the war. Placing their futures on the scales, Hector's side fell with a clank, bringing Patroclus' final words closer to fruition.

Alone and outside the walls of Troy, the two great warriors clashed spears once again. Knowing Hector's armor, Achilles was able to quickly exploit a weakness in the neck when Hector charged him. Fallen and struggling through his wound, Hector asks that Achilles gives him a proper burial, but the Achaean was still in a mind of vengeance and told him that his body would be for the birds and dogs before driving his spear through the Trojan prince's chest. Watching from atop the city walls, Priam, Hecuba, and Andromache looked helplessly on as Achilles tied Hector's body to the back of his chariot and dragged him around the city. For days, Achilles continued to desecrate the corpse of Hector as he mourned Patroclus. Finally, King Priam himself left the walls of Troy with the help of Hermes and slipped into Achilles' tent to offer him a ransom for his son's body. He connected with Achilles' better side when he asked him to think of the love between fathers and sons and the love he holds for his father, Peleus. Achilles accepted the ransom, and Priam left to care for his son's body.

A fresco depicting the scene of Achilles's triumph. This was painted by Franz Matsch. Credit: Wikimedia Commons.

Chapter 7: The Deaths of Penthesilea, Memnon, and Achilles

While the *Iliad* ended with Hector's funeral, the Trojan War continued. Troy had lost its native hero with the prince's death, but they were about to get some help from an impressive ally: the Amazons.

Who were the Amazons?

According to Greek mythology, the Amazons were a race of warrior women who were frequently pitted against the Greeks. Their territory was somewhere around the Black Sea, and many scholars place their homeland as far north as Ukraine. A queen led these warriors, and in order to keep their society going, they would find mates – but only kept the female children. The girls would grow up to become warriors like their mothers, and the boys would be abandoned, killed, or given up depending upon the telling of the story.

A depiction of an Amazon. Credit: Wikimedia Commons.

The name "Amazon" has associations with South America today, but the Greek roots are "a-mazos," which means "without breast." That is one theory that gave rise to stories claiming that the warriors would cut off their right breast so that it could not interfere with their archery or spear thrusts. Still, artistic depictions of the Amazons show them with both breasts, leading many to believe that the Greek name for them is metaphorical, as they had shunned what the Greeks would have considered being a woman's life for that of a man's by virtue of becoming warriors. The final explanation is simpler: the Greek name probably comes from the name they called themselves, which has roots in another language less understood and further lost than Ancient Greek.

Archaeological evidence gives some further insight into the debate as to whether this group existed or were figments of the collective Greek psyche. Using DNA testing on remains in Scythian graves, archaeologists discovered that many of the bodies once thought to be men were Scythian women. What led to this misconception?

The women had been buried with their weapons and with wounds and scarring consistent with those of warriors. In other words, archaeologists found bodies decorated as warriors and assumed for centuries that they were, therefore, *men*. Plenty of the graves were indeed for men, but the egalitarian internment shows that Scythian women were just as likely to train for war.

Further, the Scythian territory is consistent with the regions described as *Amazon territory* by the Greeks. Scythians were also a horse culture credited with the innovation of a saddle, both things that would have further leveled the playing field of war by removing many of the size and strength retorts that are common – even today – when discussing female soldiers. Coming this far, it is not ridiculous to assume that there was egalitarian leadership as well or even (*gasp*) a matriarchy in power during this period.

A matriarchy would support the practice of choosing to raise the girls and sending the boys to be raised by their fathers, not killing them. Their portrayal as man-haters is also undone, even by the Greeks themselves. They are described as man-killers, naturally, since that is primarily who they would have been fighting against. Being further described as fierce warriors, they would have been very good at it. But they were also highly sexualized in Ancient Greek stories, as can be seen in the Labors of Heracles.

The Amazons and the Ninth Labor of Heracles

Pre-dating their entry into the Trojan War, the Amazons were part of the story of Heracles' twelve labors. (In case you are wondering, the story is also called the Labors of Hercules; in one version, Hercules is a god. In this version, Heracles is a mere mortal.)

His ninth labor was to retrieve the belt of Hippolyte, the Queen of the Amazons at the time. According to the story, he arrives and informs her of his quest, to which she consents. However, Hera was dismayed at the ease with which he was about to accomplish his task and disguised herself as one of the Amazons to engage in a misinformation campaign. She told her fellow warriors that the Greeks had come not for the belt but *war* and that they would soon be killed if they did not stand and fight. As Heracles was about to receive the belt from Hippolyte, his soldiers were attacked by the Amazon forces, and he drew his sword and killed their queen, removing her belt once she was dead.

That is one way of telling the story, but it does not make much sense at face value. Why did Hera task Heracles with getting a queen's belt? As usual, symbolism matters here. In Ancient Greek culture, obtaining (or *taking*) a woman's belt represented a sexual conquest, especially of a virgin. What Hera truly required Heracles to do was either seduce or rape the Queen of the Amazons. Read this way, Heracles was initially successful in courting Hippolyte, which was a great surprise to Hera. With Hera's next actions remaining the same, the metaphor tells us that Heracles killed and then raped Hippolyte, symbolized by taking the belt off her body *afterward.* Our hero.

Achilles versus Queen Penthesilea

There is another version of the myth where Heracles abducts rather than kills Hippolyte after taking her "belt" and returns to Athens with Theseus, who then marries the queen. In retribution for this abduction, the Amazons, led by Hippolyte's sister Penthesilea, attack Athens to rescue her. Or they attacked Athens after Theseus discarded the Amazon queen in favor of Phaedra, the daughter of King Minos of Crete. Hippolyte, who either still loved or irreconcilably hated Theseus, was accidentally killed by Penthesilea. (Or none of that happened, and Hippolyte was killed by her sister with a spear during a deer-hunting accident.) The Ancient Greeks sometimes had difficulty keeping their stories straight. Regardless of the fate of Hippolyte, Penthesilea was Queen of the Amazons at the time of the Trojan War, and she sided with the Trojans like her father Ares had.

The Achaeans were devastated by her arrival, and she cut through their forces with more tenacity than even the recently dispatched Prince Hector had. Once again, it was up to Achilles to prove his status as the greatest warrior of the conflict and challenge the queen to single combat. The Greek storytellers once again have a hard time agreeing on what happened next. In some rarer but still prevalent versions, Penthesilea shocks everyone, including the gods, by slaying the mighty Achilles. Zeus decided that this could not be the end for the hero, so Achilles was resurrected and promptly killed Penthesilea. There was no mercy resurrection for the fallen queen, and everyone was allowed to overlook such an embarrassing almost-moment. Most versions, however, are more straightforward and tell of Achilles slaying Penthesilea fair-and-square and then falling in love with her when he removes her helmet and sees her face.

Achilles versus Memnon

Yet another challenger to Achilles was Memnon, King of Ethiopia. As a nephew of Priam, Memnon decided to come to the Trojans' aid late in the war, bringing with him a strong army and providing renewed hope for Troy. Memnon himself was the son of the Titan Eos and was described in the echelon of Achilles, Hector, Ajax the Great, and Penthesilea as a warrior. In a battle where the Trojans had begun to route the Achaean forces, Prince Paris shot and wounded the horse pulling the chariot of the aged King Nestor of Pylos.

With Nestor stuck, his son Antilochus came to his aid and engaged Memnon, whose army was pursuing the retreating Greeks. Memnon killed Antilochus, and afterward, a grief-stricken Nestor challenged Memnon to single combat. Seeing that Nestor was too old for it to be a fair fight, Memnon refused. Nestor then approached Achilles with the task, appealing to his pride by claiming that there was another warrior many believed to be his equal.

Thetis appeared, pleading with her son to turn down this fight since a vision of hers told her that Achilles would die soon after the death of Memnon. But believing that this would prove once and for all that he was the mightiest hero, Achilles accepted and confronted Memnon outside the gates of Troy. During the fight, Memnon wounded Achilles in his arm, marking the first time blood was drawn against the seemingly invincible demigod. Still, while Memnon was able to match Achilles in strength, the Achaean's speed was too much, and Memnon fell with a spear through his heart.

Combat between Achilles and Memnon.
Credit: Ron Koopman, Wikimedia Commons.

Death of Achilles

If there is one thing to take away from the story of the Trojan War, it is that prophecies will be fulfilled. People could fight them or accept them, but they came true all the same. Heroes and even the gods themselves lived by them and often died by them.

Achilles had been told on many occasions that he would die if he fought in the Trojan War. It was on his mother's mind when he departed the island of Skyros to prove his valor. It was on the lips of the fallen Hector as Achilles stood gloating over the prince's dimming eyes. When prophecy finally came to claim Achilles, though, it came from an unlikely source. While he may have lived a warrior's life and compiled an impressive resume of kills, he died ingloriously when Prince Paris shot him from afar with a poison-tipped arrow and with the spiteful guidance of the Apollo. The combination of ambush, poison, and divine intervention leaves Paris with little credit for killing Achilles, and even in victory, he is remembered as cowardly.

In some versions, it is not even Paris, but Apollo *disguised as Paris,* who delivers the fatal shot, completely removing him from the event. Either way, portraying the downfall of Achilles in this manner allowed for the realization of the seemingly contradictory prophecy that he would be the greatest warrior (and therefore undefeated in battle) and yet still die in the war.

Achilles as he lay dying. Credit: Wikimedia Commons.

In the 1995 article titled "Achilles' Heel: The Death of Achilles in Ancient Myth," Jonathon Burgess cites evidence from ancient art and literature, arguing that Achilles was most likely killed outside the walls of Troy with two arrows. The first arrow landed on his ankle, disabling him and stripping him of his legendary speed. The second one is said to have killed him. Indeed, in the later Roman myth, he was shot in the heel while inside Apollo's temple.

The question of Achilles' manner of death is simple; the answer is complex. But that is part and parcel of mythology – it is seldom straightforward. Achilles is a fictional character (we think), so one can choose whichever story most appeals to him.

Chapter 8: Ajax's Death and the Last Prophecies

Following the death of Achilles, Ajax the Great and Odysseus fought off a horde of Trojans to retrieve the body of the fallen warrior. Ajax heaved Achilles, his armor, and his weapons atop of the brick wall that was his shoulders, and Odysseus fought ferociously to hold the opposing soldiers at bay. Achilles' armor had been forged on Mt. Olympus by the god Hephaestus, and both Ajax and Odysseus coveted it for its craftsmanship and magical protective properties.

While their intentions in hauling Achilles back to the Achaean camp may have been pure, they quickly devolved into a squabble over who deserved their comrade's armor more. Having been the one to do the literal heavy lifting, Ajax claimed that he played the more essential role – especially since Odysseus could not have managed the dead warrior's weight. Conversely, Odysseus pointed out that Ajax would have joined him as a corpse had he not been there to fight off the rabid Trojans.

Both, of course, were right.

To settle the dispute, they argued before a council of high-ranking Achaeans. The contest was, of course, over before it began, with Ajax agreeing to a battle of wits with Odysseus amid a Greek myth. Athena aided Odysseus to make his speech more eloquent and to enchant the ears of the council. The armor was eventually awarded to Odysseus, and, in grief, Ajax plunged his own sword into his chest.

This suicidal response is as famous in Greek mythology as it is confusing. The image of Ajax falling on his sword is a popular image found on Greek pottery and seemed embedded in the ancient civilization's culture. Still, the reaction seems out of proportion to what had occurred. Odysseus even finds Ajax in the underworld during his journeys, and the great warrior is still angry with him over the armor dispute! The takeaway by most scholars is that this part of the tale shows how seriously the Achaeans took their honor.

Ajax had twice fought Hector to a duel and was widely regarded as nearly as invulnerable as Achilles himself. The soldier who wore the armor was symbolically the greatest Achaean warrior, an honor which Ajax was correct in expecting to fall to him. The fact that it goes to Odysseus was a grave dishonor to Ajax but perhaps marks a turning point in the story.

Odysseus was obviously inferior to Ajax in a fair fight, but Odysseus hated fair fights and was clever enough to avoid them. Similarly, the Achaeans brought more and better warriors with them than those who were defending Troy, but after a decade, they were still camped outside of its walls. It was no longer speed, strength, and honor in battle through which the Achaeans would win – but through strategy and ruthlessness. Thus, Odysseus was the best warrior for victory in the times to come, while Ajax was merely the superior fighter in the heretofore losing effort.

Nearly on cue, Odysseus captured Helenus, a Trojan prince who had left the city for Mt. Ida following a dispute with his family and forced him to give them intelligence. Helenus was a seer as well as a warrior, something that he had used on several occasions to defeat the Achaeans on the battlefield. Now, he was forced under torture to use his ability to tell his captors how they could breach the city walls and win the war.

He told them that to do so, they must recruit Achilles's son, Neoptolemus, and that they must retrieve Philoctetes (a famous archer from Lemnos, who had survived his abandonment and was in possession of Heracles legendary bow and poisonous arrows).

A depiction of Philoctetes on Lemnos. Note Heracles's bow sitting beside him.
Credit: Marie-Lan Nguyen, Wikimedia Commons.

Recruiting the son of Achilles proved the simpler of the two, as Philoctetes and his Achaean compatriots had not parted ways on the best of terms. After receiving a mysterious, oozing wound on his foot that would not heal, his fellow warriors had simply left him behind so they could get on with their war. They feared taking him with them, not knowing if his weeping limb could somehow infect them as well.

So, he was left alone. His Bronze Age quarantine ended when prophecy dictated that he was needed. Odysseus and Diomedes headed the mission to retrieve him and were astonished to find him both still alive and still wounded. Odysseus had been the loudest voice in advocating to leave Philoctetes, a fact that both warriors were well aware of at their reunion, with Philoctetes clutching Heracles' poisonous arrows. Odysseus managed to trick Philoctetes into handing over the bow and arrow, but Diomedes stood firm and refused to leave with only the weapons and not their old friend.

Heracles himself, now a god, had to intervene to break the stalemate. He promised that if he agreed to go, Philoctetes would be healed by the son of the god Asclepius, thus becoming a great hero in the conclusion of the war for the Achaean army. He also dictated that it must be Philoctetes the wielded his former weapon. In a sign of good things to come for the Greeks, Philoctetes immediately showed his worth by using his poison arrows to kill Prince Paris, hitting him three times before landing the fourth arrow in his heel, just as he (and Apollo) had done to Achilles.

With two new recruits on hand, the Achaeans were halfway towards realizing the demands of Helenus' prophecy.

The third condition for a Greek victory was stealing the Palladium of Troy from within its walls. The Palladium was a sacred wooden statue of Athena (*Pallas* to the Trojans) that fell from the sky during the founding of Troy; the statue had since been worshipped as a protective talisman of the city. Again, Odysseus and Diomedes teamed up for the task, being the two best scalpels in an age of swords and spears.

Here, it is important to remember that Troy was not completely under siege and that people were able to come and go through certain city gates, heavily guarded as they might be. In some accounts of the story, Odysseus was able to gain entry disguised as a beggar and later let Diomedes in through a secret entrance he opened from the inside.

In other stories, they were aided by an ally inside the city, likely Antenor, who had mediated between the Achaeans and the Trojans at the onset of the war. Once inside, the two Achaeans did some sneaking and a little bit of killing before being recognized by Helen. Ever the double agent and skilled in her own survival, Helen decided to show the Achaeans where to find the Palladium. They left the city in the same way they had entered; the third condition for the prophecy to Troy had been met.

However, a larger question is posed by these events. If they were able to enter the city to steal the Palladium, then what need was there for the theatrics and, frankly, the unnecessary risks of the Trojan Horse?

There is no end to sussing out history from the metaphor and entertainment inherent in Greek myths, and this is one of the more interesting points to linger on. One possible answer is that the theft of the Palladium was not a literal theft. If the Palladium was a symbol for the protection of Troy, then perhaps this story is about the symbolic theft of the safety the walls afforded them when the Greeks found (or were aided in finding) a way into the city. Troy falling after the Greeks had an entry point through their walls makes a lot more sense, at least to modern readers, than Troy falling because they lost a statue.

The final task of Helenus' prophecy was to bring the bones of Pelops to Troy. Pelops was the grandfather of Agamemnon, who was buried in Pisa, so the Mycenaean king immediately dispatched a ship and crew tasked with digging up his relative and bringing back his remains.

However, as they returned, the ship was lost in a storm, and the bones never made it to Troy. This is another odd development, as it prevents the Achaeans from fulfilling the prophecy. Anyone who has been paying attention knows that prophecies were *law to* the Achaean Greeks, and the Greeks were still able to win despite their failure. Additionally, why include it in the prophecy if they do not achieve it? Do prophecies matter, or not? Unlike the story of the Palladium (seemingly creating a fantastic tale that confounds the reader), this one needs a fantastic tale *to help it make sense.*

Let us start from the beginning. The story of Pelops opens with his murder. His father, Tantalus, killed his son as part of his plan to test whether the gods were actually omniscient.

Tantalus cut Pelops into pieces, serving him in a stew offered to the god. Most of the gods knew something was amiss with the meal and refused to eat. Demeter, however, she ate Pelops' left shoulder. Later, the gods reassembled Pelops, brought him back to life, while the blacksmith god Hephaestus created an ivory shoulder to replace the one eaten by Demeter.

Hold on; it gets better.

Poseidon then made Pelops his apprentice in Olympus, teaching him how to steer the divine chariot. After going to Greece, Pelops entered a chariot race against Pisa's king Oenomaus – who feared a prophesy that he would be killed by his son-in-law. Oenomaus killed all his daughter's potential suitors – who were his challengers in the chariot races - to thwart the prophecy.

Pelops, hearing of this, asked for Poseidon's help. They convinced the king's charioteer to replace the bolts of his chariot wheels with fake ones. It worked. Oenomaus' chariot was destroyed during the race, and Oenomaus was dragged to death by his horses. Pelops was declared the winner, made king of Pisa, and married Oenomaus's daughter.

Back to one of Heracles labors . . . many believe, therefore, it was not his *bones,* but his *bone* that was required to be brought to Troy. This story makes much more sense, as there would be nothing special about the dead king's bones except for *the one that a goddess created.*

Specifically, Demeter – the one who ate Pelops in her stew – was the goddess of the harvest and had remained neutral through the war, unlike her more excitable brothers and sisters. Demeter's support would have likely come in the form of a good harvest for the Achaeans in a time of need, or by depriving the besieged Trojans of a harvest. The ivory bone was a gift from Demeter, so perhaps this was what they needed; not the brittle remains of a long-dead king, but generosity from the goddess of the harvest.

Bottom line: the fates either said that three out of four was not bad, or they counted the fourth task symbolically, and the Greeks hatched their final scheme to take the city.

Chapter 9: The Trojan Horse and the Sack of Troy

There is almost universal agreement that the city of Troy existed, though debate might still rage regarding its scale and whether Homer was prone to embellishments in his poetic descriptions. Likewise, the war between the Achaean Greeks and the Trojans is thought to have occurred even if there is ongoing deliberation in academia about its length and significance.

The Trojan Horse, on the other hand, is almost entirely dismissed by scholars as a complete invention.

Still, it is as iconic as a symbol for the fall of the Trojans as it is a testament to the Achaean's victory, and the tale cannot be concluded without it. Through scheming, it accomplished what even Achilles could not do through brawn when it finally allowed the Greeks to breach the walls of Troy.

A depiction of the Trojan Horse by Giovanni Domenico Tiepolo. Credit: Wikimedia Commons.

The Legend of the Trojan Horse

According to the legend, Odysseus devised the scheme to build a giant, hollow wooden horse that an elite force of Achaean soldiers could hide inside of. The trick would be getting the Trojans to bring this horse into the city, so the first thing they had to do was convince the Trojans that they had left. To do this, they departed in the night for the island of Tenedos, where their fleet could remain nearby but not a present threat to Troy. The horse, therefore, was to remain as a gift to the Trojans, whom the Achaeans were declaring the victors.

The Trojans sent a party to investigate the newly deserted beach and the large wooden structure left where – for a decade – the Greek armies had camped. Among those sent to scrutinize the unexpected trophy was a priest named Laocoon. He famously claimed, upon reaching the horse, "I don't trust the Greeks even bearing gifts." He suggested that they light the equine sculpture on fire and be done with it, but Athena intervened by sending serpents that leaped out of the sea and killed Laocoon and his two sons that had accompanied him. Fearing now that refusing or burning the gift would anger the gods, the Trojans decided to bring the wooden horse through the gates and throw a commemorative feast in honor of the gods and their victory. Cassandra, cursed with prophecies that no one would believe, also advised her father, Priam, against bringing the gift inside the walls, declaring that the Achaeans would destroy them if they did so. Her advice was not heeded, and the wooden horse remained an object of celebration as the Trojans ate and drank deep into the night.

Meanwhile, Odysseus, Diomedes, Menelaus, Philoctetes, Ajax the Lesser, and about twenty other Achaeans were inside the horse. They waited in a dreadful, cramped silence for days as the Trojans debated between burning them alive, pulling them through the gates, or leaving them to starve on the beach. Eventually, they brought them into the city and threw a feast in honor of the gods and their victory. As dawn approached, the streets finally quieted, and they were alone. Odysseus and his gang had little trouble fighting their way to the gates through the surprised and largely inebriated Trojans. There, the Achaean army met them after having returned unseen in the night. A fire signal had tipped them off that it was time to return and had stealthily anchored their boats outside the city once more. After ten years, the Trojans had let their guard down for one night, and the storming Achaeans saw to it that their mistake was fatal.

A Contemporary Explanation

That is the typical story, with slightly different versions obligatorily splintering towards infinity. Historians and archaeologists take issue with it because it does not quite mesh with what they know of warfare in the region in the late Bronze Age. That is not to say that the Greeks would have been incapable of building the horse but rather that it was not a very good trick; an opponent such as the Trojans would have been well-aware of structures built to hide soldiers and breach walls. From the perspective of the Achaeans, the plan carried an incredibly high risk of failure and horrific death for those attempting to smuggle themselves.

It is worth noting, however, that Homer, Greek dramatists, and Greek historians have had a surprisingly impressive track record of archaeological evidence corroborating their claims, so perhaps it is wise not to discount the horse legend completely. If the gift were to have been used as a decoy rather than transportation, most of the story would still hold together. After all, Odysseus had already managed to sneak into the city on several occasions. Perhaps he could have done so again with a few of his friends while King Priam and the Trojan forces were thoroughly preoccupied with the elaborate and suspicious gift left on the beach. Regardless, what is generally agreed upon is that after a protracted war (lasting up a decade), the besieged Trojans were tricked into lowering their defenses, and the Achaeans made them pay.

The Sack of Troy

The tables had turned. The same walls that had kept the Achaeans out and the Trojan citizens safe for many years were now trapping them inside for slaughter. In accordance with warfare of the time, the sack of Troy was brutal. The Achaeans, fueled by a decade of frustration and defeat, slaughtered Trojan men, women, and children in their sleep. Those who were not killed were raped or abducted – and often both. The Trojan soldiers, though surprised, were certain to have put up a fierce fight through the night and into the next day, but they were never able to recover. The Achaeans were also happy to let fire do what their swords and spears could not. Fire was their ally, as it brought Trojan warriors out of ambush and the Trojan structures to the ground. To escape the fires, many affluent Trojans suddenly became propertyless refugees. In the ruins of Troy, precious metal jewelry has been found in people's homes, indicative of their rapid and thoughtless flight for their lives.

As bad as the fall of Troy was for ordinary Trojans, it was perhaps worse for the Trojan royalty, who were singled out for destruction and vengeance. King Priam was found by Neoptolemus, the son of Achilles, at the altar of Zeus, where he was executed without pomp. Odysseus, fearing that the same cycle of violence could one day repeat upon the Achaeans, found Hector's child son, Astyanax, and threw him to his death from atop the city walls. Hector's wife Andromache was taken by Neoptolemus and his sister Cassandra by Agamemnon. Each returned with the Achaeans to Greece to live as concubines to the warriors. Princess Polyxena, who some stories say was betrothed to Achilles before his death – was sacrificed on the demigod's grave. Helen, for whom the war was begun, awaited King Menelaus in her chambers. After the death of Paris, Helen had married one of his brothers, Deiphobus, whom Menelaus had slain moments earlier during the sack of the city. However, upon seeing her, he was overcome by her beauty and dropped his sword, and the two went back to Sparta as king and queen.

The Burning of Troy *by Johann Georg Trautmann.*
Credit: Wikimedia Commons.

The Flight of Aeneas

Among the refugees of Troy was Aeneas, the son of a Trojan prince, Anchises, and the goddess, Aphrodite. Until the age of five, Aeneas was raised by nymphs on Mt. Ida before being returned to his father, who had sworn never to tell that he had lain with a goddess. He was widely regarded as one of the best Trojan warriors in the war, though he was not as mighty as the likes of Hector or in the ranks of Achilles, Ajax, or Diomedes on the Achaean side. A better comparison may be Odysseus, though perhaps a little less cunning and a little more honorable.

Like Odysseus, Aeneas was favored by the gods, who twice rescued him from battle when it seemed that death was inevitable. Also, like Odysseus, Aeneas would face a long and arduous trip after the Trojan War. With his home destroyed, he fled the city with his son, father, and many other companions after receiving instructions to do so from the gods, who did not want to see the legacy of Troy completely forgotten.

Aeneas Flees Burning Troy *by Federico Barocci.*
Credit: Wikimedia Commons.

Aeneas and his crew were tasked with founding a new city that would eventually birth another great civilization: Rome. Predictably, much of this story is fleshed out by a Roman poet rather than a Greek one, centuries after Homer wrote his *Iliad* and *Odyssey* tales. The Roman poet was named Virgil, and in the *Aeneid*, he told of the meandering adventure that Aeneas and his crew undertook. Their travels took them all around the Mediterranean, with notable stops in Crete, Sicily, and Carthage, where he met and fell in love with Queen Dido. Aeneas had to be reminded by the gods of his mission, and after he secretly absconded from Carthage, a heartbroken Dido uttered a prophecy and curse that would pit their descendants in Carthage and Rome against one another in the Punic Wars (before killing herself upon a sword left to her by Aeneas).

When Aeneas arrived in Italy, he was initially welcomed by Latinus, king of the Latins. However, all did not remain well when Latinus received a prophecy that his daughter, Lavinia, would marry a man from another land. Interpreting this as Aeneas, Latinus heeded the prophecy, which enraged neighboring King Turnus of the Rutuli. Allied with the Etruscans, Turnus marched to war against the Latins and their new Trojan allies. Aeneas himself killed Turnus to win the final battle, but Latinus was killed in the war.

Aeneas founded the city Lavinium, named after his wife, and stayed there with his people for the remainder of his life. When he died, Aphrodite negotiated with Zeus to grant him immortality. He was cleansed by the river god Numicus and given nectar and ambrosia by his mother so that he could ascend to the pantheon. Many generations later, his legendary descendants Romulus and Remus would found the city of Rome, but it is Aeneas and Lavinia who are seen as the progenitors of the Roman people.

When looked at anthropologically, this story makes a lot of sense. As a story written by Romans, it connected them to antiquity and gave their leaders more legitimacy in the eyes of their subjects.

The alliance with the Latins and the conflicts with the Rutuli, Etruscans, and Carthaginians all serve to explain the historical relationships between the people of the region. The relationship between Rome and Carthage that led to the Punic Wars mirrors that of the rivalry between the Greeks and Trojans before them. Roman historians even write admiringly of the Carthaginian general Hannibal, much the way that the Greeks honored the might and dignity of Prince Hector of Troy.

The Surviving Achaeans

Arguably, many of the surviving Achaeans had a more difficult time than Aeneas. Predating the road-trip fiasco movie genre by several millennia, Odysseus had the most famous bad trip of all time. Homer tells of this ill-fated journey in his sequel of sorts to the *Iliad* called the *Odyssey*.

In Homer's *Odyssey*, Odysseus – though still protected by Athena – had angered Poseidon by defeating his favored Trojans. Because the horse ruse was his idea, the god of the sea sent a storm to throw his fleet off course, landing them on the island of the lotus-eaters. Having been fed the magical herb, Odysseus' men forgot where they had come from, what they were doing, and where they were going. Odysseus had to drag them back to their ships, where they were once again sent off course and landed on an island they thought was uninhabited.

There, they found a cave that had stores of meat and cheese, which they ate freely until its inhabitant returned. Polyphemus, a cyclops and a son of Poseidon, discovered the Achaeans eating his food and promptly began eating *them*. He rolled a boulder in front of the mouth of the cave, trapping the Achaeans to their fate. After losing many of his men, Odysseus got the cyclops drunk and blinded him with a wooden stake once he had passed out. Awaking angry and in pain, Polyphemus groped around the cave but could not find the surviving Achaeans, who were sensibly remaining quiet. However, they were still trapped, and Odysseus hatched the plan of attaching themselves to the undersides of the cyclops' sheep he was keeping inside.

Eventually, Polyphemus had to let his sheep out to graze. He inspected each sheep as they passed through to make sure it was, in fact, a sheep, but he failed to thoroughly check their bellies, to which the Achaeans were clinging. In an attempt to hide his deeds from Poseidon, Odysseus halted his escape to call to Polyphemus, telling him that his name was "Nobody" and that all the world would know that *Nobody* had blinded the cyclops.

This is precisely how Polyphemus responded to his father.

"Who blinded you, son?"

"Nobody! Nobody blinded me!"

Odysseus was alternatingly too clever for his good and not nearly as clever as he thought. In this instance, it was a bit of both. Poseidon was a god, after all, and he knew what Odysseus had done to his son. Even more enraged than before, Poseidon agreed to Polyphemus' curse that Odysseus and his crew would wander the seas for ten years before returning to Ithaca. All of Odysseus' fleet but his own ship was soon destroyed, lost, or sunk.

Odysseus and Polyphemus *by Arnold Böcklin.*
Credit: Wikimedia Commons.

When they again made landfall, all of Odysseus' men were turned into pigs by Circe when she provided them with drugged cheese and wine. Only Odysseus remained in human form, having been warned by Hermes and given an herb called *moly* that prevented his transformation. Odysseus managed to convince Circe to return his crew to their original forms by agreeing to stay with her as her lover. After a year, with Circe's help, they were able to continue their journey. She told them that if they ate the sacred cattle of Helios on the island of Thrinacia, they would never make it home to Ithaca. She also gave them many warnings of what they were going to encounter. She told them that their journey would take them past the deadly and beautiful sirens of the sea, whose enchanting songs made sailors jump from their ships, seeking the source only to find their own watery graves. Odysseus and his crew prepared for this by jamming beeswax in their ears. That is, all *except for Odysseus.* He ordered his men to tie him to the mast and guard him, but he wanted to hear the song of the sirens for himself. When the time came, Odysseus begged and pleaded to be let down so that he could find the music, but his watchful crew stayed true to their orders and defied him until his wits returned. Afterward, Odysseus boasted that he was the only man ever to hear the sirens and live to tell about it.

Next, their journey took them through narrow straits, where on one side they had to avoid a terrible maelstrom called Charybdis that would suck their ship to the bottom of the sea, and on the other side, they avoided the Scylla, a six-headed monster that fed on passing mariners. Six of the crew were taken, one by each head, before the ship had safely passed. Like many of the obstacles faced in the journey, they probably represented something more realistic but equally deadly.

Shipwrecks were a part of early Mediterranean life. There were many tight squeezes for ships trying to avoid both being pulled into whirlpools or lost in the open sea if they ventured too far from land, risking the unknown shorelines and barely submerged rocks if they got too close.

Regardless, the survivors now sought refuge on the island of Thrinacia. Odysseus advised against this, remembering Circe's warning, but agreed when the rest of his crew urged him to go. Here, Zeus sent a storm that prevented them from leaving for a very long time, and they ate their way through the food that Circe had set them off with. Facing starvation, the crew slaughtered and ate the sacred cattle of Helios while Odysseus was away praying for the storm to end. Helios demanded that they be killed, so Zeus relented the storm for long enough to convince them it was over, only to start it up again while they were at sea. The ship sunk, drowning all the crew except for Odysseus, who washed up on the shore of Ogygia.

Now the lone remainder of his own crew, Odysseus stayed on Ogygia with the nymph Calypso as her lover for seven years. It has been speculated that this was truly all that happened, and the rest was a tale made up by the always (too) clever Odysseus to explain his long absence to his wife, Penelope.

Regardless, by the time he left Ogygia and returned to Ithaca, twenty years had passed since he left and ten since the end of the war. He had been presumed dead, so he showed up to find that many suitors had arrived seeking marriage with his widow. In order to gain information, he disguised himself as an old beggar, a trick that Penelope should have remembered from before the war. He questioned her about the suitors and observed how she responded when he told her that he had met a man named Odysseus on the island of Crete. Once he was convinced that she was still true to him, he revealed himself to his now-grown son, Telemachus. Together, they devised a competition among the suitors that only Odysseus could win, where his bow was strung, and he shot an arrow cleanly through twelve rings. After watching each try and fail, Odysseus, still disguised as a beggar, proves his strength by stringing the bow and sending the arrow flying through the loops.

For the suitors' perceived treachery against Odysseus, he and Telemachus slaughtered them all and even killed many of the palace caretakers who had aided or lain with the would-be grooms.

Odysseus, thanks to his enduring wit, had defied the gods, heard the song of the sirens, bested a cyclops, was the sole survivor of a shipwreck, and was loved by both a sea nymph and a sorceress. Or at least, so he said.

Agamemnon had a less convoluted return to Mycenae than Odysseus had to Ithaca, but it proved more troublesome. He had left his throne as the most powerful of the Achaean kings, but old family troubles had returned in his absence. The feud between his father Atreus and his uncle Thyestes proved to be only temporarily settled as now Aegisthus, the son of Thyestes, had married Agamemnon's wife Clytemnestra and installed himself on the throne. This mirrored Thyestes' affair with Aerope, who was Atreus' wife and Agamemnon's mother.

Clytemnestra had abandoned Agamemnon due to his willingness to sacrifice their daughter, Iphigenia, in the name of his precious war. She took her revenge by conspiring with Aegisthus to murder him, along with Cassandra – who had returned as his concubine. Aegisthus ruled for seven years until the cycle claimed him, too. Agamemnon's son, Orestes, returned from exile and killed both Aegisthus and Clytemnestra (his own mother) for their treachery against his father. In the eyes of justice, Orestes seemed to take one step forward and once step back by avenging his father yet killing his mother. As a result, he was pursued by the Furies, who were goddesses of vengeance and retribution that drove men insane.

Apollo and Athena took his side, though, and Apollo told them that if he went to the barbarous island of Tauris to retrieve a statue of Artemis, he could end the torment of the Furies. He was captured and brought to a priestess, who turned out to be his long-lost sister, Iphigenia, who he had believed to be dead. She told him that Athena had saved her, and then she helped Orestes' escape and found the statue of Artemis. This turn of events broke the cycle of vengeance that had cursed the family, and the Furies stopped their pursuit of Orestes. He returned to Mycenae, took

Hermione as his wife (the daughter of Menelaus and Helen), and ruled as king.

This series of unfortunate events that befell Agamemnon and his kin was part of what is called the *Curse of the House of Atreus.* A curse that was "contagious" in ancient Greek mythology was called a *miasma.* It began with Agamemnon's great-grandfather, Tantalus, who tried to trick the gods into eating his son as a test of their omniscience. He was discovered and sent to the underworld where he endured a truly Dante-esque torture for his arrogance. He stood in a pool of water, but every time he bent to take a sip, the water evaporated before he could reach it. Likewise, he was positioned beneath a tree that bore fruit, but if he reached to pick one, a breeze would blow the branch just out of his reach. The miasma spread to his children, where it morphed into fratricide, patricide, incest, and human sacrifice until it was broken by Agamemnon's children, Iphigenia and Orestes.

Other notable Achaeans that survived fared better. Nestor, who did not participate in the looting of Troy, enjoyed a safe and speedy journey home. Eventually, he would leave again to create the colony of Metapontum in southern Italy.

Diomedes made it home to find his wife had moved on without him, so he, too, decided to start a colony in southern Italy.

Philoctetes also joined the Italy club, where he founded a sanctuary for Apollo the Wanderer, dedicating the bow of Herakles that he had carried since his injury and abandonment.

Neoptolemus returned to Phthia with Andromache, where he followed Peleus, his grandfather, as king. The pair had a child named Molossus, and their lineage is said to be traced to Alexander the Great of Macedon. The Macedonian kings also claimed to be descended from Herakles, but it is probably fair to say that what really mattered to them was linking their family to a nearly invincible demi-god, *whichever one that may be.*

However, Ajax the Lesser did not fare well and was almost immediately killed by the gods on his journey home as retribution for his destruction of the Temple of Apollo and the rape of the priestesses. The gods were very inconsistent about when things like arson, rape, slavery, and murder were and were not okay. Mostly, they just did not like Ajax.

PART THREE: THE IMPACT OF THE TROJAN WAR

Chapter 10: The Literature: Ancient Greek Writers on the Trojan War

Homer's *Iliad* is the oldest and most complete account of the events surrounding the Trojan War, and his *Odyssey* fleshes out some of the events after the funeral of Hector. In fact, these two books are among the oldest texts in the world that can still be read today. As old as they are, they were still written between four and five hundred years after the events of the Trojan War, a period which not inconsequentially spanned a dark age in Greek history.

What texts or information made it to Homer would have survived through a combination of oral tradition and some scattered records. Homer himself lived in Anatolia, nearer to the site of Ancient Troy than to that of Ancient Mycenae, Athens, or Sparta. This may be both the reason for the seeming sympathies to a Greek enemy in his poems and his access to more information about the events after several hundred years. The *Iliad* and the *Odyssey*, though, were not complete accounts of the conflict.

The *Iliad* is especially paltry, covering less than two months of the ten-year war. At one point in the series of books, the Epic Cycle existed, detailing the whole ordeal from beginning to end in epic dactylic hexameter. In chronological order of the war (though not necessarily in chronological publishing order), these epic poems were *Cypria, Iliad, Aethiopis, Little Iliad, Sack of Troy, Return from Troy, Odyssey,* and *Telegony.* The fragments that have survived from the other books in the Epic Cycle are usually lines that have been found quoted elsewhere, usually by later Greek historians. The original works themselves are lost to history

Cypria

Cypria was written either by Homer, Stasinus of Cyprus, Hegesinus of Salamis, or Cyprias of Halicarnassus. Fifty scattered lines survive, and they tell of the initial events that led to the Trojan War. They describe Zeus' plan to depopulate the world of his demigod children, the judgment of Paris, the gathering of the Achaean forces and the prophecies of Calchas at Aulis, the death of Protesilaus at the hands of Hector, and Greek envoy to negotiate the return of Helen and the treasure stolen by Paris.

The *Iliad* (see Chapter 6)

Aethiopis

The third poem in the Epic Cycle was written by Arctinus of Miletus and begins after Achilles' victory over Hector. *Aethiopis* tells the story of the continued challenges faced by the Achaean hero and his insatiable desire to prove that he was the greatest warrior in the world. At least, that is the presumption from its scant five lines that survive about his battles with Penthesilea and Memnon.

Little Iliad

This epic poem is attributed to either Homer, Lesches of Pyrrha, Cinaethon of Sparta, or Diodorus of Erythrae. Thirty lines of the original text survive, and while not quoted, it is widely referenced by many more texts, making it one of the better-understood works of the Epic Cycle.

It tells the story of the argument between Odysseus and Ajax over Achilles' armor, the prophecies of Helenus after his capture, the infiltration of the Troy by Odysseus and Diomedes to retrieve the Palladium of Troy, the construction of the Trojan horse by Epeius, and the emergence of the Achaean soldiers once inside the walls of Troy. Because this work is often referenced but not always quoted, there are many discrepancies and contradictions, with no single definitive version from its derivative texts. For example, Helenus' prophecy that the Achaeans must retrieve Philoctetes from Lemnos in order to win the war is in some texts given to Calchas. This Philoctetes arrival and the death of Paris earlier in the story and leaves only three prophecies for the Trojan seer to give the Achaeans.

Sack of Troy

The *Sack of Troy* by Arctinus of Miletus backtracks slightly in the narrative to start with the Trojans discovering the Trojan Horse on the beach and debating what to do with it. The death of Laocoon and his sons, the flight of Aeneas and his party, and the fates of the Trojan royal family at the hands of the Achaean conquerors. Only ten lines survive, making this one of the more anemic remnants of the Epic Cycle.

Return from Troy

Written by either Homer, Eumelus of Corinth, or Agias of Troezen, only five and a half lines remain from this contribution to the story. More can be inferred through other texts that do not quote it directly, and its contents told of the stories of most of the Achaeans after the war (save for Odysseus, who gets his own book). The Italian colonies of Nestor, Diomedes, and Philoctetes were covered in this text as well as the murder of Agamemnon and Cassandra at the hands of Aegisthus and Clytemnestra.

Odyssey (see chapter 9)

Telegony

The final installment of the Epic Cycle is *Telegony* by Cinaethon of Sparta, and it is a weird finale. It begins with Odysseus and Telemachus burying the bodies of the slain suitors.

However, the story shifts to a son that his lover Circe had given birth to after he and his crew left her island. His son, Telegonus, left the island after growing to adulthood, and unwittingly landed in Ithaca when a storm blew his ship off course. Not knowing that he was on his father's land, he began stealing and slaughtering cattle to eat. An aged Odysseus came to defend his property and was abruptly killed by Telegonus in an ensuing fight. Telegonus and Odysseus were able to recognize each other in his final moments, and he lamented what he had done.

Telegonus then found Penelope and his half-brother, Telemachus, and returned to Circe's island. Telegonus married Penelope, Telemachus married Circe, and Circe made all of them immortal. So close to the ultimate conceit of outwitting death, Odysseus died as a mortal while his family lived forever.

During the Classical Age of Athens, Greek dramatists also contributed to the growing cacophony of heroic but often conflicting accounts of the then nearly millennium-old war. For context, a Trojan War play for Classical Athenians was akin to a modern audience watching Robinhood. Still, they were captivated by the characters, who had morphed to become more complex and less brutal over time. The three main dramatists whose works have survived are Aeschylus, Sophocles, and Euripides.

Aeschylus and the Oresteia Trilogy

Aeschylus is known as the father of Greek tragedy, though only seven of his approximately seventy to ninety plays survived the ravages of time. Despite most of his work being lost to history, three of the seven surviving plays represent a trilogy about the late days of the House of Atreus.

His play *Agamemnon* starts with the titular character's return home from the Trojan War. However, Agamemnon is mostly seen through the eyes of other characters. The townspeople fear the curse on the house and worry about retribution for his sacrifice of Iphigenia. His wife, Clytemnestra, is appalled that he has brought home a Trojan concubine. Cassandra foresees the murder of Agamemnon and herself but walks towards her fate, knowing that no one will believe her, and she will not be able to escape it even if she tries.

In the next book, *The Libation Bearers*, Agamemnon's son, Orestes, meets his sister, Electra, at their father's tomb to plan vengeance against their mother and Aegisthus, whom she has taken as her new husband. They succeed, but the final installment, *The Eumenides*, describes his guilt and the torment inflicted on him by the Furies for his kin slaying. In the end, Orestes is forgiven for his actions against his mother, and the Furies are renamed The Eumenides or *The Kindly Ones*.

Sophocles: Electra, Ajax, and Philoctetes

While Sophocles is most known for his *Oedipus Rex* and *Antigone* tragedies, he also contributed to the legend of the Trojan War through three of his plays, though these are not a trilogy. His play Ajax attempts to somewhat rescue the reputations of Ajax the Great and Odysseus, who each had some confusing moments in the aftermath of Achilles' death. Electra is another telling of The Libation Bearers where she and Orestes plot the death of their mother and Aegisthus – but with Electra as the protagonist rather than Orestes.

In Sophocles' version, Ajax did not immediately kill himself after Achilles' armor was awarded to Odysseus, but rather swore vengeance upon Agamemnon and Menelaus, who had each voted against him. In a rage, he gathered his weapons and non-Achilles' armor and went in search of the maligned brothers to kill them. However, Athena clouded his vision so that he ended up killing the Greek's cattle and herdsmen instead. When Ajax regained his senses and realized what he had done, the shame drove him to suicide. While this attempts to explain a little bit more about what drove the hero to impale himself, it completely changes the rationale. In the original, he chose death over the dishonor brought on him by the judgment of others. However, in this version, he chose death rather than deal with the disgrace he had brought on himself. Odysseus, for his part, argued to have a proper burial for Ajax despite his recent actions, which Agamemnon and Menelaus reluctantly agreed to. Finally, *Philoctetes* begins with Odysseus and Neoptolemus (instead of Diomedes) going to Lemnos to bring the wounded archer to Troy after languishing for nearly a decade on the island by himself with an oddly festering foot. The morality and motivations behind each of the options play out, as Odysseus and Neoptolemus consider taking the bow and arrows but leaving Philoctetes, and Philoctetes is reluctant to join them ever after learning how the prophecy needs him to return for the Achaeans to win.

Euripides' Nine Plays

Euripides was the last of the great dramatists of the classical era, and he wrote the most prolifically of the three about the Trojan War. His nine surviving plays about the war are Andromache (wife of Hector), Hecuba (wife of King Priam during the Trojan War), Cyclops, Electra (daughter of King Agamemnon and Queen Clytemnestra of Mycenae), The Trojan Women, Iphigenia in Tauris, Helen, Orestes, and Iphigenia in Aulis.

Andromache

At the palace of Neoptolemus, Orestes sees his friend Pylades. Neoptolemus is shielding Astyanax in order to earn favor with Andromache, so the Greeks have dispatched him to fetch him. Orestes, who is madly in love with Hermione, makes his requests to Neoptolemus, who snubs them. But his refusal is conditioned on Andromache's love. Hermione intends to return to King Menelaus, her father.

Okay, stay with me here...

Neoptolemus, irritated by Andromache's coldness, concedes to Orestes. Enraged at the course of events, Orestes organizes the kidnapping of Hermione. After failing to persuade Hermione to preserve her son, Andromache turns to Neoptolemus, who wants her hand in marriage in exchange for his protection.

Andromache resolves to succumb to Neoptolemus after consulting Hector's spirit at his tomb but prepares to murder herself immediately after the wedding ceremony. Hermione demands that Orestes kill Neoptolemus at the altar in retaliation for Neoptolemus' rejection. Hermione is torn furiously between love and hate after Neoptolemus' departure. When Cleone, her confidante, informs her of Neoptolemus' insulting happiness at the wedding ceremony, resentment wins over. When she hears Orestes' narrative of how the Greeks avenged her by killing Neoptolemus at the altar, she curses him and stabs herself in the body of Neoptolemus. Orestes is overcome by despair, followed by lunacy.

(True to their reputation, Greek and Roman mythology reads like episodes of the late 70s television show, SOAP.)

Hecuba

The Greeks have conquered Troy. The women of Troy have been divided among the Achaean victors, but they have returned home. Strong winds are holding up the Greek fleet. The ghost of Achilles has requested the sacrifice of Polyxena was the daughter of Hecuba and Priam, Troy's ruler. Odysseus, the Greek hero, arrives to take her away. He was unmoved by Hecuba's anguish or her reminder that he once owed her his life. On the other hand, Polyxena would rather die than be enslaved, and she accepts her fate. Hecuba is bereaved yet again as she prepares for the burial. Polydorus, her youngest son, had been sent with a portion of Priam's fortune to Polymestor, ruler of the Thracian Chersonese (where the Greek fleet is now held).

When Troy fell, Polymestor murdered the youngster, Polydorus, and threw his body into the sea to capture the treasure for himself. It has been washed and transported to Hecuba. She seeks retribution from Agamemnon, the Greek king, but he is cautious, despite his sympathies. Hecuba then takes matters into her own hands and seeks vengeance. Polymestor and his boys are lured to her tent, where her servants slit his eyes and murder his sons. Agamemnon sends the blinded king to a secluded island and prophesies that Hecuba would change into a dog for what she has done.

Cyclops

This is an oddly familiar take on the more common version of Odysseus' encounter with the cyclops in the *Odyssey*. Here, Odysseus visits his friend, Silenus, on Mount Etna in Sicily and offers him food in exchange for his wine. As a Dionysiac servant, Silenus cannot help himself from obtaining the wine, despite the fact that the food is not his to liking. Cyclops arrives shortly after, and Silenus accuses Odysseus of taking the food, vowing to the gods and the nearby Satyrs that he is telling the truth.

Cyclops takes Odysseus and his crew inside his cave after a dispute and consumes some of them. Odysseus manages to escape and is taken aback by what he sees. He devises a plan to get the cyclops drunk and then burn off his eye with a big poker while he is unconscious.

When Cyclops gets inebriated, he claims to be seeing gods and begins referring to Silenus as Ganymede. The Cyclops then kidnaps Silenus and takes him to his cave, and Odysseus begins the next stage of his plan. When the time comes, Odysseus enlists the help of the Satyrs, who burn out the cyclops' eye. His name was "Noman," as he had informed the Cyclops before. As a result, when the Cyclops cries out who blinded him, it sounds like he is saying, *"No Man blinded me."*

Trojan Women

One of Euripides' most moving tragedies, this play depicts the predicament of the Trojan women after their men have been slaughtered and they are at the mercy of their Achaean captives. They wait for their fate, sad and worried. The herald, Talthybius, says that they will be divided among the victorious. The Trojan queen Hecuba will fall into the hands of the despised Odysseus; her daughter Cassandra will be given to Agamemnon, and her other daughter Polyxena will be slain on Achilles' grave.

Cassandra, the tragic figure, appears. As a prophetess, she foretells the conqueror's doom, but, as usual, no one listens or believes her. Andromache arrives with her son, Astyanax, to be the prize of Achilles' son, Neoptolemus. Talthybius reappears to abduct Astyanax, who has been sentenced to death by the Greeks.

Menelaus and Helen meet next; Menelaus is hell-bent on destroying her, and Hecuba fuels his hatred. On the other hand, Helen pleads her case, and their reconciliation is hinted at when Helen and Menelaus depart. Talthybius reappears with Astyanax's broken body, and Hecuba prepares the funeral. Troy is set on fire, and the city's towers crumble as the women flee into slavery.

Iphigenia in Aulis

When Iphigenia was going to be sacrificed at Aulis, Artemis interfered and substituted her with a deer on the altar, sparing the girl and whisking her away to Tauris. There, she became a priestess in the temple of Artemis, where she must ritually sacrifice foreigners who land on King Thoas' coasts.

Iphigenia despises her forced religious slavery in Tauris and is desperate to let her family know she is still alive. In addition, she had a premonition about her brother, Orestes, which leaves her feeling that he had died. Meanwhile, Orestes has murdered his mother, Clytemnestra, and is enraged by the Furies. Despite the fact that he was judged not guilty in Athens, some Furies continue to hunt him. As a result, Apollo orders him to take a sacred statue of Artemis and return it to Athens, where he will be set free. As per local custom, he is arrested by Taurian guards and taken to the temple, where they will be executed.

Orestes and Iphigenia recognize each other and rejoice, and Iphigenia tricks King Thoas into letting Orestes live by telling him that her brother's matricide has contaminated the Artemis statue. She recommends letting them both go, as she has disgraced herself and is also disgraced through her family. They flee while King Thoas is still deciding, bringing the statue with them. Thoas pledges to track down and slay the fugitives, but Athena intervenes and allows them to escape.

Helen

Helen never ran away to Troy with Paris in this alternate history but rather was carried away to Egypt, where King Proteus safeguarded her. After Proeteus' death, his son Theoclymenos planned to marry Helen, who remained faithful to her husband, Menelaus. When news reached Egypt that Menelaus had drowned, Helen became eligible for marriage. To be certain, she visited the king's sister, Theonoe, who was a seer. She learns that Menelaus survived and that a stranger would soon arrive in Egypt. This stranger turned out to be none other than Menelaus himself! Needing to find a way out of Egypt, she told King Theoclymenos that Menelaus was, in fact, dead and that she needed to perform a burial at sea in order to be free to marry him. Menelaus, still in disguise, snuck onto the boat with her, and they fled back to Greece.

Electra

In Euripides' telling of *Electra*, she was married off to a farmer because she was afraid that if she stayed in the royal household and married a noble, their children would try to avenge Agamemnon's death one day. Electra resented her exile and her mother's dedication to Aegisthus, despite his kindness towards her. Orestes, the son of Agamemnon and Clytemnestra, was fully exiled and sent to the king of Phocis, where he became friends with the king's son Pylades.

Once grown, Orestes and Pylades returned to Mycenae in search of vengeance and found Electra and her husband. Despite trying to conceal their identities in order to gain information, a servant recognized Orestes by a scar. Electra agreed to help her brother on his mission of revenge. They decide to lure Clytemnestra away from the house so that Orestes could kill Aegisthus. Having done so, they struggled over the decision of killing their mother. In this version, both Orestes and Electra kill their mother together and are both immediately torn by guilt. Shades appear to tell them that although their mother deserved her death, they had still committed a shameful act for which they must atone.

Orestes

Orestes and Electra had fled to Sparta in search of Menelaus' protection after Clytemnestra's murder. Helen emerged from the palace under the guise of making an offering at her sister Clytemnestra's grave, blaming Apollo for the House of Atreus' misfortunes. Orestes awakened after Helen had left, still enraged by the Furies. When Menelaus arrived at the palace, he and Orestes talked about the murder and the torment that followed them ever since. Tyndareus, Orestes' grandfather, and Menelaus' father-in-law entered and discussed humanity's interference in divine justice.

Later, Orestes and Pylades argued their case in front of the town assembly, but Orestes and Electra were sentenced to death. In an interesting turn, they decide to plot against Menelaus, Helen, and Hermione, who they feel have now wronged them. Helen vanished into thin air when the siblings went to kill her, so they moved next to Hermione. Menelaus entered just in time, and before more bloodshed could occur, Apollo appeared to inform Menelaus that Helen had been set among the stars and that Orestes must stand trial in Athens. He assured Orestes that he would be acquitted and that he was to marry Hermione.

Iphigenia and Aulis

The play opens with Agamemnon already having agreed to sacrifice his daughter, Iphigenia, in order to appease Artemis, but he is beginning to have second thoughts. He attempts to send a letter to her to turn around and return to Mycenae, but Menelaus intercepted it before it could reach her and leans into a fierce argument with his brother for changing his mind.

Strangely, as a result of the debate, each brother wins by changing the other's mind, and they switch sides! Menelaus would now prefer to disband the Achaean force and give up on retrieving his wife rather than see his innocent niece die, and Agamemnon strengthened his resolve that the sacrifice was painful but necessary to their cause. Still in disagreement, neither brother manages to warn Clytemnestra to turn back, so they arrive in the camp believing that Iphigenia was coming there to marry Achilles. This ruse was short-lived and served primarily to infuriate Achilles. As Agamemnon's wife and daughter learn the truth, they are terrified and argue with Agamemnon, who is by now completely convinced that it is the right thing to do. Achilles was ready to defend Iphigenia, but the girl agreed to be sacrificed when she saw how it was tearing apart the Achaean army to stay there with no wind to carry them to Troy. At the very last moment, Artemis had mercy and switched the girl for a deer.

Yes, these versions are very different – but such is mythology. Through generations of telling and re-telling – combined with cultural changes requiring a change in the narrative – these stories become somewhat of a Frankenstein; bits and pieces substituted here and there, and occasionally, an entirely foreign element is added. And while many are difficult to follow, the resounding themes are ones of plotting, revenge, escape, and forgiveness.

Chapter 11: The Legend: How Ancient Greeks Viewed the Trojan War

This chapter will cover the period when the *Iliad* and the *Odyssey* were written, how they were passed from generation to generation, what the Ancient Greeks believed about the war (whether it was a myth or not), and *when it took place* according to the ancient scholars.

Much debate still rages about the lines that historians and scholars should draw between the history, religion, and outright entertainment present in these stories. But what about the Greeks themselves? How much stock did they put into their own stories, and how much – if any – did they greet with an eye roll and/or dismiss as embellishment?

There is obviously no single correct answer to this question.

Like people today, the Ancient Greeks were not a monolith. The myths of the Ancient Greeks were firmly embedded within their culture. While many may have taken their stories quite literally, others sought them out for their metaphors, poetry, and punchlines. For the Greeks who lived during Homer's time,

Classical Athens, or the empire of Alexander the Great, the Trojan War was ancient. The city of Troy had gone, and the Achaean Greeks bore little resemblance to their modern Greek culture. As seen through the dramas of Aeschylus, Sophocles, and Euripides, much of the tweaking of the stories was to humanize the characters and align them more with their fifth-century BCE values.

So, the question becomes more complicated: not only, "Did the Greeks believe their stories *literally*?" but also, "Which versions of their myths were most believed and disbelieved, and how did that change over time?" There is perhaps a better way to approach this question obliquely, and that is to ask, "What did the Greeks think about their heroes?" This is a far more relatable and far more answerable question.

After all, it is not silly to ask people what they think about Luke's journey in Star Wars or debate what makes Thor and Steve Rogers "worthy" in the Avengers franchise. They reflect values, and these values can really get historians into the heads of the Ancient Greeks. The Greek myths about the Trojan War were a conversation that everyone could have with one another; not like a language, but like a consciousness.

So, let us dig deep into a few of the characters (or *historical figures* – if that is your belief).

Regardless of which one is used, what is important is that to Ancient Greeks, they represented *archetypes*. Achilles, Odysseus, Hector, Agamemnon, and Helen all stood for something that they more or less agreed on, even if that "something" was subject to some evolution over time. Their stories are about many things, but they revolve around the character's representation of an ideal, and how their nature is both often excused and ultimately leads to their downfall.

Achilles

Achilles was clearly everything that a Bronze Age Greek man was supposed to be and is, therefore, the archetypal hero of the war. He is strong, fast, and skilled in battle. Though not overly bright, he was no brute and remained his own man during the Trojan War, commanding his own Myrmidons and frequently asserting his independence, causing Agamemnon and other Greek leaders to continuously court him to the battlefield.

He was also handsome, and he had a strong sense of justice. Sometimes that sense of justice came in the form of traditional fairness, like when he was prepared to defend Iphigenia from her forced sacrifice. Sometimes, however, that came in the form of absolute rage and the irrational justice that was exhibited when he required not only the death of Hector by his own hand but also his eternal humiliation for killing his lifelong companion, Patroclus. The reader is aware that Hector did little wrong in his slaying of Patroclus in battle, but still, the vengeance of Achilles is terrible. This marks one of the lesser discussed aspects of the archetypal hero; *they get people to make exceptions for them.*

The actions of Achilles did not diminish his standing in either Greek or modern minds. Greeks especially knew the end of the story and did not abandon their idyllic warrior when he dragged Hector behind his chariot and left his body for the dogs. For that matter, his status does not drop when he casually sacrifices people to the gods, as he did after the death of Patroclus, or kidnaps and rapes local women, as he did at the beginning of the *Iliad*.

Agamemnon is held accountable for these things, though. In fact, his sacrifice of Iphigenia and his abduction of Cassandra as his concubine are the two main reasons Clytemnestra turned against him in Aeschylus' Oresteia trilogy. Repeatedly throughout the tales of Achilles, his arrogance is explained away by Homer as him just being "great in his greatness." This is both a fancy way of saying he is an archetype for greatness and hinting at the final aspect that makes his archetype complete: his downfall.

While he is the one person in history who literally had an Achilles heel (a phrase now used synonymously with someone's weakness or downfall), this small, unknown vulnerability was not what truly killed him. For characters like Achilles to remain in the collective consciousness, there must be a complete circle. In other words, if he is great because of his greatness, his greatness must also undo him. This aspect of the story is what makes Achilles' story memorable.

He was presented with the choice of being the greatest warrior in the world but dying young or living a long, happy life but being forgotten. He was also given repeated opportunities to turn around – even after making his initial choice to face greatness and death in the Trojan War.

In Greek myths, prophecies are typically law, but Achilles' situation is somewhat unique in the sense that he is essentially given two prophecies that he must choose between. The debate may still go on about whether he really had a choice (given his nature), but it remains a narrative choice not typical for the genre. His duels with Penthesilea and Memnon – after he slew Hector – further illustrate that near the end of his life, proving his greatness has become more of an obsession or a compulsion than a virtue to him.

Having made his choice to be a warrior, he becomes a slave to that choice, even when warned yet again of his impending death if he were to make a certain choice, this time choosing to fight and kill Memnon. Of course, the great warrior hero cannot die by being bested in battle, so his long-foreseen death comes at the hands of what is essentially an assassin in the form of Paris. Further, Paris needs poison on his arrow and the guidance of Apollo to kill Achilles in a way that he did not know he was vulnerable and therefore had not prepared for. In dying this way, all that he was is preserved.

Odysseus

That hero at the end of the war is undoubtedly Odysseus. Though he possessed many qualities of other Greek heroes, such as skill in battle, he represents a different archetype: the *maverick*. By making his cleverness and quick thinking his greatest attribute, he becomes an important representation of the strategy (and often ruthlessness) needed to be victorious through the theft of the Palladium of Troy and the ruse of the Trojan horse.

Through Odysseus, Greeks saw the flaws of brute strength and conventional mores. While duty binds Hector to meet his almost assured death by single combat, Odysseus has no qualms about stealth, backstabbing, and the brutal murder of Hector's child. As Ajax chooses death over dishonor when he is passed over for Achilles' armor, Odysseus is very comfortable with dishonorable actions such as lying and cheating so long as it means he wins.

Lastly, the shift to Odysseus contrasts Achilles by choosing a different representation of his glory: his survival. Where Achilles needed to die in order to be great, Odysseus needed to live. His *Odyssey* ends with him as the sole survivor of the voyage home to Ithaca, and the lone suitor of Penelope left standing.

As already detailed, the cleverness of Odysseus and his need to survive are in his nature, and much of his unsavory behavior is forgiven in that context. His murder of Astyanax, the child son of Hector and Andromache, is explained away because it would prevent future vengeance and further war against the Greeks. His complete abandonment of Philoctetes (almost twice) on Lemnos was also forgiven, as he did it in the name of Greek victory and prevention of plague, perhaps even leprosy, among the Achaean armies. Even the deaths of his entire crew are justified to show both their lack of caution and Odysseus' talent for survival.

Like Achilles, Odysseus was not killed by having been bested in his own strengths but through an *unknown weakness*. His lack of knowledge about his son through Circe led to a miscalculation of who – and how dangerous – the cattle-stealing stranger he met in Ithaca truly was. Left to an unplanned conventional fight many years past his physical prime, Odysseus was killed.

It is also notable that Odysseus was only able to be killed once he stopped adventuring and settled down. In other words, he died when he *stopped* being who he was. Where Achilles would have faced a symbolic death by being forgotten had he decided to settle down, Odysseus met his literal death by doing so, further contrasting the two Homeric heroes of the *Iliad* and *Odyssey*, respectively.

Hector

Hector is the honorable protector of the Trojan War epic. While he possesses mostly the same physical traits and skills as Achilles, he uses them to defend his family and his people rather than to seek glory or remembrance. This honorable trait was first seen in his decision to back his brother, Paris, despite thinking of him as a fool and disagreeing with what he had done. His strength as a warrior is honed and focused by this loyalty, which gives him the power to fight the Achaeans for a decade over something that he agreed with them about. This is how Homer (and the Greeks who read his work) were able to relate to the enemy side of the battle; he did not make them antagonists; he made them contrasting archetypes.

The *Iliad* and the *Odyssey* are stories that have no true antagonists, except for prophecies and perhaps the gods and goddesses. Therefore, the Greeks could get behind Hector and feel conflicted over the principles and outcome of the war in favor of the Achaeans, their own ancestors. It allowed Hector to become a *rival*, or honorable foe, to the Greek cause. He represented many of their own values, simply on the other side of the wall, rather than being a *nemesis* that was seen as their opposite.

And much like his Greek counterparts, much violence was done in the name of his loyalty and honor that the audience is encouraged to overlook. Defending his brother's actions that he knows to be wrong is perhaps his cruelest act towards the city of Troy. In essence, he is more willing to be honorable than to be right, and the nature of Hector is perhaps the most tragic because it leads not only to his own downfall but to the senseless deaths of thousands. He fights the Achaeans on principle, which is something that the two other heroes would have never done.

Thus, this trio competes for the crown of who the "true" hero of the Trojan War was, which is the most important part of the stories for the Greeks. Whether they believed that Achilles was a demigod or simply an incredibly fast and skilled warrior is far less important than whether they believed that made him superior to Odysseus and Hector.

Similarly, who they were more likely to excuse for their faults and bad behavior demonstrates the archetype they associate with more strongly. If impetuousness and vanity can be overlooked by someone being the absolute best at what they do, then that is a vote for Achilles. If ruthlessness and deceit are forgivable when they are accompanied by cunning and big-picture planning, then Odysseus is the protagonist of choice. And if the sacrifice and death of the masses can be justified by the principle for which one fights, then Hector is the central figure of the saga. There are also other important characters who, while not seen as the saga's ultimate heroes, are important for understanding Ancient Greek thinking about the Trojan War.

Agamemnon

The most powerful Achaean king and the leader of the Greek armies for the duration of the Trojan War is not among the central heroes but is still prominent in Greek thinking as the archetype for a ruler and (absent) father. Even the House of Atreus; curse, while named after his father and begun by his great-grandfather, runs through Agamemnon. Tantalus, Pelops, and Atreus are described as his ancestors, and Orestes, Electra, and Iphigenia are his children, making him the focal point of his own family's saga within the events of the Trojan War.

As the ruler archetype, he puts his own power ahead of his family, which was most exemplified by his willingness to sacrifice Iphigenia, even if he waffled for a while. The action was needed in order for the Achaeans to set sail for Troy, and the defeat of Troy was needed to make Agamemnon and Mycenae the main seat of power in the Aegean regions. All of this was done at the expense of his family, which makes it significant that his house's curse is related to a lack of loyalty to one's own family. The cycle of vengeance and murder among their own kin is what consistently brings about their suffering, and it only ends when his son Orestes is mournful and seeks forgiveness for killing his mother.

Agamemnon's nature was to seek power, and while he is the only one of his kin that does not literally kill a member of his own family (on a technicality), he was certainly willing to do so and did so symbolically through his neglect and absence. There was no sense of family in his actions, which is a direct contrast to Hector, who would have inherited the Trojan throne and been considered the most powerful leader of the Aegean's had his defense of his family and people been successful.

Agamemnon, victorious, returns home only to be killed just as he achieves the height of his power. While containing the same sort of tragic flaw as the other heroes, Agamemnon is not granted the same forgiveness by the audience. He is widely seen as going too far and letting his ambition get the better of him and is a cautionary tale rather than one to emulate or admire. This downfall sets him apart from the heroic trio of Achilles, Odysseus, and Hector.

Helen

Another cautionary tale is that of Helen, though it is a far different kind than that of Agamemnon. Her story begins in Sparta with Menelaus winning a competition for her betrothal, which was granted by her father, King Tyndareus. At no point did she choose Menelaus, though many revisions of her story, such as those of Euripides, try to make her more loyal to her first husband. Nor did she really choose Paris, either, as she was promised to him not by her father but by the goddess Aphrodite for naming her the victor in a contest of beauty. In order to enforce the "prize," Helen was shot by a magical arrow of Eros (later Cupid, to the Romans) so that she would run off with Paris to Troy. When it comes to Helen, interpretation is very important and divergent, which is what makes her one of the most controversial and enigmatic figures in the epic. Like the three heroes, the way that the Greeks chose to see Helen betrayed their own values, just as it is in today's society.

For those that believe Helen was a dutiful wife who was manipulated and enchanted by the gods to make her run off and act against her nature, she represents the Jungian archetype of the "Everyman." *(Or, in this case, the "Everywoman.")* It is not so much that she has a character of her own making, as it is that she provides an entry point into the story for the audience and a justification for the war that follows. This interpretation is supported by the continued treatment of Helen as a bargaining chip, starting with her betrothal to Menelaus and following her to Troy, where a group of men discuss her as property of her husband (whichever one they side with) and then make decisions on her behalf. It was not her choice to marry Menelaus, it was not her choice to fall in love with Paris, and it was not her choice to stay in Troy or return to Sparta.

A depiction of Helen. Credit: Wikimedia Commons.

The second interpretation is the Helen married Menelaus because it was expected of her as a princess of Sparta, but that she truly fell in love with Paris and decided to leave with him of her own accord. This reading turns Helen into the archetype of the lover, who seeks happiness, intimacy, and experience above all else. Supporting this is the description of Helen as the most beautiful woman in the world, rather than the most dutiful. While she could certainly be both, the emphasis on the former holds it as the most important and implies that she would seek the beauty and intimacy in others rather than simply doing what was expected of her. The fact that she and Paris are at odds with one another further supports this view since a dutiful wife would have supported him no matter what went on in the Ancient Aegean world. She falls out of love with Paris over their dispute, which would be more consistent with a passionate personality and more likely than the magic of the gods suddenly wearing off. This would also make her downfall in keeping with that of the other characters. If her passionate nature led her to run off, it was also likely to lead to death and destruction, and her eventual return to a loveless and imprisoning marriage to Menelaus in Sparta would be a suitably tragic fate.

A final interpretation of her character is that she was a true actor in the events of the war and played both sides for an outcome that was for her own betterment. In this narrative, she would have taken the archetype of the magician, the type of person that catalyzes change and seeks the improvement of their station through their own initiative. Her betrothal was not necessarily a bad thing, especially since her betrothed was something of a dimwit – and the union would allow her to remain in Sparta.

However, through Paris' diplomatic visits to Sparta, Helen at some point came to believe that Troy held better promise for her. Perhaps it could have been because she believed them more powerful, or because she saw an opportunity to compound her wealth by running off to Troy with Sparta's fortune stowed in the ships, or because there was more equity for women in politics and society – or *all of the above.*

This version does not exclude love, power, wealth, or equity as motivations but requires some leaps about Trojan culture. The latter option is especially interesting, as Andromache is seen as a valuable advisor to Hector, and the Amazons of central Asia figure prominently as fierce warriors on the level of their male counterparts. Still, they are not very large leaps. Homer and the Greek dramatists wrote their stories after hundreds of years of dark ages, and even Classical Greece in its golden age was not so golden for women. It is not difficult to imagine that Helen would have been more of her own agent than the later Greeks were able to grasp properly.

Helen would have needed to change sides back to the Achaeans as her better bet at a certain point in the war. The deaths of Hector, Penthesilea, and Memnon could likely have been the impetus for the change, which is confirmed by her assistance to Odysseus when he and Diomedes entered the city to steal the Palladium. If the symbolic rather than the literal translation of the theft of the Palladium is used, then that means that the ally who showed the Achaeans how to breach the walls could have been Helen rather than Antenor. If she's given even the slightest bit of agency, she is the more obvious choice since she had recently been widowed by the death of Paris and is mentioned explicitly in the tale for helping with the theft of Troy's protective charm. Her final manipulation of Menelaus, who she convinces to take her back rather than kill her, is her final victory, though a tainted one as she would have been a visionary deprived of her dreams of autonomy and forced to rule by stroking the ego of a powerful dope for the rest of her life.

Carl Jung wrote about many of these archetypes in the twentieth century, but it is not revisionism to apply his thinking to people who lived thousands of years before him. He was, after all, trying to get at something that was universal. This was the same thing that the Greeks were doing with their myths and histories, regardless of the overlap between the two genres. So, did the Greeks believe that the Trojan War was real? Yes, obviously. And no, of course not.

Chapter 12: The Legacy: Modern-Day Findings and Interpretations

In the absence of much convincing archaeological evidence, the city of Troy was believed to have existed in the area referred to as the "Troad," found in northwest Turkey on contemporary maps. Enthusiasts, fascinated by the Homeric legends or the later works of the Greek dramatists, would frequently embark on pilgrimages so they could stand on the same shore that Achilles spilled so much blood on and that Hector gave his life to defend. It was not until the late nineteenth century, though, that there was much to support this until an unlikely duo took their copies of Homer and their spades to Asia Minor.

Frank Calvert lived in the Troad near Hissarlik Hill. He was not a professional archaeologist but had enough knowledge to be effective in his archaeological work. His research led him to believe that this was a good place to begin his dig, and in 1868 recruited another enthusiast-turned archaeologist named Heinrich Schliemann to dig alongside him. Their findings were staggering and took the world by storm. Despite being amateurs, they unearthed ancient heroes along with ancient walls and shards of pottery and brought legitimacy to the nascent discipline of archaeology. Upon finding jewelry, Schliemann famously speculated that he had found the accouterments of the fabled Helen. A new generation inspired by the legends of Homer was soon to take up their torch and carry it into modern times to answer one of history's most nagging questions: Was the Trojan War real?

The excavations began to show that Troy had been occupied, in one form or another, since around 3,000 BCE. They lived in a difficult area that often would have made life challenging for its inhabitants. Archaeological evidence supports that both war and natural disasters such as earthquakes were responsible for the ebbs and flows of Trojan power. In times of affluence and power, such conditions led the Trojans to build fortresses to protect themselves and to store food against the threat of famine or siege. In fact, northwestern Turkey would have been one of the most heavily trafficked bottlenecks in antiquity, and its strategic position at the entrance to the Dardanelles would likely have been utilized to grow their wealth through trade and tariffs. They would, of course, need military strength to make payment a more sensible option than war for the traders and fleets passing through. Setting up a marketplace at this crossroads would have also been of great interest to them, as such win-win profitability would have further discouraged war and violence as a viable strategy, much like modern economic arrangements among EU member states have disincentivized a third world war.

What is left of Troy's temple to Athena. This temple would have been constructed after the Trojan War.
Credit: Carole Raddato, Wikimedia Commons.

The archaeological record, though, is not one of constant growth. It shows periods of expansions and contractions as their population swelled in times of prosperity and hunkered down through more destructive or deprived cycles. The arrow of time, though, moves just one way. In archaeological terms, this means "up." The deeper the artifacts, walls, or evidence, the longer ago it happened. Troy was rebuilt not in the same place, but each on top of the last one. This stratification, along with tools such as carbon dating, has given archaeologists a pretty good idea of when Troy was strong, weak, or in between. The naming convention has been to use Roman numerals to label from the bottom up, so the oldest settlement of Troy is Troy I, the second oldest Troy II, and so on.

Troy I was small but prosperous, and by the time it had grown into Troy II from 2550 through 2300 BCE, it had become very wealthy for its size, as evidenced by the quality of materials and living conditions compared to their contemporaries. The construction of the city's first walls marks the transition from Troy

I to Troy II, with a citadel built on Troy's famous strategic hill, one hundred feet above the surrounding plain.

Still, even with this feature as a constant, much of the rest of the topography would have looked different. The biggest difference from today is that the city would have been much closer to the sea than it is today due to the accumulation of silt in river deltas that have pushed the shoreline further and further away. Its position directly on the shore was significant, as it allowed the city to be by the sea while maintaining a strategic location along land routes. In a lot of ways, Troy was an early version of what the city, now called Istanbul, would be (the city was first called Byzantium, then Constantinople, and finally, Istanbul.) A further advantage for the Trojans came from the nature of sea travel in their day, which saw ships often need to port for days or weeks while they waited for favorable winds. Providing safe harbor and lodging for them would have created a captive market and contributed to their reputation as a trading hub.

By the late Bronze Age – when the Achaeans showed up – Troy had grown grander and wealthier than the inhabitants of Troy II would have believed. In fact, evidence suggests three things. First, that Troy was larger than historians expected. Second, that the descriptions of Troy by Homer were likely highly accurate. And third, *it was likely the largest city Bronze Age city in the Mediterranean*. Troy VII was the final iteration of the city that would be burned and leveled by the Greek forces, but the evidence increasingly shows that the Achaeans came at a bad time. Troy was at its absolute peak, undimmed by any kind of dark age, drought, recent war, or recession. In fact, as time goes on and the slow unearthing of the city continues and even accelerates with modern technology, there is an increasingly strong argument that the Achaeans were scrappy underdogs who had no business taking on such an important center of commerce. Sparta, by comparison, looks more and more like a backwater that Helen may have been fleeing in order to live her life in a more cosmopolitan and fulfilling civilization. Troy was not just a citadel but a city-scale complex with outer and inner walls protecting not just the royalty and nobility – but the entire population. This growth and the movement of the walls further out to encompass the lower town marks the cities final transition, from Troy VII to Troy VII.

The larger agricultural area had been carefully cultivated under the protection of Troy's military might and the leadership of Hector, who was nicknamed the "Tamer of Horses." This also implies that much of the Trojans' wealth came from horse husbandry. Domesticated horses bred for war were much less common in the late Bronze Age than they would be even by the time of Classical Greece and were therefore that much more valuable. Sheep farming was the foundation for a burgeoning textile industry centered in Troy, which they exported all around the Mediterranean and Asia Minor through their dual access and control of water and land routes. All these details have been recent revelations, as modern equipment has allowed for an analysis of the artifacts not available to the archaeologists even of the twentieth century.

These revelations paint a slightly different picture against the backdrop of the main Aegean powers of the Bronze Age: the Achaeans, the Trojans, and the Hittites. While the assessment of the Hittites as the mightiest of the three has remained unchanged, the leveling of the Achaeans and Trojans might be in the process of revision. Troy's actual territory was small, yes, but the increasing evidence of their prosperity, power, and influence has raised many an eyebrow. It may be that the Achaeans saw this and realized two things.

First, if left unchecked, their "friendly rival" could soon outpace them. Troy's neutrality between the Greeks and Hittites had allowed them to grow to a problematic point. If they did not do something soon, the Achaeans could quickly have two powerful enemies on their hands. By this interpretation, the Trojan War occurred at the height of Trojan power for that exact reason: they were a dangerous ascending power that needed to be kept in check. History has taught nothing if not that leaders prefer the status quo, and Troy was about to disrupt that for the Achaean kingdoms.

In addition, or perhaps extending this line of thinking, the Achaeans may have been driven by greed. Seeing the wealth and power that Troy had accumulated through their strategic position, they coveted the land that they sat on and saw the growth of their own power if they were able to control it. This line of thought provides a much sounder geopolitical explanation for why Achaean leaders other than Menelaus would have gone to war. Agamemnon, perhaps, could have been bound by loyalty to his brother, but loyalty was also not a trait commonly held by the cutthroat members of the House of Atreus. All of this is supported by Hittite tablets that refer to a war around 1180 BCE between the Wilusa, their name for the Trojans, and the Ahhiyawa, their name for the Achaeans.

For some counterevidence as an antidote for getting carried away and claiming proof, Troy was not alone in the Aegean world for its fall around 1180 BCE. For reasons that remain unclear, most of the Mediterranean powers descended into dark ages and ruin around this time, including the Achaeans and Hittites. It was a large reset button, and the "Greeks" who emerged from the dark age around Homer's time were ethnically and culturally different from the Achaeans, even if they still shared a common or related language.

Similarly, the "Hittites" of Asia Minor in the Bronze Age are not the same Hittites that are likely the ancestors of the biblical Hebrews. Troy, as has been documented thoroughly, was hit the hardest. The title of "most strategically located city" passed to Byzantium, and the only way to see a rebuilding of Troy is to place it in Lavinium with the resettlement of Aeneas in Italy, though the historicity of that legend is suspect at best.

Had the Achaeans been more able to capitalize on their victory, historians would likely know more. But after being sacked by the Achaeans, Troy was not rebuilt as a *Greek city.*

Archaeology indicates plenty of trade with the Greek kingdoms but does not place it as Greek itself in any of its iterations. Had there been a Trojan War and had a city as powerful as the one described by Homer been sacked by the Achaeans, there should be some evidence that they attempted to control and resettle the city and its surrounding lands. Perhaps the strangest and least believable part of the Epic Cycle is that everyone just went home after the war or resettled in Italy.

Why Italy? If Nestor, Diomedes, or Philoctetes were looking to start new colonies, why abandon the incredibly lucrative one they had just conquered. In the end, something just does not smell right. What seems most likely is that Homer and the epic poets were left with the same question. What happened in the Mediterranean world after the Trojan War? Some cataclysmic event would have explained the synchronized drop-off, but evidence for such a thing is still wanting. Still, if the authors of the Epic Cycle were indeed left without source material or a clear idea of what happened, then it makes sense that they would try to look forward rather than backward. Expansion into the western Mediterranean was the new frontier of Archaic and Classical Greece, so sending their heroes into the "new world" made more sense than having them vanish with the rest of the old.

These questions – and others – leave historians in an odd place regarding the Trojan War. There is overwhelming archaeological evidence that the city itself not only existed but existed to the standard described by Homeric legend. Yes, the ensuing dark age wiped out any evidence that could have existed about whether such a war between the Achaeans and that civilization was real or invented. That said, Greek historians, poets, and dramatists have proven themselves to be oddly dependable over time, despite their frequent inclusion of the supernatural.

As a result, most historians do believe that war occurred between the Achaeans and the Trojans, a war that is supported by contemporary Hittite texts and the stories of later Greeks. Still, the scale of the war, its participants, and its outcome remains in question by many skeptics. It seems to them too unlikely that such a massive war occurred without leaving a trace of direct evidence beyond a few scant lines of Aramaic and a city that fell into ruin at the same time that many other cities also fell into ruin. These more conservative historians will allow for a short war of an unknown outcome and significance to take place, and that both civilizations fell into ruin shortly afterward.

Still, it is important to gather all that we can out of the emerging archaeological evidence. The ruins that are being exposed and studied through modern excavations could indeed have withstood a ten-year siege, especially if the invading army were not large enough to completely surround the city, a detail corroborated by Epic Cycle texts. Additionally, the battles and technology described are consistent with Homer's tales, though this could always be ascribed to the poet's own understanding of history.

The evidence has also unearthed a more compelling reason for the war than exists in the Epic Cycle. A city with Troy's affluence and strategic location would have created both the dedication required on the part of the Achaeans to take it and the investment in its defenses by the Trojans needed to keep it. Further, the later significance of Byzantium and even more recent battles of the First World War illustrate the militaristic importance of the site. Famously, over 130,000 soldiers died in the Battle of Gallipoli, a twentieth-century equivalent of Troy, geographically speaking. This importance would again support the necessity of an economically and militarily concentrated civilization that would have likely had many "Trojan Wars" in addition to the one fought against the Achaeans. This would mean that people had been fighting and dying over Troy for thousands of years before the Achaeans attacked it; who is to say if the Trojans of their time were themselves the original inhabitants or merely the most recent foreign conquerors?

If there was a Trojan War against the Achaeans, much of what has been previously assumed might be wrong. The war was probably not decided by a few important showdowns where one warrior called out another warrior. It was more likely the most recent series of skirmishes in a history of routine skirmishes with armies attempting to control the strategic city-state. There would have been fewer full-scale assaults than Homer described and more guerilla campaigns from each side: the Trojans against the Achaean encampments, and the Achaeans against the Trojan countryside. In short, it would have been more ugly than glorious. In a word, it would have been *just a war.*

Like many wars, it could have very well hinged on something tricky or clever that gave the Achaeans the edge at just the right time or caused the Trojans to let their guard down. It could have been something hatched by someone who resembled Odysseus, or it could have been the fatigue of war for the Trojans and good luck for the Greeks.

In the end, it is very tempting to believe as much as possible about Homer's Trojan War and its heroes, but it is just as dangerous as deifying any war effort. By putting it on the plain of virtue, its cancerous elements are swept under the rug to metastasize in our world as much as it did in theirs. Achilles is a fascinating character but would make a terrifying person. Worshiping someone like him is as much an appreciation of the human ability as it is to our tendency to forget the far greater number of "little people;" the civilians, peasants, and regular folk who all died in the name of his glory. In the end, this was at best a war about the honor of a handful of people, and at worst, *simply politics.* Heroism can always be displayed, but in response to – not as a cause of – war.

Did the face of Helen launch a thousand ships? Did the rage of Achilles kill a thousand people? The record tells us probably not, on both accounts and for different reasons. But there was very likely still a terrible war, with much senselessness and some heroism, though probably on the part of those who never sought it. The sad reality is that we're still asking the wrong questions.

What would we say of Helen if she were more than a marriage device? And what great deeds might Achilles have accomplished if not made a tool of Agamemnon? These questions put the war in its place as a hindrance to greater acts. Achilles would likely agree, as all he did in the end was to destroy other great warriors because it made him look good. Perhaps, though, the Greeks layered their myths deep, and this was *exactly* what Homer was saying. Achilles was not made great through the war; he was diminished by it. It consumed him and became him. He kept trying to leave (and wanting to leave) but kept getting drawn back by vanity and arrogance.

Remember, Achilles was one of the few heroes in Greek mythology who was given a choice.

Perhaps he chose against his better nature, ignoring his mother's advice, his own dislike of Agamemnon, and the independence he so desperately needed to assert by doing what everyone wanted and expected him to do. He had to have known that a talent for death was lonely, and a legacy of death was perhaps not very glorious of an achievement. Or maybe that is just transposing modern ideas onto a Bronze Age mind that had a very different moral code. Who is to say? The point is that the interpretations, symbolism, and meaning in Greek myths are as varied as the readers, *and that is exactly the reason why they persist.* Much like the Greek constellations, the unclear outlines are a feature, not a bug, and they allow people to see what they saw because of, *not in spite of,* their vagueness. Or something like it, anyway.

Conclusion

Despite its many interpretations, thousands of class or research hours, and many archeological surprises supporting its assertion, Homer's *Iliad* remains one of the world's most-read and discussed works of all time. Though many would assess its importance from a historical perspective, an equal number of readers would likely draw its most important conclusions from a psychological standpoint.

Regardless of perspective, the Trojan War presented by Homer is still being debated from all angles today. This simple fact belies the continuing importance of understanding our past to assess our future.

Many historians posit that the Trojan War itself was not as important as the Homeric epic that followed, as the *Iliad* became somewhat of a Bible to the ancient Greeks. His account inspired thousands of people – not to mention the great warrior, Alexander the Great – and became one of the earliest and most-studied pieces of literature.

Still, history is not supported only by that one literary work. We have contemporary texts that support the fact that the Trojan War was not a small war – or one without significance. Mycenaean Greeks from much of the world united to attack Troy, garnering from 70,000 to possibly 130,000 men, traveling on an estimated 1,200 ships! This expedition was a huge undertaking for that time in history.

The fall of Troy likely triggered the Greek Dark Ages, lasting from about 1200 BCR to 800 BCE - no small occurrence in Greek history. Homer's *Iliad* was not only a recounting of a war story; it served as a unifying call for a rise from the ashes, clarity of purpose, and a patriotism that had all but been lost to the prior 400 years. The story - as told by Homer - helped the Greeks remember the myths and history of their past while also linking them to a common enemy during the period of the Persian Wars. In this way, the *Iliad* brought the past into their present, garnering national pride and a sense of destiny.

Notwithstanding that important influence, the Trojan War inspired the Greeks to invent the phonetic alphabet; they determined which vowels and consonants coexist to reproduce the sound of spoken words. Without this, the *Iliad* may not have been transformed from its oral story to its written form. Before this important time, cuneiform or pictographs were used for writing - and were unable to record human stories with power, majesty, and emotion. After all, the first word in Homer's epic poem? "Rage."

We would do well today to remember that apt word when approaching the potential for war.

Here's another book by Enthralling History that you might like

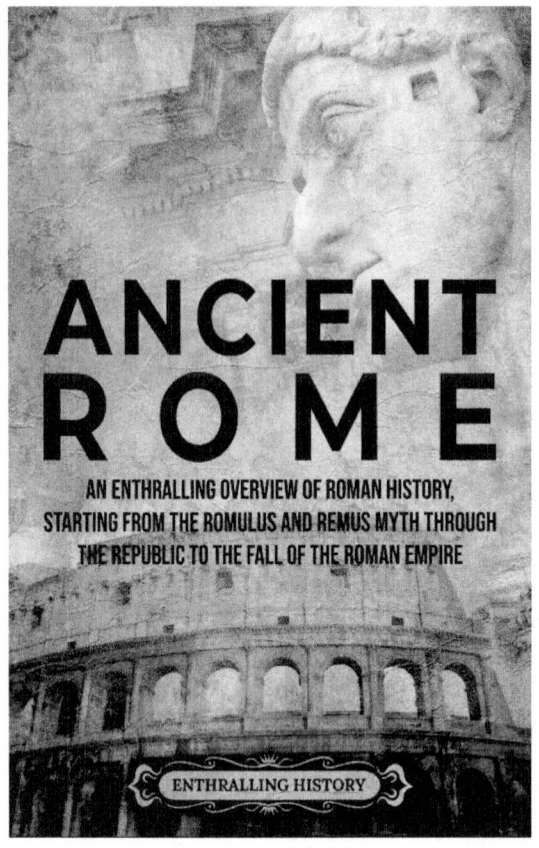

Free limited time bonus

Stop for a moment. We have a free bonus set up for you. The problem is this: we forget 90% of everything that we read after 7 days. Crazy fact, right? Here's the solution: we've created a printable, 1-page pdf summary for this book that you're reading now. All you have to do to get your free pdf summary is to go to the following website:

https://livetolearn.lpages.co/enthrallinghistory/

Once you do, it will be intuitive. Enjoy, and thank you!

We forget 90% of everything that we've read in 7 days...

Get the free printable pdf summary of the book you've read AND much, much more... shhhh...

Enter Your Most Frequently Used Email to Get Started

DOWNLOAD FREE PDF SUMMARY

© Enthralling History

References

(2021). Retrieved 23 October 2021, from https://www.theoi.com/articles/what-was-the-cause-of-the-trojan-war/

(2021). Retrieved 23 October 2021, from https://www.greekmythology.com/Myths/Mortals/Philoctetes/philoctetes.html

(2021). Retrieved 23 October 2021, from https://www.greekmythology.com/Myths/Heroes/Achilles/achilles.html

(2021). Retrieved 23 October 2021, from https://www.greekmythology.com/Myths/Figures/Amazons/amazons.html#:~:text=The%20Amazons%20were%20a%20race,the%20god%20of%20war%20Ares.

(2021). Retrieved 23 October 2021, from https://www.masterclass.com/articles/writing-101-the-12-literary-archetypes#12-archetypal-characters-to-use-in-your-writing

(2021). Retrieved 23 October 2021, from https://www.baltimoresun.com/news/bs-xpm-1993-02-22-1993053194-story.html

Achaeans (Homer) - Wikipedia. (2021). Retrieved 23 October 2021, from https://en.wikipedia.org/wiki/Achaeans_(Homer)

Achilles - Wikipedia. (2021). Retrieved 23 October 2021, from https://en.wikipedia.org/wiki/Achilles#Death

Achilles | Myth, Meaning, Significance, & Trojan War. (2021). Retrieved 23 October 2021, from https://www.britannica.com/topic/Achilles-Greek-mythology

Aeneas - Wikipedia. (2021). Retrieved 23 October 2021, from https://en.wikipedia.org/wiki/Aeneas

Agamemnon - Wikipedia. (2021). Retrieved 23 October 2021, from https://en.wikipedia.org/wiki/Agamemnon

Amazon Warriors Did Indeed Fight and Die Like Men. (2021). Retrieved 23 October 2021, from https://www.nationalgeographic.com/history/article/141029-amazons-scythians-hunger-games-herodotus-ice-princess-tattoo-cannabis

Amazons - Wikipedia. (2021). Retrieved 23 October 2021, from https://en.wikipedia.org/wiki/Amazons

Ancient Troy: The City & the Legend. (2021). Retrieved 22 October 2021, from https://www.livescience.com/38191-ancient-troy.html

Apollo - Wikipedia. (2021). Retrieved 22 October 2021, from https://en.wikipedia.org/wiki/Apollo#Anatolian_origin

Brouwers, J. (2021). The suicide of Ajax. Retrieved 23 October 2021, from https://www.ancientworldmagazine.com/articles/suicide-ajax/

Cassandra - Wikipedia. (2021). Retrieved 22 October 2021, from https://en.wikipedia.org/wiki/Cassandra

Epic Cycle - Livius. (2021). Retrieved 23 October 2021, from https://www.livius.org/sources/content/epic-cycle/

Epic Cycle - The Center for Hellenic Studies. (2021). Retrieved 23 October 2021, from https://chs.harvard.edu/primary-source/epic-cycle-sb/

Epic Cycle - Wikipedia. (2021). Retrieved 23 October 2021, from https://en.wikipedia.org/wiki/Epic_Cycle

Expedition Magazine - Penn Museum. (2021). Retrieved 23 October 2021, from https://www.penn.museum/sites/expedition/the-hittites-and-the-aegean-world/

Fall of Troy: the legend and the facts. (2021). Retrieved 22 October 2021, from https://theconversation.com/fall-of-troy-the-legend-and-the-facts-92625

First Sacking of Troy in Greek Mythology. (2021). Retrieved 22 October 2021, from https://www.greeklegendsandmyths.com/first-sacking-of-troy.html

Geology corresponds with Homers description of ancient Troy. (2021). Retrieved 22 October 2021, from https://www1.udel.edu/PR/UDaily/2003/troy030303.html

Greek & Roman Mythology - Homer. (2021). Retrieved 23 October 2021, from https://www2.classics.upenn.edu/myth/php/homer/index.php?page=trojan

Hancox, D. (2021). The Archetypal Father. Retrieved 23 October 2021, from https://corecounselling.ca/the-archetypal-father/#:~:text=The%20Father%20archetype%20combines%20the,to%20put%20ideas%20into%20fruition.

Hector in Greek Mythology. (2021). Retrieved 22 October 2021, from https://www.greeklegendsandmyths.com/hector.html

Hercules' Ninth Labor: Hippolyte's Belt. (2021). Retrieved 23 October 2021, from http://www.perseus.tufts.edu/Heracles/amazon.html

Hippolyta in Greek Mythology. (2021). Retrieved 23 October 2021, from https://www.greeklegendsandmyths.com/hippolyta.html

Idomeneus of Crete - Wikipedia. (2021). Retrieved 23 October 2021, from https://en.wikipedia.org/wiki/Idomeneus_of_Crete

Iphigenia - Wikipedia. (2021). Retrieved 23 October 2021, from https://en.wikipedia.org/wiki/Iphigenia

Judgement of Paris - Wikipedia. (2021). Retrieved 23 October 2021, from https://en.wikipedia.org/wiki/Judgement_of_Paris

Lindberg, T. (2021). Achilles and Patroclus: Archetypal Heroes. Retrieved 23 October 2021, from https://warontherocks.com/2015/12/achilles-and-patroclus-archetypal-heroes/

Memnon: the African warrior who made Achilles bleed. (2021). Retrieved 23 October 2021, from https://thinkafrica.net/memnon-african-in-troy/

Menestheus - Wikipedia. (2021). Retrieved 23 October 2021, from https://en.wikipedia.org/wiki/Menestheus

Mike Greenberg, P., Mike Greenberg, P., & Mike Greenberg, P. (2021). Diomedes: A Hero of the Trojan War. Retrieved 23 October 2021, from https://mythologysource.com/diomedes-trojan-war/

Mycenaean Greece - Wikipedia. (2021). Retrieved 23 October 2021, from https://en.wikipedia.org/wiki/Mycenaean_Greece#Political_organization

Neill, C. (2021). Understanding Personality: The 12 Jungian Archetypes. Retrieved 23 October 2021, from https://conorneill.com/2018/04/21/understanding-personality-the-12-jungian-archetypes/

Nestor | Greek mythology. (2021). Retrieved 23 October 2021, from https://www.britannica.com/topic/Nestor-Greek-mythology

NPR Cookie Consent and Choices. (2021). Retrieved 23 October 2021, from https://www.npr.org/templates/story/story.php?storyId=6117459

Original Sources - Discover Trojan War. (2021). Retrieved 23 October 2021, from https://www.originalsources.com/Discover.aspx?ID=363

Original Sources - Fragment #1. (2021). Retrieved 23 October 2021, from https://www.originalsources.com/Document.aspx?DocID=SFSAGL8BJN6SDXM

Original Sources - Fragment #1. (2021). Retrieved 23 October 2021, from https://www.originalsources.com/Document.aspx?DocID=HNLSDCYI215BPWW

Original Sources - Fragment #1. (2021). Retrieved 23 October 2021, from https://www.originalsources.com/Document.aspx?DocID=CFYALH4C4RY16CA

Palladium (classical antiquity) - Wikipedia. (2021). Retrieved 23 October 2021, from https://en.wikipedia.org/wiki/Palladium_(classical_antiquity)

Peleus - Wikipedia. (2021). Retrieved 23 October 2021, from https://en.wikipedia.org/wiki/Peleus

Penthesilea. (2021). Retrieved 23 October 2021, from http://www.hellenicaworld.com/Greece/Mythology/en/Penthesilea.html

Philoctetes - Wikipedia. (2021). Retrieved 23 October 2021, from https://en.wikipedia.org/wiki/Philoctetes

Priam - Wikipedia. (2021). Retrieved 22 October 2021, from https://en.wikipedia.org/wiki/Priam

Scythians. (2021). Retrieved 23 October 2021, from https://www.worldhistory.org/Scythians/

Strauss, B. (2006). Strauss Offers Fresh Look at 'Trojan War'. Retrieved 22 October 2021, from https://www.npr.org/templates/story/story.php?storyId=6117459

Strauss, B. (2008). *The Trojan War*. London: Arrow.

The Final Labors of Heracles. (2021). Retrieved 23 October 2021, from https://www.greecetravel.com/greekmyths/argos8.htm

The Mythology of Tenedos. (2021). Retrieved 23 October 2021, from https://www.cointalk.com/threads/the-mythology-of-tenedos.332304/

The search for the lost city of Troy - British Museum Blog. (2021). Retrieved 23 October 2021, from https://blog.britishmuseum.org/the-search-for-the-lost-city-of-troy/

There could be surprising findings in Troy: Excavation head. (2021). Retrieved 22 October 2021, from https://www.hurriyetdailynews.com/there-could-be-surprising-findings-in-troy-excavation-head-136425

Thetis - More than Achilles's Mom. (2021). Retrieved 23 October 2021, from https://www.thoughtco.com/thetis-not-just-a-greek-nymph-116707

Trojan War - Wikipedia. (2021). Retrieved 23 October 2021, from https://en.wikipedia.org/wiki/Trojan_War#Gathering_of_Achaean_forces_and_the_first_expedition

Trojan War - Wikipedia. (2021). Retrieved 23 October 2021, from https://en.wikipedia.org/wiki/Trojan_War

Who Was Agamemnon? (2021). Retrieved 23 October 2021, from https://www.thoughtco.com/agamemnon-116781

Winkle, C. (2021). The Eight Character Archetypes of the Hero's Journey. Retrieved 23 October 2021, from https://mythcreants.com/blog/the-eight-character-archetypes-of-the-heros-journey/

Herodotus. *The Histories with an English translation by A. D. Godley.*

(1920). Cambridge: Harvard University Press. At the Perseus Project of the Tufts University.

Fields, N. *Thermopylae 480 BC*. Osprey Publishing, 2007.

Ctesias. *Persica* (excerpt in Photius's epitome).

Diodorus Siculus. *Library in Twelve Volumes with an English Translation by C. H. Oldfather. Cambridge, Mass.; London.* (1967). At the Perseus Project of the Tufts University.

Herodotus. *Herodotus.* Penguin Classics, 1996.

Hornblower, Simon & Spawforth, Antony & Eidinow, Esther. *The Oxford Classical Dictionary.* Oxford University Press, 2012.

Kinzl, Konrad H. *A Companion to the Classical Greek World.* Wiley-Blackwell, 2010.

Plutarch. *Aristides.*

Xenophon. *Anabasis.*

Burn, Andrew Robert. *The Pelican History of Greece.* Penguin. 1974.

Aristotle. *Politics.*

Berve, Helmut (1937). *Sparta.* Meyers Kleine Handbücher, 7. Leipzig: Bibliographisches Institut AG.

Cicero. Tusculan Disputations.

Delbrück, Hans. History of the Art of War Vol I. ISBN 978-0-8032-6584-4.

Holland, Tom. Persian Fire. Abacus, 2005. ISBN 978-0-349-11717-1

Campbell B. (ed). The Oxford Handbook of Warfare in the Classical World. OUP, Oxford, 2013.

Kinzl K.H. (ed). A Companion to the Classical Greek World. Wiley-Blackwell, 2010.

Salisbury, J. E. Encyclopedia of Women in the Ancient World. ABC-CLIO, 2001.

Snyder, J. M. The Woman and the Lyre. Southern Illinois University Press, 1989.

Spencer, C. Homosexuality in History. Harcourt, Brace & Company, 1995.

Simon Hornblower. The Oxford Classical Dictionary. Oxford University Press, USA, 2012.

William Shepherd. Plataea 479 BC. Osprey Publishing, 2012.

Xenophon. Constitution of the Lacedaemonians.

Burg, B. R. Gay Warriors: A Documentary History from the Ancient World to the Present. NYU Press, 2001.

Cahill, T. Sailing the Wine-Dark Sea: Why the Greeks Matter. Anchor Books, 2004.

Cartledge, P. The Spartans: The World of the Warrior-Heroes of Ancient Greece. Vintage Books, 2004.

Crompton, L. Homosexuality and Civilization. Belknap Press: An Imprint of Harvard University Press, 2006.

Forrest, W. G. A History of Sparta: 950-192 BC. W. W. Norton & Company, 2000.

Thucydides & Strassler, R. B. et. al. Thucydides Histories. Cambridge University Press, 2013.

Xenophon. The Whole Works of Xenophon. Andesite Press, 2015.

Aristotle & McKeon, R. Aristotle's Politics. Clarendon Press, 1999.

Cartledge, P. The Spartans: The World of the Warrior-Heroes of Ancient Greece. Vintage Books, 2004.

Lefkowitz, M. R & Fant, M. B. Women's Life in Greece and Rome. Johns Hopkins University Press, 2016.

Plutarch. Plutarch's Lives. Palala Press, 2016.

Plutarch. The Age of Alexander. Penguin Classics, 2012.

Xenophon. The Landmark Xenophon's Hellenika. By Robert B. Strassler. 2010.

History of Sparta

An Enthralling Guide to the Spartans and the Trojan War

Printed in Great Britain
by Amazon

10148864R00183